MAN MEETS GRIZZLY

Encounters in the Wild from
Lewis and Clark to Modern Times

MAN MEETS GRIZZLY

Encounters in the Wild from
Lewis and Clark to Modern Times

───────

GATHERED BY F. M. YOUNG
EDITED BY CORALIE BEYERS

Foreword by Frank C. Craighead, Jr.

BOSTON
Houghton Mifflin Company
1980

Library of Congress Cataloging in Publication Data

Main entry under title:
Man meets grizzly.

1. Grizzly bear — Legends and stories. I. Young,
Francis Marion. II. Beyers, Coralie.
QL795.B4M34   599.74′446   80-13844
ISBN 0-395-29194-1

Printed in the United States of America

S 10 9 8 7 6 5 4 3 2 1

To
H. WARD AND ARDIS YOUNG MCCARTY
who made this book possible
and
TO THE BEAR THAT BEGAN IT

ACKNOWLEDGMENTS

APPRECIATION IS DUE to many people who encouraged and otherwise assisted in the preparation of this book. Of those to whom F. M. Young was indebted, almost none are now left. Besides his family, he would have wished to thank the authors and copyright holders of the stories he was kindly permitted to use, and also old friends, for their advice.

My own gratitude goes most especially to John, Ardis, Lousje, Susan, and Nancy, for the trust and confidence that only a family can give; to Austin and Alta Fife, for their early and continued encouragement; to Frank C. Craighead, Jr., for invaluable help; to Dean William F. Lye, Kenneth B. Hunsaker, and others at Utah State University, including the indispensable Library Services, for the means to complete the book; to Ann Friedli and Elaine Davis, for their generous and skillful help in the preparation of the manuscript. And to Joan.

FOREWORD

Frank C. Craighead, Jr.

F. M. YOUNG'S unique collection of bear stories makes a thrilling and fascinating book, revealing the grizzly as it was known and visualized by the explorers, hunters, mountain men, and settlers of the West. Though these pioneers both admired and feared the grizzly, they relentlessly destroyed him wherever his presence conflicted with their aims and objectives, whether these were exploring, trapping, or ranching.

Prior to the entrance of the white man on the primeval stage of North America, the grizzly and the American Indian managed to coexist, competing with one another for food and living space and each taking a toll on the other when they clashed. Neither could, or desired to, exterminate the other. Once the white man had obtained a dominant position with his repeating rifle, however, he showed the grizzly no quarter. In face-to-face encounters there could be none. Only one opponent was likely to walk away. This book is a record of these encounters. These narratives, thrilling and at times saddening, vividly picture conditions as they once existed between bear and man. The outcome was inevitable. Man's dispersion into every conceivable habitat, nook, and cranny, along with his continuing population increase, made this so.

The tales in this collection form a substantial part of the lore of grizzly bears. They emphasize the bear's ferocity and cunning. Almost none of these encounters resulted from an attempt to study the bear, to come to know his habits and understand his behavior. Efforts in this direction did not take place until the grizzly was generally recognized to be well on the way to extermination. Not until the early part of the twentieth century did a few pioneer wildlife students, such as William H. Wright and

Enos Mills, observe grizzlies with the intention of contributing to the body of knowledge about them.

A rewarding part of my professional career has been spent in making a long-range, systematic study of the grizzly bear in the Yellowstone ecosystem, where the largest remnant of the nation's grizzlies, excluding those in Alaska, found a home within the protection afforded by Yellowstone National Park. The research began in 1959 and involved my brother John, myself, and a team of colleagues. Our study was aimed at filling gaps in the body of scientific knowledge about the grizzly. Prior to our study, reliable scientific information was limited. There are good reasons why this was so, reasons these tales illustrate. The grizzly is naturally shy of man, tends to be nocturnal, and roams a wild and rugged habitat. Many difficulties can arise for the investigator who gets close enough to the bear to study him.

To provide continuing protection for the Yellowstone grizzlies, a more complete picture of grizzly ecology was necessary. Such data was also needed in order to ensure the proper management of the bears, whom concerned people regard as a diminishing natural resource. Today there are perhaps only 600 to 700 grizzlies left in the original 48 states. What these numbers signify is startlingly tragic; for before the settlers arrived, California alone was inhabited by an estimated 10,000 grizzlies.

The Craighead grizzly-bear study, conducted between 1959 and 1971, yielded information that could not have been obtained earlier, because sophisticated modern technology provided valuable assistance to our methodology. To gather our data, we captured bears in culvert traps and immobilized them, using tranquilizing darts. This gave us a period of relative safety in which to mark the animals with coded ear tags. We collared some bears with the aid of miniature radio transmitters, which made it possible for us to readily locate and observe grizzlies, follow their movements at night, when they are most active, and do so over extensive areas of rugged terrain. We developed and perfected this method, with the result that an observer could track a single bear through its daily wanderings, from season to season, even year to year. One bear, to whom we are indebted for much information, was observed in this way for eight consecutive years.

This study provided what earlier encounters could not: information about the size of the bear population, the extent of the area over which it roamed, and the composition of that population; information about the grizzly's social organization, feeding habits, seasonal movements, breeding age, frequency of breeding, litter size, and causes of mortality; and information about prehibernation and hibernation behavior. Much of this work has been published in technical papers, and a popular account appears in my book, *Track of the Grizzly* (Sierra Club Books, 1979). Data from this and other studies contribute not only to the fund of scientific wildlife information, valuable for its own sake, but are also necessary for proper management of the remaining grizzlies, whose occasional contacts with people continue to pose a threat to the preservation of this animal.

There is always an element of risk, a chance of conflict, in the coexistence the Yellowstone ecosystem provides. But by understanding this great bear and by adjusting management practices to reflect what we know and are still learning about it, we can minimize the risk. There are hopeful signs that we may do so before the grizzly's steady decline reaches zero on the population graph.

It is rare in our busy and complicated modern lives for a granddaughter to acquire the interest and find the time and energy to carry on and complete the unfinished work of a grandfather. This book is a credit to both F. M. Young and his granddaughter, Coralie Beyers.

CONTENTS

IV. HARD TIMES

V. SUNDOWN

VI. AFTERGLOW

VII. NIGHTFALL

EDITOR'S NOTE

F. M. YOUNG admired bears, especially grizzlies, as the most interesting and intelligent animals in the wild, and he admired mountain men for the same reason. This collection of bear stories is drawn from his stock of lore concerning the men and movements that opened the West — a fund he added to with interest and love almost until the day he died, in 1949, at age seventy-nine. The oral tradition from which these tales originated is perceptible in the simple and direct manner of their telling; nearly all of them came firsthand from the men who experienced the adventures. Growing up in the Utah Territory in the closing years of the nineteenth century, F. M. Young was familiar with many of these tales.

He was naturally drawn to the stuff of legend, for his own heritage was touched by it. His father, a younger brother of Brigham Young, was in the first company of Mormons who entered the Salt Lake Valley, in 1847. His father was an intrepid man who confronted the wilderness with a calm determination to create a home in the valleys of the mountains. His mother, Johanna (Anna) Larson Young, was a youthful convert from Sweden, who in 1862 took passage to America by six-weeks' steerage, then walked across the plains with a handcart company, a long and hard journey, but endured with all the buoyancy of the early converts. Shortly after her arrival in the valley of the Saints she became the fifth wife of Lorenzo Dow Young, a serious man nearly fifty years her senior. While Lorenzo Dow farmed and developed herds of cattle and sheep, he sent Anna, along with two other wives, to manage a ranch and run a stagecoach stop for the miners of the Oquirrh Mountains, in the desert thirty miles southwest of Salt Lake City. There, in 1870, Francis Marion Young, my grandfather, was born. He spent his early childhood on several ranches belonging to his father or older half-brothers, tending cattle and sheep and acquiring a hearty respect for the landscape.

When Frank was seven years old his father bought a relinquishment on a piece of land in the sagebrush country near Leamington and sent Frank's mother and her three small sons to homestead it for a year. They lived in a rude dugout shelter, vacated only the day before they moved in by the trapper who sold it to Lorenzo Dow. Their dwelling was a long mile from the nearest neighbor, of which there were only a handful in the entire Sevier Valley. In an age of extensive journal-keeping, Anna Young wrote nothing. But her son Frank remembered and later recorded the time she battled bullsnakes on the rafters with a pitchfork; the time she calmed and comforted the boys when they were frightened by the drumming of horse hoofs overhead, as stolen horses were driven across their sod roof by an outlaw band; and the night she pursued a chicken-stealing wolf, with brandished broom, far along the trail, until he grew tired of the chase and finally gave up the booty. Only after the incident that nearly cost young Frank his life, when an entire wall of their rude home caved in following heavy rains, did she inform Lorenzo Dow it was time the family moved closer to the settlements in Salt Lake Valley.

Frank's father taught him to bud trees, and with a cherished half-sister he planted many Carolina poplars, lilac bushes, roses, and peonies on his father's properties, hauling by hand the water to nourish the young plants, and in a material way establishing the garden setting that the Mormons came to value so highly. As he grew older, his father sent him to help with his sheep herds in the primitive Uintah Basin country of northeast Utah.

Grandfather's lifetime interest in bears resulted from a boyhood experience that occurred while he was tending his father's sheep. True, he was confronted by a black bear, not a grizzly, and an indifferent bear at that, but he felt all the emotions one associates with the grizzly, and a strong imprint was made. Though he later laughed about his first encounter, he never forgot how small and defenseless man is, alongside a bear in the bear's own territory.

F. M. Young became a well-known Utah educator, long and

affectionately remembered by his students, and a notable horticulturist of irises, peonies, and roses. The idea for this volume, and the serious work of collecting stories for it, began after his retirement from teaching in 1931. Active in the Oregon Trail Society and, later, the American Pioneer Trails Society, he collaborated with LeRoy Hafen, then of the Colorado State Historical Society, on a history of Fort Laramie and the fur trade of the West.* While doing research for that book, he began collecting published stories and accounts concerning bears, to supplement the narratives he had gathered from family, friends, and acquaintances and had stored and told for many years. However, I am inclined to believe that the germ of the idea for this book of bear stories came even earlier, with the death of Old Ephraim in 1923, while my grandfather was teaching in Logan, Utah. He heard the story of this adventure firsthand from Frank Clark, the man who shot Old Ephraim, when he visited him at his sheep camp the summer following the bear's death. Of all the tales he ever read or heard, he liked this one best, he often told me.

After publication of *Fort Laramie*, F. M. Young worked seriously on the bear book, traveling widely to do his collecting. Wherever he went he had an uncanny ability to strike up conversations with men who had encountered bears. His colleagues in the Oregon Trail Society, which awarded him an honorary life membership, called him "Grizzly Frank"; and he was proud to be associated with those historians who early articulated the significance of the American West.

In his last years, world war and failing health slowed his work, and he died without completing the book. Because as a child, listening to Grandfather's stories, I had come to love the bears, I worked on the manuscript with him during my college years, and he asked me to finish the book for him. It has taken many years for me to complete all that he had envisioned for this volume. But I have tracked him, finally, through all the notes he gathered, adding only those pertinent materials that I feel sure he would approve of, had he the occasion to become acquainted with them.

It is obvious that since Frank Young's death in 1949 new

* LeRoy Hafen and F. M. Young, *Fort Laramie and the Fur Trade of the West* (Glendale, Calif.: A. H. Clark, 1938).

studies have added much information to that which was available for his investigations. How he would have valued, for instance, the exhaustive, pioneering ecological research of Frank and John Craighead, who have focused overdue attention on the grizzly bear, his habitat, and man's relationship to him. However, I have included in this book only materials describing events that occurred before or during the active years of Young's life — published accounts selected from records, journals, diaries, and histories, a few of which have become familiar classic tales, such as Hugh Glass's saga; and personal narratives F. M. Young gathered that are nowhere else available — his contribution to the literature of the West and a fair reflection of his admiration for man, bear, and environment.

Encounters between bear and man were the ultimate adventure the West could provide, Young thought, for their outcome turned not as much on the grizzly's superior brawn or man's superior brain as on resourcefulness, courage, and luck — qualities that could be possessed by either adversary. The encounter usually happened by chance, the by-blow of some other activity such as trapping, hunting, traveling, ranching, or soldiering. Occasionally it was deliberately sought, but there were few madmen in the mountains. In my childhood I often heard Grandfather tell of these adventures, admiring the wild creature as well as man, recognizing the savage dignity of the bear and the ingloriousness of man's encroachment upon the wilderness domain. He told me many times that in James Oliver Curwood's story of Thor and the Golden Rule he found the ideal conclusion to a century of depredation. I think now, after long immersion in the subject of this book, that the story of Old Ephraim cuts even nearer to the bone, dramatizing the fundamental inability of man and grizzly to coexist; for, though they are dangerous to each other, man is ultimately more dangerous to the bear.

Since Frank Clark's adventure with Old Ephraim in 1923, little remains from the early period. The West that Grandfather's generation knew and saw rapidly disappear is gone forever. F. M. Young knew the Old West, lived to see it fade, and longed to communicate something of its essence to descendants who could never experience it. Because his lifetime coincided with the westward movement, "westering" was a natural part of him; to later generations it is only an idea. These stories embrace that legendary time. If they succeed in communicating, it is because they are factual and have an authentic voice; hence the modest tone and the almost offhand recollection of supreme excitement that marks them.

Perhaps the auspicious moment for publication of this volume is the present. Today we know of the Old West only through story; our world is becoming more tenuous and limited, and the prodigal resources have diminished. Where previously, like heedless children, we squandered what was plentiful, we are now forced to confront the notion of depletion and gird ourselves to accommodate it. These stories sound the knell of one of our lost resources. To F. M. Young, the whole point of Frank Clark's remarkable adventure with Old Ephraim was not that the cunning survivor of so many years' marauding was finally brought down, but that Clark never boasted of his exploit. The simple sheep herder sensed that something wild and dangerous, yet vital and somehow admirable, had been stilled. Something was gone that the West would never see again.

The sense of loss grows on us today, fifty years after the grizzly disappeared from the Wasatch Mountains and almost all other mountains as well. Grandfather's stories serve to remind us not only that the king is dead but that there is none to take his place.

CORALIE M. BEYERS

I

MEET THE GRIZZLIES
F. M. Young

INTRODUCTION

THIS BOOK is a collection of bear stories, mostly concerning the grizzly, which have been selected from books on exploration and hunting, early periodicals, journals, and diaries, or unpublished recollections: stories of trappers, traders, travelers, hunters, and settlers in the Great West; stories of the kind of adventure that has long since gone the way of the grizzly.

It has been my intention to select the tales for their own interest and excitement and also for their illustration of the dangers and difficulties attending the development of the West. Taken together, these narratives constitute a record of human drama unmatched in other endeavors; they serve as footnotes to the grand chapters of western history. Seen from a different perspective, they record, as well, the saga of the grizzly bear in his century of contact with the white man, and in that respect constitute an elegy to a vanquished monarch. For the white man must dominate his environment and all creatures in it; of these, the grizzly has yielded most slowly and under greatest duress. These bear tales record a conflict that inevitably led to pursuit and destruction, similar in many respects to the fate of the wolf, buffalo, and Indian. The grizzly's day was tragically brief, and as a result of his history we are forced to think and act differently today, for the surfeit of killing has brought us perilously close to an imbalance in nature. The inscription at the base of the large bronze sculpture of a standing mother bear with cubs, at the Museum of Natural History in Denver, expresses my own view succinctly: "When the Grizzly is gone we shall have lost the most sublime specimen of wild life that exalts the western wilderness." *

The idea for this book took shape during my researches into

---

* Reprinted by permission of J. A. McGuire, the donor.

the fur trade of the West. I became fascinated by reports of incidents buried in more important data, descriptions of encounters with the grizzly, the most dread animal of the lands beyond the Missouri. Humorous or tragic, the episodes were stated matter-of-factly, for the most part, and I was struck by the unsentimental mention of high adventure. Recalling the men I had known who had also met the grizzly, some terribly disfigured as a consequence, whose experiences paralleled those in the early histories, I resolved to preserve, from the documents and from the recollections of old-timers of my acquaintance and others, all the accounts I could find of meetings with bears. Here, then, accurate and authentic, are narratives that, in most instances, would otherwise be lost to the generations for whom the West is only a legend. Some of the tales are familiar, such as the history of Hugh Glass, or have appeared in many versions, such as the story of Utah's Old Ephraim; but many others would have languished indefinitely in dusty volumes on library shelves or in obscure historical archives, or simply would have perished with the men who lived them, being nowhere else recorded.

Reading these narratives, I am filled with a sense of change. In my long lifetime I have seen much, and I think myself fortunate in the extreme to have been part of that historical moment we call the Old West, as well as part of the new. Many grizzlies still roamed the Utah Territory when I was born there in 1870, but I never had the desire to hunt or kill one, although as a boy I cured the hide of a huge grizzly that had killed one of my father's sheepherders. From earliest boyhood I heard stories of the exploits and prowess of this lordly animal, which is, to my way of thinking, the most intelligent and interesting animal in the wild. And I have known several men who grappled in solitary combat with him, whose tales thrilled me as a boy and thrill me yet. I learned early to respect both the men and the bears.

I would like this collection to be my modest tribute to all that has gone before. The grizzly bears of these tales are gathered under one cover in a variety of guises: objects of curiosity or sport, menaces and marauders, challenges and trophies; but all are ghosts from an epoch whose like we will never see again; their stories create a remembrance of what once was and can be no more. To this end, the grizzly is an appropriate symbol.

My purpose has been to present the various phases of the white man's contact with the largest and fiercest of North American mammals, in stories which portray the intelligence and determination of man pitted against the instinct and strength of the bear. This was a contest for dominance in the wilderness that has been concluded only in the present century, and not many years ago. Were it not for the modern repeating rifle, the struggle would have lasted longer and the antagonists would have been more evenly matched. Most of these stories are from the earlier times, when man and bear met on relatively equal terms; the days of muzzle-loaders and small-bore firearms, which were not entirely reliable, when man as well as bear had to rely on cunning, strength, endurance, and luck.

Adventures with bears were common in the early days when there were few men and many bears. In those morning years of the nineteenth century, all was plenitude. Prairies and mountains beyond the Missouri River teemed with wildlife of every sort, a prodigality of riches that invited casual slaughter by the white men venturing there. The journals of Lewis and Clark note the great abundance of deer, buffalo, elk, geese, ducks, and prairie chickens, as well as bears, which the party quickly found to be as dangerous as the Indians had warned. This expedition gave the world its first scientific information about the grizzly bear, providing data for the Smithsonian Institution. Not long after Lewis and Clark's landmark trek, Lustig's company, on a single journey up the Missouri by boat in 1812/13, killed, by my count of their records, 81 buffalo, 116 deer, 14 bears, 20 elk, and 11 turkeys; many of these animals were shot from the boat and the rest were slaughtered in brief forays along the nearby range.

A steady stream of enterprising and expectant men went westward. The 1830s were the heyday of the mountain men, those adventuresome wanderers who plied the arduous fur trade, men such as Charles Larpenteur on the upper Missouri and Zenos Leonard in the Rocky Mountains. Many of these men had been fired by the tales of those returning to civilization laden with pelts. The older trappers had taken their share of the bounty, but much remained for younger ones. Zenos Leonard's narrative provides a clear sense of the available game in 1831, when, at the onset of his journey across Kansas, he marvels at the numbers of buffalo, elk, deer, and antelope visible on the prairie. On the Laramie River he found some places literally covered with game, among these the "Grizzly, Red and White Bear." The way west, it would seem, was crowded with animals. Yet Leonard and his men found game scarce in harsh mountain country, where they had to kill such meat as they could, not as they chose. But no man in all the western territories could travel very far for very long without seeing the grizzly bear, and until this time there were more sightings than meetings.

As the pressures of man increased, however, wildlife populations decreased, with beaver, buffalo, and grizzly bear sharing the fate of being hunted to near extinction in the span of a man's lifetime. It was not unusual or considered wasteful for a hunter to bring down a bull buffalo in order to take only the tongue or a cut of choice hump meat. Many mountain men, whose appetites became omniverous (like the grizzly's, by necessity), favored cub meat as a delicacy, and of course they usually had to kill the mother bear in order to obtain it; but to them this only made one less varmint of which to be wary.

Typical of those men of the mountains was the guide Captain John Gunnison took on in southeastern Colorado in 1831, a man of Spanish extraction who had spent his entire life in the wilds of the mountains as trapper, trader, hunter, scout, and guide, who knew the mountains well from Colorado to the Pacific, and who claimed to have lived nine years on meat alone, without tasting bread or salt. This man, Messalino, killed all he ate and said he never saw a grizzly bear but that he took a shot at him. "I try to hit in the right spot," he said, "but if I miss it I have to run." According to Captain Gunnison, there were not many such hunters, courageous enough to charge the grizzly bear without a well-equipped companion to assist; for the animal is dangerous even when fatally shot. In his journey west in 1846, Francis Parkman also came to know a redoubtable mountain man, Henry Chatillon, a man of quiet temper yet great courage, who was reliably reported to have killed more than thirty grizzly bears.

In California during the 1850s, a man who kept his eyes sharp for a few days could spot a hundred grizzlies roaming the hills above Monterey. In 1848, the account of Henry Tinsley reports, a party of five hunters spent a year looking for grizzlies in Oregon and brought back 700 scalps to Sutter's Fort, from whence they started. And as late as 1861 California officials offered a ten-dollar bounty for each grizzly bear scalp, several hunters garnering more than a hundred scalps in a year.

In spite of all the killing that had gone before, grizzlies were a frequent hazard during the years of intensive settlement in the Rocky Mountains in the 1860s. So numerous were they in the valleys of northern Utah that they threatened even the most peaceable and settled resident. An incident remembered even to this day occurred in Cache Valley in 1864, when a man was literally torn apart by a bear he surprised in a thicket as he went to collect firewood one November day. His killing prompted a form of reprisal much used in those days. Many of his neighbors from Mendon Fort swept out in a posse in pursuit of the bear, some on horseback and some afoot. They followed the tracks of the bear and its two yearling cubs. One man carried his gun butt-end forward as he trudged over the snow. When the bear suddenly rose on its hind feet not ten feet in front of him, he tried to turn his gun around but could not because the bushes were so thick. Another man ran forward and shoved the muzzle of his big gun into the bear's mouth and tried to shoot, but the gun did not fire. Several other men, crowding close to the bear standing by a tunnel in the thicket, shot her, then shot one of the cubs that came out of the tunnel. The other cub ran off to the mountains. It was a hard winter, so the poor settlers of Mendon Fort dressed both bears and ate fairly well for the winter. Fortunately no men were injured in that melee, but across the valley to the east that same year another man was not so lucky. A grizzly was spotted plundering a squash patch. When the irate settler summoned his neighbors, some of them, grabbing up whatever weapon came first to hand, were armed with only cudgels and scythes. One man thrust the muzzle of his gun into the bear's mouth, and his gun, like the Mendon Fort settler's, failed to fire. But this man was raked by hind claws and killed by the bear who stood at bay. It requires great bravery or foolhardiness to put one's body needlessly close to an enraged grizzly. Hunters who do are fortunate indeed to escape with their hides intact. In those days, firing the charge into the bear's mouth was thought to insure a fatal shot. But on occasion it was the man who died.

Where bears proved to be a continuing menace or nuisance to growing communities, the men would mount "bear-sweeps" from time to time, as they did in Salt Lake Valley, and rid an area of bears by means of close-ranked, intensive hunting. In this manner the "varmints" were driven into the mountains and the valleys made safe for the settlers. But neither were the bears spared in the mountains, for the stockmen increasingly used these for ranges. As the mountains filled up with sheep and cattle it was difficult for a grizzly bear to make his vast circuits without bumping into sheep camps or range cattle. Proximity brought its own rewards, however, and occasionally a bear would acquire a distinct preference for mutton or beef or both and deliberately seek out his meals.

As a boy I spent several summers tending sheep for my father and older half-brothers in the Uintah Mountains, and I often saw bears there, always more blacks than grizzlies. I knew several herders who had met the grizzly personally, or whose herds had been molested by him. The old sheepherders were very casual about him. One of these, John Oliver, worked for my brother. One day John, a determined man from Missouri, looked out of his tent and was surprised to see three bears on the bed-ground — an old she-bear and two half-grown cubs. John sat down and put four cartridges, which I had just recently loaded, into his gun and calmly stepped out to greet the bears. With the four shells, he shot the old one twice and also killed the two cubs. Of course they were going about their bear business and not attacking. But John was absolutely fearless, and I think he was typical of the herders in those mountains, whose lonely job made them vulnerable to injury or death, often caused by marauding bears. Bears often visited the sheep camps. In the night, whenever the dogs barked and the sheep ran, old John would put on his shoes, take the .45–.70, and go out through the timber and round them up. It just happened that he never ran into any hungry grizzlies. But other of my brothers' herders were not as lucky.

One of the most unusual stories of bears molesting sheep came from my brother Fera, who as a young man moved three thousand head of ewes from the Uintah Mountains to Carter Station, Wyoming, to be delivered to a buyer. He had just one companion, so progress was difficult and slow. Making camp at dusk one day, they noticed the sheep crowding down toward the creek. Fera ran below the sheep and saw a big black bear. When the bear saw Fera he raised up on his hind legs and showed his teeth. Fera yelled to Rob to bring the gun. The bear dropped to all fours and ran away. So Fera returned to camp. In the night he heard horse bells and the horses running in their hobbles. He dressed quickly and ran out of the tent, shouting over his shoulder to Rob to bring the gun, as the sheep were all gone. Fera worked his way among the sheep, trying to determine the trouble, and in the light of the full moon he observed four bears boxing at the sheep and roaming after the outsiders, in the manner that a bunch of pups would play. Down in the hollow below was the other part of the herd, milling and running, with five more bears romping after them. Fera yelled as loud as he could, and to his surprise all the bears ran for the timber. He rounded up the sheep and brought them back to camp. When he went into the tent he found Rob still sound asleep, the rifle leaning against the tent pole. Next day no dead sheep were found anywhere, and my brother always maintained that bears, at least black bears, play with sheep first and then kill them. Possibly these bears were unfamiliar with sheep, because they were still young bears and were enjoying their first meeting before an anticipated feast.

I have no reports of grizzlies making sport of their victims. It is the black bear that has the reputation for playfulness, not his cousin. Even the biggest black bear makes tracks when the grizzly king hoves into sight. The difference in reputation between these two varieties of bears is nowhere more clearly indicated than in their generic names: The black bear is called *Ursus americanus,* but the grizzly is *Ursus horribilis.*

The concluding episodes in the story of the grizzly bear concern the "outlaw" bears who ravaged the herds in the ranges between 1880 and 1915. They were killer bears, but their threat was principally to range stock, not ranchers. Though they made their kills frequently, in the areas chosen as their territories, they were seldom sighted. Encounters with these bears had to be deliberately sought, and sometimes were, when stockmen posted large bounties for their destruction. Capturing the bear required weeks, months, and sometimes years of patient tracking and repeated efforts. The plentiful bears of early days shrank into solitary phantom creatures whose pawprints or handiwork was the single evidence of their existence.

Joaquin Miller said at century's turn that the grizzly went out as the American rifle came in. Hounded out of his domain, he hid by day and pillaged by night. One of the last of the California bears, which had been the object of a standing reward posted by a number of interior counties for several years, finally, in his old age, was discovered by hunters. They crept into the lair where the old grizzly king lay, nearly blind and dying of old age, and dispatched him with a volley from several Winchesters. They found him to be almost toothless, his paws terribly mutilated from the cruel bites of numerous steel traps, and his carcass bearing enough lead, Miller reported, to sink a small ship.

Some of these last, tenaciously troublesome bears acquired a personality and legend of their own, bears such as Old Mose, Old Clubfoot, Three Toes, and Old Ephraim, to name only those of local fame when I was raising my family and beginning my teaching career in Utah. These were all bears who had acquired an appetite for freshly killed lamb or steer, and they killed with the same discriminating taste shown by the early buffalo hunters, disemboweling a lamb to taste the liver or taking but a few morsels from a felled steer. They prowled the vicinity for many years, some of them survivors of earlier scourgings whose pawprints showed the effects of traps, and they demonstrated uncanny intelligence in eluding their hunters.

Old Ephraim was one of the very last of these. When his career ended in 1923, the day of the grizzly bear effectively came to an end. Even he was something of a relic, his long career lasting between thirty and forty years of *noticed* activity. Some people who have written about Old Ephraim have asked, "How came he among the Wasatch Mountains? And why did he live out his wandering life alone?" These writers may not have known that though many bears have been killed in the Wasatch Mountains, even more have lived there. As to his living a solitary life, we do not know for a fact that he did. Frank Clark, the man who shot Old Ephraim, showed my son and me the tracks of another grizzly in the same hollow where Old Ephraim was killed, three years after the event.

The Indian alone held the grizzly bear in reverential awe and seldom attacked him single-handedly. In the Southwest the Spanish conquistadors met him with their long spears. The earliest expeditions of Americans regarded him with curiosity and fear. In Old California the vaqueros and Spanish dandies lassoed him and forced him to fight bulls to the death in strong corrals, while wagers were laid on the outcome. Trappers many times were forced to use Bowie knives in hand-to-hand encounters with him. Kit Carson allowed he was never so frightened as when two grizzly bears kept him up a small quaking aspen for two hours. Many an unsuspecting pioneer settler was knocked cold by a blow from the grizzly's powerful paw, or died in his embrace. Stockmen and hunters reduced the remnants of the once great tribe of Old Ephraim to near extinction. Today a traveler to the West must visit Yellowstone or Glacier Park, the established wildlife preserves, to see a bear, and of those seen very few are grizzlies.

Perhaps it is not wise to speculate too imaginatively; even so, Wasatch forests are large and deep and may still hold a few surprises; I would like to think that those pawprints Frank Clark showed me were a sign that there is yet, somehow, a descendant of the descendants of Lewis and Clark's "white bears," roaming the timbered flanks of the Utah mountains, free and unperturbed by encroaching civilization, self-sufficient and solitary. It has been quiet on the high ranges all the years since Old Ephraim's death. Most men take this to mean there are no more bears, but I prefer to think it means only that there are no bears with an appetite for mutton on the hoof.

F. M. YOUNG
1947

The Bear on the Trail

I have spent a fair share of my life in the Utah mountains, which I know and love well, and have seen many bears in the woods. Utah at one time had a very large bear population, both black and grizzly, particularly in the settled valleys where willow growth along the streams invited succulent forage. Even after the bears were driven into the mountains they were still numerous and a common hazard to herders on the ranges there. So numerous were they that as late as 1925 I saw bear prints like cow tracks in the dust of aspen and alder glades in the Wasatch mountains. Although I have seen many bears, I never had much desire to hunt and kill one. An experience I had as a boy cured any bloodthirstiness I may have had. In itself nothing remarkable, the experience has stayed with me as a reminder of the fear man has traditionally felt for the wild animal. My courage faltered then because fear overmastered sense. The meeting with the bear on the trail gave me a lasting appreciation for the men who have acted with cool resourcefulness in the face of grizzly attack. And I think, too, that when a bear is savage to man it is because he recognizes man as the only creature dangerous to him.

I RECALL when I was fifteen years old. The farm work was pretty well up, and it was hot. Somehow I got courage enough to ask Father if I could have a week's vacation and take two of my friends and the farm team and go up to Weber Canyon, where my older brother George had a sheep camp. To my surprise, Father said we could go, provided that we bring home a load of dry aspen logs for kindling. So we got ready, taking Old Gray and Boley, the wagon, bedding, and grub, and away we went as happy as larks. I took a long-barreled rifle — Father's gun, but he let me keep it — which had been bored out to make a shotgun. Of course it was a muzzleloader. With it I occasionally shot quail for Father. I also carried a powder horn and a leather pouch and looked, I thought, like Daniel Boone or Davy Crockett.

We journeyed a day and a half and arrived at the summer supply camp in the late afternoon and found George there. He took my friends and the team to his camp and had me accompany a herder on horseback to a camp two or three miles further up the canyon. I took the gun. On the way a deer jumped up near the trail. I dismounted and fired at the fleeing animal. Nothing came of it, but it was exciting. I reloaded and soon saw a pine hen, which I shot and was very happy. That night for supper, Albert (the herder) and I had trout, which he had caught in the Weber River that day, and my chicken, so we ate well. Next day he was going to another camp to get a part of mutton, for the herders divided their mutton in warm weather, so he left me with his companion, Mr. Parks. Albert said he would be back about noon. Mid-morning next day I walked down the hollow to meet him and ride back to camp. I sat down by the trail to rest, and I heard a jaybird making a lot of noise in a bunch of trees nearby. I sat drowsily, my head resting on hand, elbow, and knee. Soon I thought I heard something approaching. Thinking it was Albert returning, I looked up and to my amazement and horror saw a large bear coming up the trail, no more than twenty steps away. His mouth was open and drooling, and I could see his white teeth and red tongue. I lost no time getting to my feet and starting for camp, up the canyon and a steep climb. I ran, shouting for Mr. Parks. He was deaf and I was a mile away, but fright or panic prompted the calling. I wondered why the bear didn't rush me and make an end of it all. I wondered why bears wanted to eat children — the story of children being eaten by bears in Second Kings came to me with frightful clarity. I felt very much a child. I keep looking over my shoulder at that bear. Once I fell down and lost my powder horn. I grabbed it up and kept on running. The bear just kept the same distance between us — I straining and panting, he ambling along the trail. He walked easily, and I ran hard; soon I was only walking, but I put into that effort all the strength I had.

For a mile the bear followed me. At last, after what seemed a very long time, I came to a rise of ground about 150 yards below camp, from which I could see Mr. Parks chopping wood. I shouted to him, "Bear!", tripped and fell flat. Parks saw me, and must have heard "Bear!", for he grabbed his rifle and hurried to me.

"Where is the bear?" he asked.

I pointed down the trail.

He scouted for a short distance, then came back and asked me to come and show him. I got up, poured a handfull of shot in my gun barrel and rammed it home. Fortified by the gun, I showed him the tracks. The bear had followed me just to the rise of ground below the camp, then turned up the hill into the timber. I looked for him and saw his dark coat partly hidden by a pine; he moved slowly up into the trees, stopping occasionally to look back at us with what I now know was benign curiosity. I didn't think so at. the time. The bear moved into the shadows, and I could not point him out to Mr. Parks, who, besides being mostly deaf, could not see well. So he never did catch sight of the bear, and soon the bear was gone.

I have thought many times about that bear. If a tree had been near when I first spotted him, I might have attempted to climb it. I did not know then that black bears can climb trees with ease. I know that bear intended me no harm, since it would have been an easy matter for him to overtake me. At the time, however, I felt enough fear for both of us.

That night the sheepherders said they could hear my heart beating across the tent. Well, I was very frightened. Never so frightened before or since. I had always been a timid boy. As I scrambled up the long trail back to camp that day, I made a vow that if the bear spared my life I should never again be afraid of the dark or of any man. I think that resolve, which I have always remembered, has helped me many times. I used to think that man, because of his reason, would not harm other men without good cause, but experience has taught me that bears can be less dangerous than men.

That bear marked the beginning of my high regard for bears in general, and grizzly bears in particular, and to him I dedicate this book of bear stories.

Characteristics of Bears

GRIZZLY BEARS usually mate in June or July, and the gestation period is about seven and a half months. After mating, the male and female go their own ways, the female finding her own cave or bed for winter. For the most part, the grizzly chooses a spot near the timber line or on some rather remote hillside in a ravine or canyon. During its long sleep, or dozing, the bear lives on the accumulation of fat stored during the feeding season.

Cubs are born any time from January to March. They are very small and helpless, weighing only ten to twenty ounces, about the size of a ground squirrel, with practically no hair or fur, blind (the eyes open in about fourteen days), no teeth at birth, and small, sharp claws. From one to four babies are born at a time, though usually the number is two or three. The mother bear keeps her little ones warm and well nourished. She seldom leaves the den during the early nurture and not at all while the cubs are very young.

It is the mother bear's responsibility to care for the new generation alone. She will fight and drive away any male bear or other animal that might attempt to molest her or her young ones. A naturalist at Yellowstone Park told me of seeing a male grizzly trying to attack two cubs. The mother drove her cubs up a tree for protection, then fought the male. Whenever he attempted to go up the tree after the cubs, the mother would pull him down.

Occasionally, after the cubs have grown a bit and are able to care somewhat for themselves in the den, she will venture out for short periods. It is then that the fisher (called the black cat) or fox will steal into the den and carry off a baby bear. These animals are the principal enemies of the young grizzly. If the mother returns while these pillagers are in the cave or den, she makes quick disposal of them.

When the cubs are about two months old, weighing between ten and twenty pounds, and of a size with a mountain hare, the mother leads them forth to learn the art of making a living. A good teacher but a strict disciplinarian, she teaches her little ones how to play and how to work; how and when to travel and when and where to lie low; what herbs are good and where to find them; how to meet and treat other animals. There is not a more sagacious animal than the grizzly bear, or a more concerned mother. Hard-pressed victims of attack have more than once found occasion to be grateful for this concern, when the mother, in the midst of administering a mauling, pauses in her fury in order to cuff her cubs to keep them out of danger.

Though the grizzly's eyesight is its poorest sense, its ears and nose are among the very best in all nature, and the mother grizzly teaches her young how to use the knowledge that comes through these senses to good advantage. Grizzly cubs are apt pupils. Enos Mills found them to be the most energetic, alert, and individualistic of all the wild young he was familiar with. Their senses, instinct, and intelligence grant these animals extraordinary curiosity and powers of concentration.

The young remain with the mother during the first season of their lives, ever learning how a bear makes a living and protects itself. Then they go into hibernation with her, thus learning how to make a comfortable den for the long winter sleep. I am confident the mother bear instructs her cubs in useful matters on warm days while they are lying in shady nooks or basking in the berry patches on sunny hillsides, and also as cold approaches and they withdraw into the dry, dark recesses of their winter shelter. When the cubs emerge the second season they are husky, active creatures weighing around two hundred pounds, approaching independent status and nearly able to fend for themselves.

At the end of the second feeding season, the old bear gives the youngsters a good farewell cuffing and sends them on their way to carve a life of their own in the wild. Because of the extended maternal period, mother grizzlies as a rule bring forth young only every second year.

The young bears stay together another year or more, a dominant one usually assuming leadership. When a hunter runs onto three or four grizzlies in a group they may be all of one family. Although at one time it was thought to be the case, grizzlies are not, according to best authority, naturally gregarious. When a number of bears are seen together it is most likely because of a common feeding ground and not because they care for company. Joaquin Miller saw grizzlies far up the Sacramento feeding together in numbers under the trees, "as tranquilly as sheep." The grizzly bear's ferocity is easily exaggerated.

During their first year young grizzlies have been known to climb trees, but after the second winter their claws have grown so long that tree climbing is not for them. An interesting observation about grizzlies climbing was given by General Fremont, who thought the grizzly a gregarious creature. In his report to the government in 1847, he told of observing what he took to be a family of grizzly bears gathering acorns on a grassy hill set with oaks. They appeared to be having a commotion, and when Fremont and his men approached cautiously to see better, he noticed that several huge grizzlies stood under the boughs gathering and eating the acorns that grizzly cubs threw down from the branches above. When the cubs, seeing the men on horseback, began backing down the tree, the older bears, which had not yet discovered the men, drove the young bears back up the tree as if they had been children.

When mature, a grizzly has claws from four to seven inches long; not curved and sharp like the black bear's, but large, slightly curved, and somewhat concave on the underside, very much resembling a chisel, and well-adapted for digging, tearing logs apart, and fighting, when necessary. With these unique tools the grizzly will remove huge quantities of earth and rocks quickly in pursuit of a rodent morsel or dig a pit large enough to bury the carcass of a range bull, which he carefully covers up to insure a future meal for himself. And of course the claws are formidable weapons in combat, cutting like razors and strong as steel.

The walk or run of a grizzly is peculiarly his own. It resembles the movement of a rocking horse; front and hind legs of one side move together, giving the animal the appearance of shuffling along, but he can shuffle very rapidly when need be. He has a sort of loping run, half again as fast as that of the black bear, and he can outrun a man, as many have discovered to their grief; it takes even a fast horse to keep up with him, not to mention outdistance him, in a short chase.

This member of the great bear family continues to grow larger and stronger until he reaches maturity, in the seventh or eighth year. At that time he varies in size from four hundred to one thousand pounds. A grizzly bear at the Chicago zoo was weighed at 1153 pounds. The biographer of James Capen Adams says that Adams's Old Sampson tipped the hayscales at 1500 pounds. Many hunters have estimated grizzlies they have killed to weigh from one thousand pounds to one ton; but a bear may look very large to a man out in the wilds.

Much has been written concerning the size of grizzlies. It was long a custom of mountaineers and hunters to speak of the size of bears in terms of the size of their tracks. Enos Mills gave the measurements of the largest grizzly track he had seen as slightly more than thirteen inches long and seven and a half inches wide. This length did not include the claws, which are sometimes seven inches long. Townsend's grizzly had a lateral footspan of ten inches and claws of seven inches. Than Galloway measured the foot of a Colorado grizzly at a little more than fourteen inches. Yet tracks do not always indicate the size of a bear, any more than footprints do the size of a man.

There have in fact been many huge grizzlies. Than Galloway, the Utah bear hunter, reported killing one so large that its skin, when stretched to dry, covered one end of a good-sized cabin. A bear is measured from the tip of the nose to the root of the tail; not that it would do much good to measure to the end of the tail, for this appendage is notoriously short. In early days it was a standing joke among the otherwise dignified Indians to induce one unacquainted with the grizzly bear to take hold of its tail. Despite the size of its tail, the grizzly is commonly a large bear, and many of the stories in this collection comment on its great size. An interesting footnote to the tale of Old Ephraim is that when his skull was presented to the Smithsonian Institution by the Boy Scouts of Cache Valley, the year following his death, the curator reported that it was the largest grizzly specimen they had had an opportunity to examine — a statement that the Smithsonian recently confirmed.*

The age to which the grizzly lives is not definitely known, but

* The Smithsonian corroborated this record in 1960, when I wrote to them concerning Old Ephraim's reputed size. In 1978 the skull was returned to Utah State University in Logan, Utah, on permanent "loan." [Editor's note]

informed estimates vary between twenty-five and forty years. Old Mose, the Colorado cattle killer, is said to have been at least forty-five years old. The Pine Valley marauder, Old Clubfoot, was known to have been engaged in his pastime for thirty-five years and may even have been full-grown before he began killing. Old Ephraim roamed nearly thirty years in the mountains above Bear Lake. These animals all had characteristic tracks, so there is some basis for their alleged longevity. Grizzly accounts often stress the age of the bear, perhaps giving it an exaggerated importance. Still, it is a little strange that I know of no tales concerning Young Mose, Young Ephraim, or Young Three Toes. This emphasis suggests something about the relationship between bear and man. It may be that the grizzly's hoary appearance invests him in early life with the semblance of age. More likely, it results from man's assumption that the longer the years of wilderness living, the more the bear is endowed with wisdom and cunning; longevity thus makes him a worthier adversary, a fitter foe for man, and man's triumph is therefore sweeter. This is true, I believe, for both the Indian and the white man.

Originally the home of the grizzly bear extended from the barren lands of the Far North southward through Alaska and down the spine of the Rocky Mountains, even into Mexico; and from the foothills east of the Rockies it extended west to the Pacific coast. There was some variance of species in this large range; in fact there were probably several such, among them the California grizzly, the Wasatch grizzly, the Rocky Mountain grizzly, and the Kodiak bear of Alaska.

James Capen Adams, the grizzly hunter of California in the 1850s, said that the California bear was larger than the Rocky Mountain or Wasatch grizzly, but not so ferocious. Adams hunted more extensively in California than in the Rockies, but he found that in both areas the grizzly male selected his own range and maintained preemption rights thereon. Old Mose, for instance, was credited with a range of seventy-five miles in diameter. Old Ephraim's territory, though narrow, was at least fifty miles in length. Ernest Thompson Seton also holds to the idea of grizzly estates. It may be the case that grizzlies mark the boundaries of their territories as do wolves, for it was early noted that old male bears have a habit in the late spring and early summer months of biting the bark of certain trees at the highest point they can reach when standing on their hind legs. To the experienced observer, these "bear signs" are precise indicators of the size of the bear. Some have thought these marks are made while the animal is sharpening his teeth, but others think it probable that he leaves his mark as a challenge to rivals in amours or territorial claims.

Grizzly bears vary in color. There is no law of coloration that I know of. Some are nearly black, others black and white, brown, or cinnamon; both grizzlies and black bears are sometimes cinnamon-colored, so color is no criterion for differentiation. Once even the experienced hunter W. H. Wright mistook a grizzly for a black bear and in trying to tree it with dogs had the fight of his life.

According to Captain Mayne Reid, an English adventurer who hunted these bears during the 1840s, the grizzly is more like the brown bear of Europe than any other species. The fur is typically long and shaggy and does not present the even surface that characterizes the coat of the black bear. Reid found it to be commonly of a dark brown color, the hair whitish at the tips, especially during the summer season when the coat is generally lighter in color. All the bears he observed had heads of grizzled gray, and it is this characteristic that has given the animal its specific name. There are also white-breasted black bears, but this condition occurs when white hairs are intermingled in the fur, and it has been noted that these odd hairs are white to the roots, whereas the hoary appearance of the grizzly is caused by only the tips of the hair being white; this gives the true grizzly his name of silver tip, a term usually applied to the Wasatch grizzly. Though the grizzly coat varies from brown to reddish brown, bay to cinnamon, as does that of the black bear, the Indians were able to distinguish him from the black bear at a glance.

All who would recognize the grizzly need take note of significant differences between him and the black bear. Size is a help, but not a certain indicator, as many black bears, especially in California, attain huge size and can weigh as much as six hundred to eight hundred pounds. Other differences are apparent in the ears, which on the grizzly are shorter, more conical, and set wider apart; the claws, which are longer and broader and lighter colored than those of other species; the huge paw, which is broader and longer than that of other bears; and the tail, which is so short and inconspicuous that it is completely buried under the fur of the buttocks. But most characteristic are the humped shoulders of the grizzly, with their roach-like hairs, and the broad, dish-faced head. Some grizzlies have measured thirteen inches between the ears. The skull of Old Ephraim was sixteen inches long, which is very large even for a grizzly, and it completely filled a bushel basket.

Few people have desired grizzly bears as pets. James Capen Adams was one exception. He captured a female cub in Oregon and named her Martha Washington. She became remarkably domesticated and followed Adams through the mountains, where on cold winter nights he would build a fire and have the bear lie down near it, then cuddle himself up very cosily between the bear and the fire. In 1854 he captured the cub Ben Franklin. To raise this cub he took two pups away from a greyhound dog named Rambler, and the grizzly, Ben Franklin, grew to maturity close chums with the dog. This bear was Adams's close companion during his later years, once saving his life from a wounded grizzly by engaging it in combat while Adams reloaded his gun. Adams would pack his camp equipment on Ben or load a deer upon his back to carry to camp. After he quit hunting, he kept a small museum where he let children ride Ben for a dime. Adams demonstrated that the monarch of the mountains, the much feared and maligned grizzly, could be wholly domesticated and become a true and loyal friend.

Yet captivity, however gentle and kindly, is not to a bear's liking, and, ironically, Adams's death resulted from the effects of a blow to the head administered by his domesticated grizzly. Most captive bears seem to resent their present condition. I knew of a bear with a long memory that resented its captor for years. Three Utah hunters at the head of Weber Canyon ran onto a mother black bear and two cubs and followed her for a considerable distance. She and the cubs crawled into her den. The hunters fired and wounded her, and she came out of the den angry and dangerous. So they killed her and the cub who followed her. The other cub stayed in the den, which was a deep hole. One of the hunters took the cub home and chained it up. The hunter who captured him visited the cub frequently as it grew older. It always showed savagery toward him but not toward the other man, and when the captor decided to take the bear to his home the animal seemed never to forgive him and showed such ferocity that he finally felt compelled to kill it. Such are the tender mercies of the hunter who would domesticate wild orphans.

James Oliver Curwood, who loved and admired bears above all other creatures of the wild, also desired to have one for a pet, but wisely forbore raising a captive cub. Though there have been several accounts of close companionship between men and bears, even of Indian women suckling bear cubs, I have never heard of exceptional closeness to a grizzly cub except for James Capen Adams's experiences.

Townsend's statement, made early in the nineteenth century, reflects the prevailing sentiment toward these wild young: "We have sometimes taken young grizzly bears, but these little fellows, even when not larger than puppies, are so cross and snappish, that it becomes dangerous to handle them, and we could never become attached to any animal so ungentle, and therefore young "Ephraim" (to give him his mountain cognomen), generally meets with very little mercy from us when his evil genius throws him in our way."

Yet Adams's remarkable success domesticating the great bear prompted Enos Mills to conclude that in this respect, as well as in other points, the grizzly resembles the dog and may in fact be a distant cousin. Mills attempted to trace the ancestry of the grizzly and advanced the idea that ancestors of the Rocky Mountain grizzly came from Kamchatka, the peninsula of eastern Siberia where large brown bears similar to the Kodiak bear still exist. Mills never makes mention of any kinship of the bear to the swine family. It is incomprehensible to me how the rangers and employees of the Federal Predatory Animal Department of the National Parks ever got into their vocabulary the words *boar* and *sow*, in reference to grizzly bears. Could it be because they wallow in mud baths? If so, why not call buffalo and hippopotamuses boars and sows as well?

By common consent, the grizzly is known as an aristocrat among animals, as much the monarch of North America as the lion is of Africa and the tiger is of Asia. He is not only the most powerful of our wild animals but also the most intelligent, and is so esteemed by the three men most capable of judging him, namely, Dr. W. T. Hornaday, Enos Mills, and W. H. Wright. These authorities paid tribute to his intelligence by citing his cunning, his prowess, his adaptability to his surroundings, his choice of foods, his woodcraft, his sensibilities, his strategy of outwitting hunters, and the development of his senses, especially those of smell and hearing. Dr. Hornaday said that except for the monkey or ape, the grizzly's facial expression and general adaptability of head and body, which it uses to express its thoughts, exceed that of all other animals. Enos Mills admired the alertness of this animal, whose nose enabled it to outwit its enemies until the repeating, long-range rifle came into use. W. H. Wright, probably the greatest of the bear hunters, had a special .45-.90 repeating rifle made for his bear hunting. He said that trailing the grizzly bear is a great challenge, one of the most difficult and demanding, for not only is the grizzly phenomenally quick to catch every sound, and not only is his sense of smell amazingly developed, but he is also unusually cunning in guarding himself against danger from the rear. Enos Mills supports this view, noting that the bear has the skill, audacity, and speed to slip around and follow interestedly along behind the individual who is trailing him.

G. O. Shields, another notable hunter, used a Winchester .50-.95. I know of several Utah grizzlies that were taken with much smaller guns, in particular the .25-.30 used in killing Old Clubfoot, Old Ephraim, and Three Toes. But in early days the muzzleloaders brought man and bear into much closer proximity, so that the bear could sniff out an intruder and quietly fade unseen into the trees. It is the conclusion of all who have studied this bear that the development of the repeating rifle, with its long range and massive power, limited the story of the white man and the grizzly bear to one century. Yet even during one hundred years of hunting and destruction of the bears, continuous and mounting conflict with settlers, and shrinking wilderness preserves, as ranchers took over the ranges, the grizzly has managed to survive by his skills. Enos Mills claims that the grizzly developed the trait of concealing his trail, and thus eluding pursuit, out of necessity, after coming into contact with the white man and the repeating rifle. There might be truth to this, because it is common knowledge that the grizzly bear fears only man and other grizzlies. His resourcefulness, historically, has enabled him to survive in areas where other animals have become extinct, as the Tar Pits of Los Angeles testify.

Bear wisdom is apparent in the grizzly's ability to be vegetarian as well as meat-eater, depending upon the kind of food available. Grizzlies eat roots, vegetables, berries, fruits, nuts, grubs, and insects. Their favorite meat may well be elk, particularly that of the young calves; fawns are also fancied. A Yellowstone Park ranger gave an interesting example of this taste for elk when he told me about something he observed near Fishing Bridge one evening. A cow elk was a short distance from where he stood, walking back and forth in the tall meadow grass but keeping her head turned toward the timber nearby. Soon a large grizzly bear left the timber and hurried toward the elk; she ran out of his reach, then stopped to look back and watch the bear, who suddenly lost interest in her. Then began a systematic search by the grizzly. He walked through the grass for twenty or thirty yards in an almost straight line, then, stepping over a few yards laterally, walked back the same distance, paralleling his first sweep. The bear, to the amazement of the ranger, kept this up for some time, ever widening the range of his search. Seeing only the bear and the elk, the ranger was puzzled about the bear's object. After four or five narrow sweeps, the bear finally left the meadow, but not without first giving a farewell glance at the cow elk, which had never left her place in the meadow or ceased watching the bear. After the bear was safely away, the elk walked out into the meadow, just beyond where the bear had so persistently searched, and roused her calf, which had been lying motionless, invisible, and apparently with little or no scent; and together they walked away whole.

There is much speculation but very little evidence that the grizzly's carnivorous preferences include human flesh. Most authorities claim that bears do not care for it. There have been reports of grizzly hunters who never returned to camp and whose skeletons later were found showing evidence that their flesh had been eaten, but one can only surmise as to what animals did the eating. More specific, but still problematical, are the two accounts cited by Dr. Hornaday, in which black bears in British Columbia are said to have eaten human flesh. In one case a man was killed and partially eaten before the bear was driven off; in the other, a seven-year-old boy was killed and partially eaten. Bear tracks convinced searchers that bears had done the killing. Yet killing and eating may have occurred separately and by different animals. In some instances of grizzly attack the flesh is so torn and rent that the body may give the appearance of having been partially eaten.

Less dramatically and more representatively, the grizzly works hard for what he eats. Though mostly vegetarian, he is willing to devote time and energy digging deep and large holes in rocky hillsides, to unearth one small squirrel. His mundane diet does not interest us as much as his exotic fare. It is an accepted part of grizzly lore that once he acquires a taste for sheep or cattle, particularly the young animal or the tender parts of mature animals, he becomes insatiable. Admittedly there have been several bears notable for their appetites for that kind of fresh meat, but their reputations have been rather more widely publicized than was necessary.

No one doubts the grizzly's strength: old-timers, trappers, and hunters tell of grizzlies killing buffalo and dragging or carrying the huge and heavy carcass some distance over rough terrain, then burying it. Many stories have been told of the grizzly catching a buffalo or steer by the head with one paw and with the other breaking its neck. One stroke of his paw can tear the hide and ribs from a victim. However, despite his great strength, the bear has not always been victorious in these encounters. One story, for which I cannot vouch, concerns a powerful bull that was charged by a bear in a forest and, retaliating, struck his horns into his assailant, pinning him to a tree. In this situation both were later found dead, the bull from starvation, the bear from wounds. I know of a Kodiak bear and a bull moose that, joined in a standoff battle, dueled each other to death. A bull or moose cannot be easily killed unless the bear surprises the animal and strikes first. All three — moose, bull, and grizzly — have a terrible tenacity that matches their strength.

Most competent writers on the grizzly agree that he is seldom the aggressor, but when wounded, closely pressed, or surprised, he becomes a juggernaut, springing to kill with all his power. There are various views on just how the grizzly attacks his foe. Some say the bear strikes for the face or head and bites the foe in these areas. Others state that the bear will hold the victim with one arm, while clawing and striking with the other and biting at the same time. W. H. Wright says he never saw a grizzly attack in an upright position or open his mouth as he charged. There may be exceptions to this, as in the instance of Old Ephraim. The standing bear probably assumes that position in order to better investigate a situation. There are reports of bears hugging and biting, or striking at the side of the head and biting when they can get a hold. There are enough stories of unfortunate men whose faces have been disfigured in this manner to support the idea that the head is a favorite target for the bear.

Yet I was much bothered on this point because of the conflicting opinions held by those who should know, until a young naturalist at Yellowstone Park, Lowell Biddulph, enlightened me. While he was on an observation trip in early spring, when there was still considerable snow on the ground, he used as headquarters a cabin near Dunraven Pass; it was built on a hillside with a window on the downhill side. He was in the custom of throwing table scraps out of that window. On an evening of full moonlight, when he could see clearly, a large grizzly bear came to eat the food. It was soon joined by another large grizzly. They began to quarrel over the food. Both rose on their hind legs and struck each other on the head, bit at the face and neck, and threw arms around each other and hugged and bit at each other's throat.

This account convinces me that a grizzly bear will use whatever means he can employ to best his antagonist and will, upon occasion, hug. To do this he stands. The strength of the bear's arms makes a very effective vise. Some of the most serious wounds hunters have received were made by a bear reaching up with his hind foot and tearing clothes and flesh from the victim, who was held by the bear's forearms. A curious thing about wounds inflicted by bears, which Hornaday and others have noted, is that bear bites and scratches almost never produce blood poisoning. Inquiry among hunters and park rangers, as well as doctors, supports this statement. This is strange, for the same kinds of wounds from wolves or lions frequently result in blood poisoning; it is all the more remarkable because bears like to scavenge garbage and stale meat, carrion even, and they dig and scratch in the dirt.

There is no question as to the courage of the grizzly bear. Yet despite all his well-documented temerity and bravery, when he is wounded or hurt he has been known to utter the most pathetic groans and whines imaginable. I would like to think that giving expression to his feelings in this way betokens his high degree of sensitivity. The wolf will suffer any agony or punishment and never make a sound.

Wright says a grizzly rushes to the fight on all four feet, with a growl and champing of teeth. A female grizzly bear is said to be one of the most ferocious of all wild animals when protecting her young, and she requires little provocation to do so, construing the actions of any intruder as a menace to her cubs. Yet even this formidable mother has been known to run away and leave her cubs when hunters have fought them.

Everyone who knows something of the nature of the grizzly bear agrees that coming upon a mother grizzly with cubs is the most dangerous kind of encounter. As illustration, a young ranger of my acquaintance had an experience of this sort in Yellowstone Park that, though he survived it, effectively terminated his career in the park service. He was surveying and counting timber in a little-frequented part of Yellowstone. Busily engaged in his work, he was too occupied to notice beforehand a slump in the terrain between his starting point and his objective. While stepping off his yardage, he suddenly came upon a large mother grizzly bear and two cubs that had been concealed from his view, in the slump. With a snap of her jaws, the grizzly charged the ranger, who, without any means of defense, ran for a fir tree and scrambled into its branches. He succeeded in springing high enough to catch a good hold on a limb, and he tried to climb out of reach of the angry bear; but before he could do so, she had caught one of his feet in her mouth. She shook his foot as a dog would shake a cat and crushed the bones of the instep and foot generally. She also clawed his leg. The ranger held on to the branch of the tree for dear life and endured the pain inflicted. After the bear was apparently satisfied with what she had done, or convinced she could do no more damage, she returned to her cubs and disappeared in the forest. The maimed ranger dropped to the ground and crawled four miles to a road, where he was picked up by a passing car and taken to a ranger station for first aid. The young man passed many months in a hospital. He never returned to his Park job. His experience with one grizzly was too much.

Some writers say that when a grizzly is shot in the body, he will bite the wound before charging. This may be true in a few cases, but I have no remembrance of any of the big bear hunters making such a statement. Some authorities, however, say a bear will rend, bite, or lick the wound when he has been hit. It is obvious, though, that the bear does not always pause for this purpose when shot, because he is too intent upon the destruction of his enemy to stop for minor actions. All accounts agree, however, that a wounded grizzly is a horror in fur and claws. He can be ravaged with bullets and still plunge forward attacking again and again, as in the case of the Wyoming bear that was riddled by fifty-four shots before dying.

Yet W. H. Wright thinks the vitality of grizzlies has been considerably overstated and the bear lore maintaining that a wounded grizzly is unstoppable, that he cannot bleed to death, and that a shot must penetrate a vital organ, preferably the brain, in order to kill is untrue. Many stories attest to the indomitable fury of the wounded bear, but all bullets that hit take their effect, though perhaps not soon enough or to a sufficient degree for some hunters' needs. For instance, while on the Powder River Expedition of 1865, Captain H. E. Palmer reported the destruction of a monstrous grizzly on the eastern slope of the Big Horn Mountains. This bear had taken shelter in a little plum patch. The trainmaster, a daring man, baited the bear by riding up to within a few rods of the patch. When the bear rushed out after him, the man would turn his mule so quickly the bear could not catch him. The men of the camp then poured a volley from their Sharp's rifles into the bear. The bear withdrew into the plum patch, was teased into the open again, and again was fired upon by the men. When the grizzly was finally downed they found his hide perforated with twenty-three balls. They estimated he weighed about 1800 pounds.

When approached too closely or suddenly, the grizzly rises immediately with a "hough, hough," a hideous noise, half grunt, half roar, which will cause even the stoutest heart to stand still and make the bravest man wish he were busy elsewhere. In the practice of martial arts, a grunt, growl, or shout can intimidate or deter an opponent. But I know of no human cry that can create as great a sense of terror as that "Woof!" of the grizzly bear.

A naturalist and a companion were once walking unarmed through a rough section of Yellowstone about three or four miles from a road, following the tracks of a large grizzly bear up a steep hill. The tracks in the light snow were over thirteen inches long. Just as the men came over the top a huge grizzly met them. He gave a loud "hough" and reared up. The ranger said the bear's eyes were plainly like ice, even in their color. The bear's mouth was open and drooling, and his big teeth showed. The men were frozen with consternation, the bear with surprise or indecision. For a few seconds the three stood thus; then the grizzly dropped to all fours and ran down the trail for about twenty yards and went off into the timber, and they could hear him crashing for half a mile.

My rancher cousin had a similar experience. While on a horsepack trip, Jack and his wrangler walked out to a grassy meadow near their camp just after daylight to bring in the horses and ran upon a mother grizzly with two cubs, about seventy-five yards away when first seen. The old bear immediately gave a "whoof" and rushed toward the two men, who carried no guns. Jack looked for trees to climb. He saw his wrangler looking intently at the nearest tree, and, since he was closer to it, the wrangler made a spring to climb up it. Jack knew they both could not get up that tree soon enough, if the bear continued her course, so he stood perfectly still to face the oncoming mother grizzly, while stories of what an angry grizzly mother might do crossed his mind. When within twenty yards, the bear came to a sudden stop, raised up on her hind legs, and gave the men a long look. She must have decided they were harmless, for she stood there a few moments, then dropped down and returned leisurely to her cubs and walked away. Both men felt their hair raise and their hearts thump and were thankful for whatever made the old grizzly change her mind.

A man who spent a lifetime in the mountains and observed

many grizzlies, Charles Hedrich, was convinced that when man encounters a grizzly in the wilds, what results — violence or indifference — depends very much upon the immediate previous experiences of the bear. As an illustration, he told of two forest rangers riding out of Jackson's Hole up Hoback Canyon, who suddenly heard a tremendous turmoil of growling and whining and crashing of brush on the hillside above them near a side hollow. They halted to listen. Soon there came rushing down the hollow and into the road a huge grizzly bear. When the bear saw the horsemen it rushed toward them with fierce growls and "houghs." The rangers turned their horses and raced down the canyon road, because, being unarmed, fleeing was all they could do in this situation. After chasing the horsemen for some distance and failing to overtake their horses, the bear stopped and went up a side ravine. The men halted, waited a bit, and then, curious as to the cause of the bear's behavior, retraced their tracks to where they first heard and saw the bear. They rode up to the little flat from which the bear had burst upon them. There they saw the ground torn up, the brush and grass crushed, and much hair and fur strewn around. From this they concluded that two grizzlies had met there and decided to settle an old grudge and had fought until the one, perhaps an old grizzly, had been beaten and driven away. The old bear, full of anger and humiliation, saw the two rangers and decided to take out his revenge on them. Hedrich says that the actions of a grizzly are very much the result of recent experiences: if he has had a good sleep or a good meal of berries or meat, he will go about his business and harm no one. If aggravated, he responds in kind and with telling force.

One cannot always predict what a bear will do, any more than one knows just what to expect from a man. Experience has proven that the grizzly mother can be a savage engine of destruction when she feels her cubs are threatened. We know, too, that surprising a grizzly of either sex is usually dangerous, as many good bear stories testify. And a hunter should always be wary in approaching his downed prey, for though the strength of a grizzly may have been overestimated, on occasion he is formidable and dangerous even when presumed dead. The downed bear is not always a dead one, as many men have discovered to their grief. Some of the most harrowing encounters, in fact, have occurred when the hunter, sure of his kill and excited, neglects to reload his gun and approaches the fallen animal too closely. The bear may still have energy and fury enough to close on the man.

I knew a rancher up near Henry's Lake, in Idaho, who had gone after a grizzly he noticed eating at the carcass of a long-dead cow. He fired, at a good shooting distance, and the bear keeled over but was quickly up and running away. The rancher, a good shot, fired his .30-.40 five more times and made that many hits. On the fifth shot the bear went down and stayed there. Supposing the bear to be done for, the rancher went up to it. When he poked it with his gun, the bear, to his surprise, sprang to its feet and attacked him. He placed one more shot. The bear, bleeding and red-eyed, gnashed him with her teeth and struck with her powerful arm, tearing him with her claws. Having thrown the man to the ground and satisfied herself that her antagonist was dead, the bear moved away. After walking about fifty yards she lay down, and later she was found dead there. The rancher was fearfully torn and lacerated and spent many months recovering.

Man feels both fear and admiration for the grizzly. He has respected and even, in some instances, as was the case with the Indians, venerated the grizzly bear's prowess and courage. The white man has on the whole been more grudging in his admiration, especially when he has felt his person or livestock to be threatened. The Indian alone has given his homage gladly. For the Indians, it was a signal honor to kill a bear in combat, when only spears, bows and arrows, or the limited rifle they had acquired from white traders were used. Chiefs sometimes wore necklaces of grizzly claws as indisputable tokens of their bravery.

There is still much to learn about this great creature of the western forests; study of his life and characteristics would surely result in our being less fearful of him and more understanding of the demands of his wandering, solitary existence. W. H. Wright said that the grizzly bear knows more about the habits of man than man knows about the bear. There must be truth in this statement, for the bear has survived somehow, despite the white man's unremitting efforts to destroy him. And the grizzly, unlike man, seems to fear nothing and no one.

II

MORNING YEARS

After Coronado: Spearing Bears

Alfred Barnaby Thomas

This account describes perhaps the first meeting of white men and grizzly bears of which we have any record, nearly one hundred years before Lewis and Clark met the white bear on the Missouri River. The bears in this account were undoubtedly grizzlies, although they were not yet known by that name and in fact had no distinguishing name.

In his excellent book reviewing the Diary of the Campaign of Governor Antonio de Valverde against the Ute and Comanche Indians in 1719, Alfred Barnaby Thomas gives us an interesting history of New Mexico and Colorado. Both the territory and the bears were new and strange to these explorers: we note the governor giving names to the various springs and campgrounds along the way.

THE EXPEDITION having set out from Santa Fe, crossed the river and went along its meadows for four leagues over level ground; his lordship gave the name of the place San Francisco. It is a cheerful spot with a beautiful view and excellent springs. On the left there is a range of mountains and on the right a very extensive plain. On this road today many deer and prairie chickens which moved about in flocks were caught to such an extent that nowhere else were more caught because of their abundance in

From *After Coronado* (University of Oklahoma Press, 1935), with the kind permission of the author.

this region. The governor hunted deer and chicken. On this day a
mountain lion and a wildcat were killed. At about sunset some
Indians came in running from a bear, which plunged into the
middle of the camp, throwing the people into confusion. With
great shouting and uproar, they killed him with many spear
thrusts and arrows. His strength and size were so formidable that
the governor was impelled to go with the chaplain to view it.

They camped at a spring the governor named Nuestra Señora
de Dolores. On the sixth of the present month of October, the
señor governor and all his camp left this spring of Nuestra
Señora de Dolores and marched over level land and through
many good pastures because it was grassy. On the road to the left
was a summit sloping to the east, heavily wooded with pines.
Having traveled some six leagues, they arrived at a spring which
had considerable water. There the camp was put up and the governor called it Nuestra Señora del Carmen. On this day before
the halt a bear was met. It was larger than the preceding ones, for
its size and height were probably greater than that of a donkey.
One of the soldiers went out and put a spear into him up to the
middle of the shaft. The brute turning around seized the lance,
and grasped the horse by the hocks. At the same time another
soldier went to the rescue and gave the bear another spear thrust.
The bear, seizing the horse by the tail, held him down and clawing viciously, tore a piece of flesh off the rump. Having tied the
bear up finally, they finished killing him. The soldiers who were
bringing up the rear guard of the cavalry met a female and two
cubs which they also killed.

The Grizzly as Lewis and Clark Found Him

Captain Meriwether Lewis

No account of the grizzly bear in early Western literature would be complete without the matter-of-fact mention of the first encounters with him by the trailblazing expedition of Lewis and Clark. In the journal of Meriwether Lewis we have a fund of information based on the first sightings of this bear by the men of the expedition. Their curiosity was scientific, and the data collected was to provide the Smithsonian Institution with its first opportunity to classify this great mammal of western America. Even these first objective observations show why legends quickly gathered around the "white bear," as he was designated to distinguish his "tipped" hair.

SATURDAY, APRIL 13, 1805. [Just above the entrance of the little Missouri into the great Missouri.] At the distance of ten miles further we passed the mouth of a large creek, discharging itself in the center of a deep bend. Of this creek and the neighboring country, Captain Clark, who was on shore, gave me the following description. "This creek I took to be a small river from its size and the quantity of water which it discharged; I ascended it one and a half miles and found it the discharge of a pond or small lake, which had the appearance of having formerly been the bed of the Missouri. Several small streams discharge them-

From *The Original Journals of the Lewis and Clark Expedition, 1804–1806,* edited by Reuben Gold Thwaites (New York: Dodd, Mead & Co., 1904).

selves into this lake. The country on both sides consists of beautiful level and elevated plains, ascending as they recede from the Missouri; there were a great number of swan and geese in this lake and near its borders I saw the remains of forty-three temporary Indian lodges, which I presume were those of the Assinniboins, who are now in the neighborhood of the British establishments on the Assinniboin river." This lake and its discharge we call Goose Egg from the circumstance of Captain Clark shooting a goose while on her nest in the top of a lofty cottonwood tree, from which we afterwards took one egg. The wild geese frequently build their nests in this manner, at least we have already found several in trees, nor have we as yet seen any on the ground, or sand bars where I had supposed from previous information that they most commonly deposited their eggs. Saw some buffalo and elk at a distance today but killed none of them. We found a number of carcasses of the buffalo lying along shore, which had been drowned by falling through the ice in the winter and lodged on shore by the high water when the river broke up about the first of this month. We saw also many tracks of the white bear of enormous size, along the river shore and about the carcasses of the buffalo, on which I presume they feed. We have not as yet seen one of these animals, tho' their tracks are so abundant and recent. The men as well as ourselves are anxious to meet with some of these bears. The Indians give a very formidable account of the strength and ferocity of this animal, which they never dare to attack but in parties of six, eight or ten persons; and are even then frequently defeated with the loss of one or more of their party. The savages attack this animal with their bows and arrows and the indifferent guns with which the traders furnish them; with these they shoot with such uncertainty and at so short a distance that (*unless shot thro' head or heart, wound not mortal*) they frequently miss their aim and fall a sacrifice to the bear. Two Minetaries were killed during the last winter in an attack on a white bear. This animal is said more frequently to attack a man on meeting with him than to flee from him. When the Indians are about to go in quest of the white bear, previous to their departure they paint themselves and perform all those superstitious rights commonly observed when they are about to make war upon a neighboring nation.

*   *   *

Monday, April 29, 1805. Set out this morning at the usual hour;
the wind was moderate; I walked on shore with one man. About
8 A.M. we fell in with two brown or yellow [white] bear; both of
which we wounded; one of them made his escape; the other,
after my firing on him, pursued me seventy or eighty yards, but
fortunately had been so badly wounded that he was unable to
pursue so closely as to prevent my charging my gun; we again
repeated our fire and killed him. It was a male not fully grown;
we estimated his weight at 300 pounds, not having the means of
ascertaining it precisely. The legs of this bear are somewhat
longer than those of the black, as are its talons and tusks incom-
parably larger and longer. The testicles, which in the black bear
are placed pretty well back between the thighs and contained in
one pouch like those of the dog and most quadrupeds, are in the
yellow or brown bear placed much further forward, and are sus-
pended in separate pouches from two to four inches asunder. Its
color is yellowish brown, the eyes small, black, and piercing; the
front of forelegs near the feet is usually black; the fur is finer,
thicker and deeper than that of the black bear. These are all the
particulars in which this animal appeared to me to differ from
the black bear; it is a much more furious and formidable animal
and will frequently pursue the hunter when wounded. It is
astonishing to see the wounds they will bear before they can be
put to death. The Indians may well fear this animal, equipped
as they generally are with their bows and arrows or indifferent fusees, but in the hands of skillfull riflemen they are by
no means as formidable or dangerous as they have been represented.

Sunday, May 5, 1805. Captain Clark and Drewyer killed the largest brown bear this evening which we have yet seen. It was a
most tremendous looking animal, and extremely hard to kill notwithstanding he had five balls through his lungs and five others in
various parts; he swam more than half the distance across the
river to a sandbar, and it was at least twenty minutes before he
died; he did not attempt to attack, but fled and made the most
tremendous roaring from the moment he was shot. We had no
means of weighing this monster; Captain Clark thought he
would weigh 500 pounds. For my own part I think the estimate
too small by 100 pounds. He measured 8 feet 7½ inches from the

most to the extremity of the hind feet, 5 feet 10½ inches around
the breast, 1 foot 11 inches around the middle of the arm, and 3
feet 11 inches around the neck; his talons, which were five in
number on each foot, were 4⅜ inches in length. He was in good
order; we therefore divided him among the party and made them
boil the oil and put it in a cask for future use; the oil is as hard as
hogs lard when cool, much more so than that of the black bear.
This bear differs from the common black bear in several respects:
Its talons are much longer and more blunt, its tail shorter, its
hair, which is of a reddish or bay brown, is longer, thicker and
finer than that of the black bear; his liver, lungs and heart are
much larger even in proportion with his size; the heart particularly was as large as that of a large ox. His maw was also ten
times the size of black bear and was filled with flesh and fish. His
testicles were pendant from the belly and placed four inches
asunder in separate bags or pouches. This animal also feeds on
roots and almost every species of wild fruit.

Saved by Three Grizzled Bears

David Thompson

Buried in this narrative is a remarkable instance of providence,
but so casually and modestly referred to that its significance can
easily be overlooked. The incident occurred in 1810 while
Thompson, an unusual and God-fearing man, was searching for
the source of the Columbia River with a small band of men,
laboriously traversing the dense snows of Athabasca Pass. His
little company was pursued by a band of Piegan warriors, who,
superior in their knowledge of the terrain, were closing the gap
between them. Suddenly, on the trail left by the fleeing men, the
Indians spied three grizzly bears. The Indians instantly perceived
the significance of the bears and dropped their pursuit. A man
who commanded bears was not to be trifled with. Thompson's
relation of the episode illustrates the need for careful readings of
these early journals, for few of the men make much of their re-
markable adventures.

HAVING NOW MADE an assortment of goods, wherewith to load
four canoes for the fur trade of the interior country, we left this
depot; and by the same route we had come proceeded to the
Saskatchewan River and continued to Cumberland House, where
we took dried provisions to keep us until we should come to
where the bisons are; after which we lived by hunting them to the
upper end of the plains; to where the river passes through forests
to the mountains. Here engaged two native men to hunt for us,

From *David Thompson's Narrative of His Explorations in Western America,*
1784–1812, edited by J. B. Tyrell (Toronto: Champlain Society, 1916).

the red deer and bisons of the woods. The manner of furnishing the men with provisions was by hunting these animals, and bringing their meat by horses to the canoes, a supply for full three days; when we appointed a place to meet them with a fresh supply; thus the canoes proceeded to within twenty miles of the east foot of the mountains; we had given them a full supply for three days, and Mr. William Henry, the two Indians and myself proceeded to the foot of the mountains, where we killed three red deer, made a stage and placed the meat on it in safety to wait the canoes. This was on the 13th October 1810, and we expected the canoes to arrive late on the 16th or early on the 17th at latest, but they did not make their appearance; our oldest hunter, of about forty years of age, as usual rose very early in the morning and looking at the stage of meat, said to me, I have had dreams, this meat will never be eaten; he then saddled his horse and rode off. Somewhat alarmed at his ominous expression and the nonarrival of the canoes, I told Mr. Henry and the Indian to proceed thro' the woods down along the river in search of the canoes, and see what detained them, with positive orders not to fire a shot but in self-defense; about eight in the evening they returned, and related that a few miles below us they had seen a camp of Piegans on the bank of the river, and that a short distance below the camp, they had descended the bank to the river side, and found where the canoes had been. They had made a low rampart of stones to defend themselves, and there was blood on the stones; they went below this and fired a shot in hopes of an answer from the canoes, but it was not returned: I told them they had acted very foolishly, that the Piegans would be on us very early in the morning, and that we must start at the dawn of the day, and ride for our lives; on this we acted the next morning, and rode off, leaving the meat: the country we had to pass over was an open forest, but we had to cross, or ride round so many fallen trees that active men on foot could easily keep up with us; the Piegans had very early arrived at the stage of meat and directly followed the tracks of the horses, and would in the evening have come up with us, but providentially about one in the afternoon snow came on which covered our tracks and retarded them; about an hour after, as they related, they came on three grizzled bears direct on the track (they were smelling the tracks of the horses); they were fully persuaded that I had placed the bears there to prevent any further pursuit; nor could any arguments to the contrary make them believe otherwise and this belief was a mercy to us: we rode on through the woods until it was nearly dark, when we were obliged to stop; we remained quiet awaiting our fortune, when finding all quiet, we made a small fire, and passed the night with some anxiety; my situation precluded sleep, cut off from my men, uncertain where to find them, and equally so of the movements of the Indians. I was at a loss what to do, or which way to proceed; morning came and I had to determine what course to take, after being much perplexed whether I should take to the defiles of the mountains and see if the men and horses were safe that were left there; or try and find my men and canoes. I determined upon the latter as of the most importance; on the second day we found them about forty miles below the Indians, at a trading post lately deserted; here after much consultations, we fully perceived we had no further hopes of passing in safety by the defiles of the Saskatchewan River, and that we must now change our route to the defiles of the Athabasca River which would place us in safety, but would be attended with great inconvenience, fatigue, suffering and privation; but there was no alternative. We therefore directed the men to proceed through the woods to the defiles of the mountains and bring down the horses to take the goods across the country to the Athabasca River, and on the 28th October they arrived with twenty-four horses and we were now in all twenty-four men; having furnished ourselves with leather tents and dressed leather for shoes, we loaded our horses in proportion to their strength from 180 to 240 pounds weight each horse, and arranged the men, four to hunt and procure provisions, two men to clear a path thro' the woods, the other taking care of the horses, and other duties; with Thomas, an Iroquois Indian, as guide; our road lay over the high grounds within about thirty miles of the mountains: the woods are mostly of a kind of cypress, of small clean growth, and not close. With occasional cutting away of few trees we should have made several miles a day, but the forests are so frequently burned and occasion so many windfalls, that the horses make very slow progress, thus the dense forests are destroyed and meadows formed. We went eight miles in six and a half hours, and put up, without any supper. The country was tolerable good with pine and aspen woods.

October 30th. The hunters, thank heaven, killed two cow bisons and a young grizzled bear. We went six miles and camped, as we had to collect the meat, the ground was wet, the horses fatigued and heavy loaded.

Captain Williams's Grizzly

David H. Coyner

This episode comes from one of the most remarkable books about the early West, David H. Coyner's The Lost Trappers, published in 1847. Coyner's narrative concerns the fate of Ezekiel Williams, who is said to have led trappers up the Missouri River in 1807. Williams's party is alleged to have reached the Yellowstone and trapped in the Rockies. According to Coyner, the party was scattered by Indian attacks, and only three of twenty companions survived. These survivors were soon separated, and Williams, it is claimed, made his solitary way down the Arkansas, reaching the Missouri in 1809.

There are many questions regarding the authenticity of Coyner's account. Coyner himself never saw the Far West. But the account persists in its detail and interest, and this portion of it, relating Williams's escape in a canoe from a hungry grizzly, could have occurred. It is one of the few tales in this collection that defies authentication or refutation. But it is a good bear story.

AS THE COUNTRY was an unexplored region, he might be on a river that flowed into the Pacific, or he might be drifting down a stream that was an affluent to the Gulf of Mexico. He was, however, inclined to believe that he was on the sources of the Red River. He therefore resolved to launch his canoe, and go wherever the stream might convey him, trapping on his descent, when

From *The Lost Trappers: A Collection of Interesting Scenes and Events in the Rocky Mountains* (Cincinnati: J. A. & U. P. James, 1847).

beaver might be plenty. The first canoe that he used he made of buffalo skins. As these kind of water conveyances soon began to leak and rot, he made another of cottonwood, as soon as he came to timber sufficiently large, in which he embarked for a port, he knew not where. The most of his journeyings Captain Williams performed during the hours of night, except when he felt it perfectly safe to travel in daylight. His usual plan was to glide along down the stream, until he came to a place where beaver signs were abundant. There he would push his little bark to the shore, into some eddy among the willows, where he remained concealed, except when he was setting his traps or visiting them in the morning. He always set his traps between sunset and dark, and visited them at the earliest break of day. When he had taken all the beaver in one neighborhood, he would untie his little conveyance and glide onward and downward to try his luck in another place.

Thus, for hundreds of miles did this solitary trapper float down this unknown river, through an unknown country, here and there lashing his canoe to the willows and planting his traps in the little tributaries around. The upper part of the Arkansas (for this proved to be the river upon which he was trapping) is very destitute of timber, and the prairie frequently begins at the bank of the river and expands on either side as far as the eye can see. Captain Williams saw vast herds of buffalo, and as it was running season, the bulls were making a wonderful ado, making the plains roll with their low, deep grunting or bellowing, tearing up the earth with their feet and horns, whisking their tails, and defying their rivals to battle. Often they would come together in fierce battle, with a fury and force that reminded the spectator of the collision of two steamboats. Smaller game was also seen by Captain Williams in great abundance. Large gangs of wild horses could be frequently seen grazing on the plains and hillsides. As it was the spring of the year, the neighing and squealing of the stallions might be heard at all times of a still night. Captain Williams never used his rifle to procure meat, except when it was absolutely necessary, and when it could be done with perfect safety. On one occasion, when he had no beaver flesh, upon which he generally subsisted, he killed a deer, and after refreshing an empty stomach with a portion of it, he placed the carcass, which he had cut up, in one end of his canoe. As it was his invariable custom to sleep in his canoe, the night after he had laid in a supply of venison he was startled in his sleep by the trampling of something in the bushes on the bank. Tramp, tramp, tramp went the footstep, as it approached the canoe. Captain Williams first thought it might be an Indian that had found out his locality, but an Indian would not approach him in that careless manner. Although there was a beautiful starlight, yet the shade of the trees and a dense undergrowth made it very dark on the bank of the river. Captain Williams always adopted the precaution of tying his canoe to shore with a piece of rawhide about twenty feet long, which let it swing from the bank about that distance. This precaution he adopted at night, so that in an emergency he might cut the cord that bound him to the shore, and glide off without any noise. During the day he hid his canoe in the willows.

As the sound of the footsteps grew more and more distinct, the captain observed a huge grizzly bear approach the edge of the water and hold up its head as if scenting something. He then let his huge body into the water and made for the canoe. Captain Williams snatched up his axe as the most suitable means of defending himself in such a scrape, and stood with it uplifted and ready to drive it into the head of the huge aggressor. The bear reached the canoe, and immediately placed his forepaws upon the hind end of it, and nearly turned it over. Captain Williams struck one of his feet with the edge of his axe, which caused him to relax his hold with that foot. He, however, held on with the other foot, and Captain Williams inflicted another blow upon his head, which caused him to let the canoe go entirely. Captain Williams thought the bear had sunk in the water, from the stunning effects of the blow, and was drowned. He saw nothing more of him, nor did he hear anything. The presumption was, he went under the water. His aim was to get at the fresh meat in the captain's canoe. The next morning there were two of the bear's claws in the canoe, that had been severed from one of his feet by Captain Williams's axe. They were carefully preserved by the resolute captain for a number of years, as a trophy which he was fond of exhibiting, and the history of which he delighted to detail.

Kidnapped by a Bear

Ross Cox

*This story dates back to the earliest trapper days on the Colum-
bia River, before American trappers reached that country. It
comes from the pen of the adventuresome Ross Cox, an English-
man, whose travels took him into the forests of British Columbia
from 1814 to 1816. His account of the unfortunate voyager is
especially interesting, because it clearly shows how need dictates
action, even in wild animals who have an instinctive fear of fire.
The bear seemed to break all the rules for self-preservation yet
was actually impelled by one of the strongest needs, that of food.
Even the grizzly bear can starve. The unusual behavior of this
bear, however, has prompted some critics to doubt its authenticity. Yet I found two accounts of the same episode in different
sources. The trappers of Cox's party did not doubt this story,
which convinces me that it could and did happen.*

BEARS ARE SCARCE about the plains, but they are found in considerable numbers in the vicinity of the woods and lakes. Their
flesh is excellent particularly in the summer and autumnal
months, when roots and wild fruit are had in abundance. They
are most dangerous animals to encounter, especially if they are
slightly wounded, or that any of their cubs are in danger, in
which case they will rush on a man, though he were armed at all

From Ross Cox, *Adventures on the Columbia River, including the narrative of a resi-
dence of six years on the western side of the Rocky mountains, among various tribes of
Indians hitherto unknown: together with a journey across the American continent*
(London: H. Colburn & R. Bentley, 1831).

points; and woe to him if Bruin should once enfold him in his
dreadful grasp.

I have seen several of our hunters, as well as many Indians,
who had been dreadfully lacerated in their encounters with bears:
some have been deprived of their ears, others had their noses
nearly torn off, and a few have been completely blinded.

From the scarcity of food in the spring months they are then
more savage than at any other season; and during that period it
is a highly dangerous experiment to approach them.

The following anecdote will prove this; and, were not the fact
confirmed by the concurrent testimony of ten more, I would not
have given it a place among my memorabilia.

In the spring of this year [1816] Mr. M'Millan had dispatched
ten Canadians in a canoe down the Flathead River on a trading
excursion. The third evening after quitting the fort, while they
were quietly sitting round a blazing fire eating a hearty dinner of
deer, a large, half-famished bear cautiously approached the group
from behind an adjacent tree; and before they were aware of his
presence, he sprang across the fire, seized one of the men (who
had a well-furnished bone in his hand) round his waist, with the
two forepaws, and ran about fifty yards with him on his hind legs
before he stopped. His comrades were so thunderstruck at the
unexpected appearance of such a visitor, and his sudden retreat
with *pauvre Louisson,* that they for some time lost all presence of
mind; and, in a state of fear and confusion, were running to and
fro, each expecting in his turn to be kidnapped in a similar manner; when at length Baptiste Le Blanc, a half-breed hunter, seized
his gun, and was in the act of firing at the bear, but was stopped
by some of the others, who told him he would inevitably kill
their friend in the position in which he was then placed. During
this parley Bruin relaxed his grip of the captive, whom he kept
securely under him, and very leisurely began picking the bone
which the latter had dropped. Once or twice Louisson attempted
to escape, which only caused the bear to watch him more closely;
but on his making another attempt, he again seized Louisson
round the waist, and commenced giving him one of those infernal
embraces which generally end in death. The poor fellow was now
in great agony, and vented the most frightful screams; and observing Baptiste with his gun ready, anxiously watching a safe

opportunity to fire, he cried out, "Tire! tire! mon cher frère, si tu m'aimes. Tire, pour l'amour du bon Dieu! A la tête! à la tête!" This was enough for Le Blanc, who instantly let fly, and hit the bear over the right temple. He fell, and at the same moment dropped Louisson; but he gave him an ugly scratch with his claws across the face, which for some time afterward spoiled his beauty. After the shot Le Blanc darted to his comrade's assistance, and with his *couteau de chasse* quickly finished the sufferings of the man-stealer, and rescued his friend from impending death; for, with the exception of the above-mentioned scratch, he escaped uninjured. They commenced the work of dissection with right good will; but on skinning the bear, they found scarcely any meat on his bones; in fact the animal had been famishing, and in a fit of hungry desperation made one of the boldest attempts at kidnapping ever heard of in the legends of ursine courage.

Fear of Grizzlies in Early Days

Washington Irving

We are indebted to Washington Irving for recognizing early the significance of the fur trade to the development of the early West. He gathered and skillfully edited the accounts of members of that intrepid band responsible for opening the frontier to settlement. In the following narrative he relates the experiences of two trappers in the employ of the Astoria Company, who encountered the grizzly bear — an expectation of almost every traveler in western parts at that time. The bear's challenge and their response have become classic ones. Irving's description of the grizzly, taken entirely from secondary sources, of course, owes as much to previous accounts as to the report from these Astorians and confirms and adds to the grand lore concerning the grizzly.

TWO HUNDRED AND FIFTY MILES west of the Ariekara village on the Missouri, skirting a mountain chain, trying to find a pass, one afternoon on a clear day we encamped in a narrow valley on the banks of a beautifully clear but rushy pool surrounded by thickets bearing abundance of wild cherries and yellow and purple gooseberries.

While the afternoon's meal was in preparation, Mr. Hunt and Mr. McKenzie ascended to the summit of the nearest hill, from whence, aided by the purity and transparency of the evening at-

From *Astoria: Anecdotes of an Enterprise Beyond the Rocky Mountains* (Philadelphia: Carey, Lea, & Blanchard, 1836).

mosphere, they commanded a vast prospect on all sides. Below them extended a plain dotted with innumerable heads of buffalo. Some were lying down among the herbage, others roaming in their unbounded pastures, while many were engaged in fierce contests like those already described, their low bellowings reaching the ear like the hoarse murmurs of the surf on a distant shore.

Far off in the west they described a range of lofty mountains — Tetons — printing the clear horizon, some of them evidently capped with snow. These they supposed to be the Big Horn Mountains, so called from the animal of that name with which they abound.

On returning to the camp, Mr. Hunt found some uneasiness prevailing among the Canadian voyageurs. In straying among the thickets they had beheld tracks of grizzly bears in every direction, doubtless attracted thither by the fruit. To their dismay, they now found that they had encamped in one of the favorite resorts of this dreaded animal. The idea marred all the comfort of the encampment. As night closed, the surrounding thickets were peopled with terrors, insomuch that, according to Mr. Hunt, they could not help starting at every little breeze that stirred the bushes.

The grizzly bear is the only really formidable quadruped of our continent. He is the favorite theme of the hunters of the Far West, who describe him as equal in size to the common cow and of prodigious strength. He makes battle if assailed, and often, if pressed by hunger, is the assailant. If wounded, he becomes furious and will pursue the hunter. His speed exceeds that of a man but is inferior to that of a horse. In attacking, he rears himself on his hind legs and springs the length of his body. Woe to the horse or rider that comes within the sweep of his terrific claws, which are sometimes nine inches in length, and tear everything before them.

At the time we are treating, the grizzly bear was still frequent on the Missouri and in the lower country, but, like some of the broken tribes of the prairie, he has gradually fallen back before his enemies and is now chiefly to be found in the upland regions, in rugged fastnesses like those of the Black Hills and the Rocky Mountains. Here he lurks in caverns or holes which he has dug in the sides of hills or under the roots and trunks of fallen trees. Like the common bear, he is fond of fruits and mast [fallen nuts] and roots, the latter of which he will dig up with his foreclaws. He is carniverous also and will even attack and conquer the lordly buffalo, dragging his huge carcass to the neighborhood of his den that he may prey upon it at his leisure.

The hunters, both white and red men, consider this the most heroic game. They prefer to hunt him on horseback and will venture so near as sometimes to singe his hair with the flash of the rifle. The hunter of the grizzly bear, however, must be an experienced hand and know where to aim at a vital part; for of all quadrupeds he is the most difficult to kill. He will receive repeated wounds without flinching, and rarely is a shot mortal unless through the head or heart.

That the dangers apprehended from the grizzly bear at this night encampment were not imaginary was proved on the following morning. Among the hired men of the party was one William Cannon, who had been a soldier at one of the frontier posts and had entered into the employ of Mr. Hunt at Mackinaw. He was an inexperienced hunter and a poor shot, for which he was much bantered by his more adroit comrades. Piqued at their raillery, he had been practicing ever since he had joined the expedition, but without success. In the course of the present afternoon, he went forth by himself to take a lesson in venery, and, to his great delight, had the good fortune to kill a buffalo. As he was a considerable distance from the camp, he cut out the tongue and some of the choice bits, made them into a parcel, and slinging them on his shoulders by a strap passed around his forehead, as the voyageurs carry packages of goods, set out all glorious for the camp, anticipating a triumph over his brother hunters.

In passing through a narrow ravine, he heard a noise behind him, and looking around beheld, to his dismay, a grizzly bear in full pursuit, apparently attracted by the scent of the meat. Cannon had heard so much of the invulnerability of this tremendous animal that he never attempted to fire, but, slipping the strap from his forehead, let go the buffalo meat and ran for his life. The bear did not stop to regale himself with the meat but kept on after the hunter. He had nearly overtaken him when Cannon reached a tree, and, throwing down his rifle, scrambled up it. The next instant Bruin was at the foot of the tree; but, as this species of bear does not climb, he contented himself with turning the chase into a blockade. Night came on. In the darkness Cannon could not perceive whether or not the enemy maintained his station; but his fears pictured him rigorously mounting guard. He passed the night, therefore, in the tree, a prey to dismal fancies. In the morning the bear was gone. Cannon warily descended the tree, gathered up his gun, and made the best of his way back to the camp without venturing to look after his buffalo meat.

While on this theme we will add another anecdote of an adventure with a grizzly bear, told of John Day, the Kentucky hunter, but which happened at a different period of the expedition. Day was hunting in company with one of the clerks of the company, a lively youngster, who was a great favorite with the veteran but whose vivacity he had continually to keep in check. They were in search of deer when suddenly a huge grizzly bear emerged from a thicket about thirty yards distant, rearing himself upon his hind legs with a terrific growl and displaying a hideous array of teeth and claws. The rifle of the young man was leveled in an instant, but John Day's iron hand was as quickly upon his arm. "Be quiet, boy! be quiet!" exclaimed the hunter between his clenched teeth, and without turning his eyes from the bear. They remained motionless. The monster regarded them for a time, then, lowering himself on his forepaws, slowly withdrew. He had not gone many paces before he again returned, reared himself on his hind legs, and repeated his menace. Day's hand was still on the arm of his young companion; he again pressed it hard and kept repeating between his teeth, "Quiet, boy! — Keep quiet! — Keep quiet!" though the latter had not made a move since his first prohibition. The bear again lowered himself on all fours, retreated some twenty yards further, and again returned, reared, showed his teeth, and growled. This third menace was too much for the game spirit of John Day. "By Jove!" exclaimed he, "I can stand this no longer," and in an instant a ball from his rifle whizzed into the foe. The wound was not mortal; but, luckily, it dismayed instead of enraging the animal, and he retreated into the thicket.

Day's young companion reproached him for not practicing the caution which he enjoined upon others. "Why, boy," replied the veteran, "caution is caution, but one must not put up with too much, even from a bear. Would you have me suffer myself to be bullied all day by a varmint?"

An Adventure with a "White Bare"

Jacob Fowler

Close in the wake of Lewis and Clark came a small army of adventurers of every description — from mountain men to princes from foreign realms — eager to see for themselves the almost endless American wilderness. Many, sensing the historical importance of their travels, kept journals. We are indebted to these tireless diarists who, often fatigued, chilled, and hungry, kept their records current and full of the detail that gives us the flavor of those early days in the great West. Irving, Kelly, Sage, Ruxton, Townsend — without these men and others like them we would never have personal records of the opening of this country.

According to Elliot Coues, this simple and harrowing narrative marks the first instance in which an American citizen died and was buried in the area that is now Colorado. Lewis Dawson, the unfortunate victim of this bear attack, succumbed to his wounds. There was little medical aid on the frontier. This collection contains several stories in which men had to wait helplessly by while their comrades suffered. The "Slut" in this story is typical of the many dogs that recklessly joined the fray in a bear attack.

[TUESDAY, NOVEMBER 13, 1821.] We Seen a Branch Puting in from the South Side Which We Sopose to be Pikes first forke

From *The Journal of Jacob Fowler, Narrating an Adventure from Arkansas through the Indian Territory, Oklahoma, Kansas, Colorado, and New Mexico, to the Sources of the Rio Grande Del Norte, 1821–22,* edited, with notes, by Elliot Coues (New York: Francis P. Harper, 1898).

and made for it, crossed and camped in a grove of Bushes and timber about two miles up it from the River. We made Eleven miles West this day. We Stoped Heare about one oclock and Sent back for one Hors that Was not able to keep up. We Heare found some grapes among the brush. While Some Ware Hunting and others Cooking, and Some Picking grapes, a gun Was fired off and the Cry of a White Bare Was Raised. We Ware all armed in an Instent, and Each man Run His own course to look for the desperent anemel. The Brush in Which We Camped Contained from 10 to 20 acres Into Which the Bare had Run for Shelter finding Him Self Surrounded on all Sides. Through this Colonel Glann With four others atemted to Run; but the Bare, being In their Way, lay Close in the brush undiscovered till they Ware Within a few feet of it, when it Sprung up and caught Lewis Dawson and Pulled Him down. In an Instent Colonel Glanns' gun mised fyer, or He Wold Have Releved the man. But a large Slut Which belongs to the Party atacted the Bare With such fury that it left the man and persued Her a few steps, in Which time the man got up and Run a few steps but Was overtaken by the Bare. When the Conl made a second attempt to shoot, his gun mised fyer again, and the Slut as before Releved the man Who run as before, but Was soon again in the grasp of the Bare Who Semed Intent on His distruction. Colonel Glanns again Run Close up and as before His gun Wold not go off, the Slut made another atack and Releved the man. The Colonel now became alarmed lest the Bare Wold pusue Him also and ran up a Stooping tree, and after Him the Wounded man, who Was followed by the Bare. And thus they Ware all three up one tree. But a tree standing in reach, The Colonel steped over on that and let the man and Bare pass till the Bare Caught Dawson by one leg and drew Him back wards down the tree. While this Was going on the Col. sharpened His flint, Primed His gun, and Shot the Bare down While it was pulling the man by the leg, before any of the party arived to Releve Him. But the Bare Soon Rose again and Was Shot by several other men who had got up to the place of action. It Is to be Remarked that the other three men With Him Run off, and the Brush Was so thick that those on the out Side Ware Some time getting threw.

I Was my Self down the Crick below the brush and Heard the

dredfull Screems of man in the Clutches of the Bare, the yelping of the Slut, and the Hollowing of the men to "Run in, Run in. The man Will be killed!" and knowing the distance So great that I cold not get there in time to Save the man. So it Is much Easeer to Emagen my feellings than describe them, but before I got to the place of action the Bare Was killed and I met the Wounded man with Robert Fowler and one or two more asisting Him to Camp Where His Wounds Ware Examined. It appeers His Head Was In the Bares mouth at least twice and that When the monster gave the Crush that Was to mash the man's Head (it being two large for the Span of His mouth) the Head Sliped out, only the teeth Cutting the Skin to the bone Wherever they touched it so that the Skin of the Head Was Cut from about the Ears to the top in Several derections. All of Which Wounds Ware Sewed up as Well as Cold be don by men In our Situation, Haveing no Surgen nor Surgical Instruments. The man Still Retained His understanding but Said, "I am killed that I heard my Skull Brake." But We Ware Willing to beleve He Was mistaken as He Spoke Chearfully on the Subject, till In the after noon of the second day When He began to be Restless and Some What delereous. And on examining a Hole in the upper part of His Right temple Which We beleved only Skin deep We found the Brains Workeing out. We then Soposed that He did Heare His Scull Brake. He lived till a little before day on the third day after being Wounded, all Which time We lay at Camp, and Buried Him as Well as our meens Wold admit. Emedetely after the fattal axcident And Haveing done all We Cold for the Wounded man We turned our atention to the Bare and found Him a large fatt anemel. We Skinned Him but found the Smell of a polcat so Strong that We Cold not Eat the meat. On examining His mouth We found that three of His teeth Ware broken off near the gums, Which We Sopose Was the Caus of His not killing the man at the first Bite, and the one not Broke to be the cause of the Hole in the Right temple Which killed the man at last. The Hunters killed two deer and Cased the Skins for Baggs, so We dryed out the Bares oil and Caryed it with us. The Skin Was also taken Care of.

The "White Bear"
of the Arkansas

James O. Pattie

Lewis and Clark recorded accounts of the strength and ferocity of the grizzly bear in the journals of their epic journey to the Pacific, 1803–06. Lewis may have been the first white man, but certainly not the last, to vow that he would rather fight two Indians than one grizzly bear.

This account from Pattie's Narrative, *describing his company's first move westward across Kansas, illustrates the legendary ferocity of the "white bear." Note also that Pattie observed 220 bears in a day. It is no wonder these early travelers gave us so many records of encounters with bears, for in those days the bears were numerous. But not for long.*

THE SUCCEEDING MORNING we crossed the ridge, and came to water in the evening, where we encamped. Here we killed a white bear, which occupied several of us at least an hour. It was constantly in chase of one or another of us, thus withholding us from shooting at it, through fear of wounding each other. This was the

From *The Personal Narrative of James O. Pattie of Kentucky, During an Expedition From St. Louis, Through the Vast Regions Between That Place and the Pacific Ocean, and Thence Back Through the City of Mexico to Vera Cruz, During Journeyings of Six Years; in Which He and His Father Who Accompanied Him, Suffered Unheard of Hardships and Dangers, Had Various Conflicts with the Indians, and Were Made Captives, in Which Captivity His Father Died; Together with a Description of the Country, and the Various Nations Through Which They Passed.* Edited by Timothy Flint (Cincinnati: John H. Wood, 1831). Reprinted in *Early Western Travels, 1748–1846,* vol. 18, edited by Reuben Gold Thwaites (Cleveland: A. H. Clark Co., 1904–07).

first I had ever seen. His claws were four inches long, and very sharp. He had killed a buffalo bull, eaten a part of it, and buried the remainder. When we came upon him, he was watching the spot where he had buried it, to keep off the wolves, which literally surrounded him.

On the 11th, we traveled over some hilly ground. In the course of the day, we killed three white bears, the claws of which I saved, they being of considerable value among the Indians, who wear them around the neck, as the distinguishing mark of a brave. Those Indians who wear this ornament view those who do not as their inferiors. We came to water, and encamped early. I was one of the guard for the night, which was rather cloudy. About the middle of my guard, our horses became uneasy, and in a few moments more, a bear had gotten in among them, and sprung upon one of them. The others were so much alarmed that they burst their fastenings, and darted off at full speed. Our camp was soon aroused, and in arms, for defense, although much confused, from not knowing what the enemy was, nor from what direction to expect the attack. Some, however, immediately set off in pursuit of our horses. I still stood at my post, in no little alarm, as I did not know with the rest, if the Indians were around us or not. All around was again stillness, the noise of those in pursuit of the horses being lost in the distance. Suddenly my attention was arrested, as I gazed in the direction from which the alarm came, by a noise like that of a struggle at no great distance from me. I espied a hulk, at which I immediately fired. It was the bear devouring a horse, still alive. My shot wounded him. The report of my gun, together with the noise made by the enraged bear, brought our men from the camp, where they awaited a second attack from the unknown enemy in perfect stillness. Determined to avenge themselves, they now sallied forth, although it was so dark that an object ten steps in advance could not be seen. The growls of the bear, as he tore up the ground around him with his claws, attracted all in his direction. Some of the men came so near that the animal saw them, and made towards them. They all fired at him, but did not touch him. All now fled from the furious animal, as he seemed intent on destroying them. In this general fight one of the men was caught. As he screamed out in his agony, I, happening to have reloaded my gun, ran up to relieve him. Reaching the spot in an instant, I placed the muzzle of my gun against the bear, and discharging it killed him. Our companion was literally torn in pieces. The flesh on his hip was torn off, leaving the sinews bare, by the teeth of the bear. His side was so wounded in three places that his breath came through the openings; his head was dreadfully bruised, and his jaw broken. His breath came out from both sides of his windpipe, the animal in his fury having placed his teeth and claws in every part of his body. No one could have supposed that there was the slightest possibility of his recovery, through any human means. We remained in our encampment three days, attending upon him, without seeing any change for the worse or better in his situation. He had desired us from the first to leave him, as he considered his case as hopeless as ourselves did. We then concluded to move from our encampment, leaving two men with him to each of whom we gave one dollar a day, for remaining to take care of him, until he should die, and to bury him decently.

On the 14th we set off, taking, as we believed, a final leave of our poor companion. Our feelings may be imagined, as we left this suffering man to die in this savage region, unfriended and unpitied. We traveled but a few miles before we came to a fine stream and some timber. Concluding that this would be a better place for our unfortunate companion than the one where he was, we encamped with the intention of sending back for him. We dispatched men for him, and began to prepare a shelter for him, should he arrive. This is a fork of Smoke Hill River, which empties into the Platte. We set traps, and caught eight beavers, during the night. Our companions with the wounded man on a litter reached us about eight o'clock at night.

In the morning we had our painful task of leave-taking to go through again. We promised to wait for the two we left behind at the Arkansas River. We traveled all day up this stream. I counted, in the course of the day, two hundred and twenty white bears. We killed eight that made an attack upon us; the claws of which I saved. Leaving the stream in the evening we encamped on the plain. A guard of twenty was relieved through the night, to prevent the bears from coming in upon us. Two tried to do it and were killed.

We arrived at the main body of the Arkansas and camped on

the 22nd. We waited there till November 4 for the arrival of the two men we had left with our wounded companion. They came and brought with them his gun and ammunition. He died the fifth day after we had left him, and was buried as decently as the circumstances would allow.

Grizzlies of the Southwest

James O. Pattie

James Pattie and his father undertook a formidable six-year jour-
ney, beginning in 1824, from St. Louis to the Pacific by way of
Santa Fe, thence back through Mexico to Vera Cruz. Their ad-
ventures and hardships were numerous in these wild regions. I
have included lively accounts of "the white bear," which Pattie
saw in great numbers. These stories are interesting for several
reasons: they illustrate the former size of the grizzly population,
emphasize the ferocity of the grizzly bear, and show the fool-
hardiness of youth. These bears were encountered in Colorado
and New Mexico.

IN THE EVENING of the same day [February 25], although the
weather threatened a storm, we packed up, and began to descend
the river. We encamped this night in a huge cavern in the midst
of the rocks. About night it began to blow a tempest, and to
snow fast. Our horses became impatient under the pelting of the
storm, broke their ropes, and disappeared. In the morning, the
earth was covered with snow, four or five inches deep. One of
our companions accompanied me to search for our horses. We
soon came upon their trail, and followed it, until it crossed the
river. We found it on the opposite side, and pursued it up a creek
that empties into the Helay on the north shore. We passed a cave
at the foot of the cliffs. At its mouth I remarked that the bushes
were beaten down, as though some animal had been browsing

From *The Personal Narrative of James O. Pattie* . . . (Cincinnati: John H. Wood,
1831).

upon them. I was aware that a bear had entered the cave. We collected some pine knots, split them with our tomahawks, and kindled torches, with which I proposed to my companion that we should enter the cave together, and shoot the bear. He gave me a decided refusal, notwithstanding I reminded him that I had, more than once, stood by him in a similar adventure; and notwithstanding I made him sensible that a bear in a den is by no means so formidable as when ranging freely in the woods. Finding it impossible to prevail on him to accompany me, I lashed my torch to a stick, and placed it parallel with the gun barrel, so that I could see the sights on it, and entered the cave. I advanced cautiously onward about twenty yards, seeing nothing. On a sudden the bear reared himself erect within seven feet of me, and began to growl, and gnash his teeth. I leveled my gun and shot him between the eyes, and began to retreat. Whatever light it may throw upon my courage, I admit that I was in such a hurry as to stumble, and extinguish my light. The growling and struggling of the bear did not at all contribute to allay my apprehensions. On the contrary, I was in such haste to get out of the dark place, thinking the bear just at my heels, that I fell several times on the rocks, by which I cut my limbs, and lost my gun. When I reached the light, my companion declared, and I can believe it, that I was as pale as a corpse. It was some time before I could summon sufficient courage to re-enter the cavern for my gun. But having rekindled my light, and borrowed my companion's gun, I entered the cavern again, advanced and listened. All was silent, and I advanced still further, and found my gun, near where I had shot the bear. Here again I paused and listened. I then advanced onward a few strides, where to my great joy I found the animal dead. I returned, and brought my companion in with me. We attempted to drag the carcass from the den, but so great was the size that we found ourselves wholly unable. We went out, found our horses, and returned to camp for assistance. My father severely reprimanded me for venturing to attack such a dangerous animal in its den, when the failure to kill it outright by the first shot would have been sure to be followed by my death.

Four of us were detached to the den. We were soon enabled to drag the bear to the light, and by the aid of our beasts to take it to camp. It was both the largest and whitest bear I ever saw. The best proof I can give of the size and fatness is that we extracted ten gallons of oil from it. The meat we dried, and put the oil in a trough, which we secured in a deep crevice of a cliff, beyond the reach of animals of prey. We were sensible that it would prove a treasure to us on our return.

On October 28th [1826], I started for the copper mines, wrought by my father. This day my course led me up the del Norte, the bottoms of which are exceedingly rich. At a very short distance from the Passo, I began to come in contact with gray bears, and other wild animals. At a very little distance on either side are high and rugged mountains, entirely sterile of all vegetation. I had no encounter with the bears, save in one instance. A bear exceedingly hungry, as I suppose, came upon my horses as I was resting them at midday, and made at one of them. I repaid him for his impudence by shooting him through the brain. I made a most delicious dinner of the choice parts of his flesh. My servant would not touch it, his repugnance being shared by great numbers in his condition. It is founded on the notion that the bear is a sort of degenerated man, and especially, that the entrails are exactly like those of human beings.

On the 30th, I struck off from the del Norte, and took my course for the copper mines directly over the mountains, among which we toiled onward, subsisting by what we packed with us, or the product of the rifle, until the 11th of November, when I had once more the satisfaction of embracing my father at the copper mines. He was in perfect health, and delighted to see me again. He urged me so earnestly to remain with him, though a stationary life was not exactly to my taste, that I consented from a sense of filial duty, and to avoid importunity. I remained here until the first of December, amusing myself sometimes by hunting, and sometimes by working in the gold mine, an employment in which I took much pleasure.

In a hunting excursion with a companion who was an American, he one morning saw fit to start out of bed and commence his hunt while I was yet asleep in bed. He had scarcely advanced a league before he killed a deer on the top of a high ridge. He was so inadvertent as to commence skinning the animal before he had reloaded his rifle. Thus engaged, he did not perceive a bear with her cubs, which had advanced within a few feet of him. As soon as he saw his approaching companion, without coveting any further acquaintance, he left deer and rifle and ran for his life. He stopped not, until he arrived at the mines. The bear fell to work for a meal upon the deer, and did not pursue him. We immediately started back to have the sport of hunting this animal. As we approached the ridge where he had killed the deer, we discovered the bear descending the ridge towards us. We each of us chose a position, and his was behind a tree, which he could mount in case he wounded, without killing her. This most ferocious and terrible animal, the grizzly or gray bear, does not climb at all. I chose my place opposite him, behind a large rock, which happened to be near a precipice that I had not observed. Our agreement was to wait until she came within thirty yards, and then he was to give her the first fire. He fired, but the powder being damp, his gun made long fire, whence it happened that he shot her too low, the ball passing through the belly and not a mortal part. She made at him in terrible rage. He sprang up his tree, the bear close at his heels. She commenced biting and scratching the tree, making, as a Kentuckian would phrase it, *the lint fly*. But finding that she could not bite the tree down, and being in an agony of pain, she turned the course of her attack, and came growling and tearing up the bushes before her, towards me. My companion bade me lie still, and my own purpose was to wait until I could get a close fire. So I waited until the horrible animal was within six feet of me. I took true aim at her head. My gun flashed in the pan. She gave one growl and sprang at me with her mouth open. At two strides I leaped down the unperceived precipice. My jawbone was split on a sharp rock, on which my chin struck at the bottom. Here I lay senseless. When I regained recollection, I found my companion had bled me with the point of his butcher knife and was sitting beside me with his hat full of water, bathing my head and face. It was perhaps an hour before I gained full recollection, so as to be able to walk. My companion had cut a considerable orifice in my arm with his knife, which I deemed rather supererogation; for I judged that I had bled sufficiently at the chin.

When I had come entirely to myself, my companion proposed that we should finish the campaign with the bear. I, for my part, was satisfied with what had already been done, and proposed to retreat. He was importunate, however, and I consented. We ascended the ridge to where he had seen the bear lie down in the bushes. We fixed our guns so that we thought ourselves sure of their fire. We then climbed two trees, near where the bear was, and made a noise that brought her out of her lair and caused her to spring fiercely towards our trees. We fired together, and killed her dead. We then took after the cubs. They were three in number. My companion soon overtook them. They were of the size of the largest raccoons. These imps of the devil turned upon him and made fight. I was in too much pain and weakness to assist him. They put him to all he could do to clear himself of them. He at length got away from them, leaving them masters of the field, and having acquired no more laurels than I, from my combat with my buffalo calf. His legs were deeply bit and scratched, and what was worse, such was the character of the affair, he only got ridicule for his assault of the cubs. I was several weeks in recovering, during which time I ate neither meat nor bread, being able to swallow nothing but liquids.

The country abounds with these fierce and terrible animals, to a degree that in some districts they are truly formidable. They get into the corn fields. The owners hear the noise which they make among the corn, and supposing it occasioned by cows and horses that have broken into the fields, they rise from their beds, and go to drive them out, when instead of finding retreating domestic animals, they are assailed by the grizzly bear. I have been acquainted with several fatal cases of that sort. One of them was a case that intimately concerned me. Iago, my servant, went out with a man to get a load of wood. A bear came upon this man and killed him and his ass in the team. A slight flight of snow had fallen. Some Spaniards who had witnessed the miserable fate of their companion begged some of us to go and aid them in killing the bear. Four of us joined them. We trailed the bear to its den, which was a crevice in the bluff. We came to the mouth and fired a gun. The animal, confident in his fierceness, came out, and we instantly killed it. This occurred in New Mexico.

Grizzlies on the Missouri

Prince Maximilian of Wied

Aristocratic European travelers were not uncommon visitors to the western American wilderness that Lewis and Clark opened as a consequence of their momentous journey. One such traveler was the German nobleman, Maximilian, Prince of Wied, who made a leisurely, lengthy, exceptionally well-documented investigation of this territory from 1832 to 1834. On the Missouri he was not disappointed in his hopes of seeing the "white bear," but was too polite to exhibit much excitement. His valuable notes and specimens, however, made a substantial contribution to the Smithsonian Institution's bear taxonomy.

AFTER OUR HUNTERS had returned, with the flesh of a buffalo, we had a favorable wind, which allowed us to use our sail. At a turn of the river we suddenly saw a couple of bears running backwards and forwards on a sand bank before the willow thickets. One of them at length went away, and the other ran along the strand, and fell on the dead body of a buffalo cow, which was half buried in the mud. While the keelboat sailed against the stream in the middle of the river, a boat was put out, into which Messrs. Mitchell and Bodmer, and the hunters, Dechamp and Dreidoppel, threw themselves, and rowed along the bank towards the ravenous animal. The sight of this first bear chase was interesting, and we that remained as spectators on deck awaited the result with impatience. Dechamp, a bold and experienced

From *Travels in the Interior of North America, 1832–34*, Part II (London: Ackermann & Co., 1843). Reprinted in *Early Western Travels, 1748–1846*, vol. 23, edited by Reuben Gold Thwaites (Cleveland: A. H. Clark Co., 1904–07).

hunter and an excellent marksman, was put on shore, and crept unperceived along the strand, till he got to the branch of a tree, about eighty paces from the bear, in order, in case of need, to intercept his retreat to the thickets. The ravenous bear sometimes raised his colossal head, looked around him, and then greedily returned to his repast; doubtless because the wind was in our favor, and these animals are not remarkably quick-sighted. The boat had got to within fifty paces, when the pieces were leveled. Mr. Mitchell fired the first mortal shot, behind the shoulder blade. The other shots followed in quick succession, on which the bear rolled over, uttered fearful cries, tumbled about ten steps forward, scratched the wounded places furiously with his paws, and turned several times completely over. At this moment Dechamp came up and put an end to his misery by shooting him through the head. The huge beast lay stretched out: it was fastened by ropes to the boat, and conveyed in triumph to the ship, where it was measured, and a drawing made of it. I much regretted that I had not taken part in the sport; but I had not believed that it was possible, in such an open, unprotected spot, to get so near the bear.

This grizzly bear was a male, about three years old, and, therefore, not the largest size: he was six feet two inches and two lines in length, from the nose to the tip of the tail; the latter being eight inches. His color was dark brown, with the point of the hair of a rusty color, but new hair already appeared of a lighter gray, with yellow tips. This bear is known to be a very dangerous beast of prey, and is willingly avoided by the hunters: if fired at, he very frequently attacks, even if not wounded, when they suddenly come too near him. If he perceives a man in time, he generally gets out of the way, especially when he has the wind. Almost all the hunters of the prairie relate their adventures with the bears, and whole volumes might be filled with such stories. It is certain that many white men and Indians have been torn to pieces by these dangerous animals, especially in former times, when they were very numerous, and lived to a great age, as may be seen in Lewis and Clark's Travels. Even last year, five of Mr. Mitchell's hunters, who had wounded one of these animals, were so quickly pursued by him that they were obliged to take refuge in the Missouri. This species of bear cannot climb, and therefore a tree is a good means to escape their attacks. The true country of these animals on the Missouri, where they are at present the most numerous, is the tract about Milk River. Here there is no wood of any extent in which they are not found, but they are likewise seen everywhere in a northwesterly direction. In these solitudes, the long claws of this bear serve to dig up many kinds of roots in the prairie, on which he chiefly subsists, but he is especially fond of animal food, particularly the flesh of dead animals. There is no other species of bear on the upper Missouri, for the black bear is not found so high up. At the place where we had killed the bear, it would have been easy to shoot many of these animals, by posting ourselves near the dead buffalo cow: the whole sand bank was covered with the prints of bears' footsteps, and trodden down like a threshing floor; but our time was too short and too precious: we therefore proceeded on our voyage till a violent thunderstorm threatened us, and we lay to, by the high bank of the prairie, where our bear was skinned. During the night, torrents of rain fell, which wetted our books and plants in the cabin.

On the following day, the 19th, we had another chase after a colossal bear, which swam through the Missouri to a dead buffalo; but our young hunters were this time too eager, and fired too soon, so that the animal escaped, though probably wounded, as fifteen rifles were discharged at him. Afterwards we saw several beaver lodges. The people towed the steamer in the afternoon, making their way along the bank, through a dense willow thicket. All of a sudden they cried that there were bears close to them; on which the hunters immediately leaped on shore. Mr. Mitchell had scarcely arrived at the head of the towers, when he perceived a she-bear with two cubs. Dechamp came to his aid, and in a few minutes the three animals were in our power. Mr. Mitchell had killed the mother, which was of a pale yellowish-red color; one of the cubs, which was brought alive on board, was whitish about the head and neck, and brownish-gray on the body; the other was dark brown. The females of these animals are generally of a lighter color than the males, which is the case with many beasts of prey, particularly the European fox. The live cub was in a great rage, and growled terribly; it was impossible for me to save his life.

III

HEYDAY

The First Saga of Hugh Glass

Washington Irving

Although Irving does not mention any names, he was told by Henry L. Ellsworth, his companion on the foray across Oklahoma, that the men in this narrative were members of Ashley's hunting party — the party to which Hugh Glass belonged. The accepted view is that Irving's is one of the first published versions of Hugh Glass's famous encounter with a grizzly bear, though it is an offhand mention in the midst of material of greater import. I have therefore included in this book two other early versions, by Rufus Sage and Frederick Ruxton, both from the pristine days of western travel and adventure, which serve to illustrate how quickly legend attaches to a good story.* Glass's experience stands out from all other hand-to-hand fights not because of the struggle itself but because of the injured man's extraordinary tenacity and endurance in crawling, alone and unaided, back to the settlement, returning, like a Lazarus of the wilderness, to amaze and confound those who had thought him dead. It is now impossible to determine what actually happened and how (or if) it came about that Glass was left for dead. Yet even critics of the alleged facts agree that Glass demonstrated a remarkable will to live and probably deserves his place as the most famous survivor of an encounter between man and grizzly.

OUR MAN BEATTE returned grim and mortified, from hunting. He had come upon a bear of formidable dimensions, and

From Washington Irving, *A Tour on the Prairies* (Philadelphia: Carey, Lea, & Blanchard, 1835).
*The scanty details of this encounter have been fleshed out by many writers since Irving, receiving their ultimate mythic use in *Lord Grizzly*, by Frederick Manfred (1954). [Ed.]

wounded him with a rifle shot. The bear took to the brook, which was swollen and rapid. Beatte dashed in after him and assailed him in the rear with his hunting knife. At every blow the bear turned furiously upon him, with a terrific display of white teeth. Beatte, having a foothold in the brook, was enabled to push him off with his rifle, and, when he turned to swim, would flounder after, and attempt to hamstring him. The bear, however, succeeded in scrambling off among the thickets, and Beatte had to give up the chase.

This adventure, if it produced no game, brought up at least several anecdotes, round the even fire, relative to bear hunting, in which the grizzly bear figured conspicuously. This powerful and ferocious animal is a favorite theme of a hunter's story, both among red and white men; and his enormous claws are worn round the neck of an Indian brave, as a trophy more honorable than a human scalp. He is now scarcely seen below the upper prairies, and the skirts of the Rocky Mountains. Other bears are formidable when wounded and provoked, but seldom make battle when allowed to escape. The grizzly bear, alone, of all the animals of our western wilds, is prone to unprovoked hostility. His prodigious size and strength make him a formidable opponent; and his great tenacity of life often baffles the skill of the hunter, notwithstanding repeated shots of the rifle and wounds of the hunting knife.

One of the anecdotes related on this occasion gave a picture of the accidents and hard shifts to which our frontier rovers are inured. A hunter, while in pursuit of a deer, fell into one of these deep funnel-shaped pits, formed on the prairies by the settling of the waters after heavy rains, and known by the name of sinkholes. To his great horror, he came in contact, at the bottom, with a huge grizzly bear. The monster grappled him; a deadly contest ensued, in which the poor hunter was severely torn and bitten, and had a leg and an arm broken, but succeeded in killing his rugged foe. For several days he remained at the bottom of the pit, too much crippled to move, and subsisting on the raw flesh of the bear, during which time he kept his wounds open, that they might heal gradually and effectually. He was at length enabled to scramble to the top of the pit, and so out upon the open prairie. With great difficulty he crawled to a ravine, formed by a stream then nearly dry. Here he took a delicious draught of water, which infused new life into him; then dragging himself along from pool to pool, he supported himself by small fish and frogs.

One day he saw a wolf hunt down and kill a deer in the neighboring prairie. He immediately crawled forth from the ravine, drove off the wolf, and, lying down beside the carcass of the deer, remained there until he made several hearty meals, by which his strength was much recruited.

Returning to the ravine, he pursued the course of the brook, until it grew to be a considerable stream. Down this he floated, until he came to where it emptied into the Mississippi. Just at the mouth of the stream, he found a forked tree, which he launched with some difficulty, and, getting astride of it, committed himself to the current of the mighty river. In this way he floated along until he arrived opposite the fort at Council Bluffs. Fortunately he arrived there in the daytime, otherwise he might have floated, unnoticed, past this solitary post, and perished in the idle waste of waters. Being descried from the fort, a canoe was sent to his relief, and he was brought to shore more dead than alive, where he soon recovered from his wounds, but remained maimed for life.

Glass and the Grizzly

Rufus Sage

Sage's version of Hugh Glass's experience, with its colorful embellishments, appealed mightily to the imaginations of the many readers who pored over his fascinating anecdotes from the security of their armchairs and sitting rooms.

SEVERAL YEARS SINCE, an old trapper by the name of Glass, with his companion, while on an excursion, came upon a large grizzly bear.

Bruin, having received the salute of two rifles, as usual rushed towards his uncivil assailants, who broke from him with all possible dispatch. But Glass, stumbling, fell prostrate in his flight, and before he could recover his feet the infuriated beast was upon him.

Now commenced a death struggle. The pistols of the hunter were both discharged in quick succession — the ball of one entering the breast of his antagonist, and that of the other grazing his back.

Smarting and maddened by the pain of additional wounds, the bleeding monster continued the conflict with the fury of desperation — tearing from the limbs and body of the unfortunate man large pieces of trembling flesh, and lacerating him with the deep thrusts of his teeth and claws.

From Rufus Sage, *Scenes in the Rocky Mountains, and in Oregon, California, New Mexico, Texas, and the grand prairies; or, Notes by the way, an excursion of three years, with a description of the countries passed through. Including their geography, geology, resources, and present condition, and the different nations inhabiting them,* 2d. ed. rev. (Philadelphia: Carey & Hart, 1847).

Meanwhile the sufferer maintained, with his butcher knife, an obstinate defense, though with fast-waning effort and strength. Finally, enfeebled by the loss of blood and exhausted from the extraordinary exertions of a desperate and unequal contest, he was unable to oppose further resistance, and quietly resigned himself to his fate.

The bear, too, with the thick blood oozing from his numerous wounds, and faint from the many stabs among his veins and sinews, seemed equally in favor of a suspension of hostilities; and, extending himself across the hunter's back, he remained motionless for two hours or more.

But now another enemy commences an assault upon his vitals — that enemy is death. In vain is defensive effort. In vain are all his struggles, he falls by the hunter's side a lifeless corpse.

The setting sun had cast his lurid glare upon the ensanguined spot, as the comrade of the miserable Glass ventured near to ascertain the result of the fierce encounter.

There lay the body of his deserted friend, stretched out, apparently lifeless and half torn to pieces; and, by its side, lay the carcass of that enemy, which had waged with it such murderous war, cold and stiffened in death!

Now, doubly terrified at his loneliness, but still governed by sordid motives, he stripped the former of his arms and every other valuable, then no longer needed (as he supposed) by their owner, and, mounting his horse, started immediately for the nearest trading post.

On his arrival he recounted the particulars of the fatal occurrence — carefully concealing, however, his own criminal conduct. The story was accredited, and the name of Glass found place upon the long catalogue of those who had fallen a prey to wild beasts and savage men.

Six weeks elapsed and no one thought of the subject of our sketch as among the living. The general surprise, therefore, may be readily imagined, on opening the fort gates one morning, at finding before them the poor, emaciated form of a man, half-naked and covered with wounds and running sores, and so torn the fleshless bones of his legs and thighs were exposed to view in places! And how this astonishment was heightened on recognizing the person of Glass in the illy defined lineaments of his countenance — the very man so long regarded as the inhabitant of another world! A veritable ghost suddenly appearing upon the spot could not have occasioned greater wonder!

But sensations of pity and commiseration quickly succeeded those of surprise, and the unhappy sufferer was conveyed within doors and received from the hands of friends that careful attention his situation so much required.

The story of his misfortunes was thrillingly interesting. When left by his companion for dead, he was in a state of unconsciousness, with scarcely the breath of life retained in his mangled body. But the soft nightwind stanched his wounds, and a slight sleep partially revived him from his deathlike stupor.

With the morning, the slight sensations of hunger he began to experience were appeased from the raw flesh of the carcass at his side; and, thus strengthened, by a slow and tedious effort he was enabled to reach a near stream and quench his thirst. Still further revived, he again crawled to the carcass at the demands of appetite.

In this manner he continued for three days, when the putrescent corpse compelled him to abandon it.

Then it was he commenced his tedious return to the fort (some seventy miles distant), which he performed during an interval of forty successive days! The whole of this long stretch he crawled upon his hands and knees — subsisting, for the meanwhile, only upon insects, such as chance threw in his way, but passing most of the time without one morsel with which to appease the gnawings of hunger or renew his wasted strength.

Yet, great as were his sufferings and intolerable as they may seem, he survived them all, and, by the kind attention of friends, soon recovered.

He lived much of his life thereafter in the town of Taos, New Mexico, and frequently repeated to wondering listeners the particulars of this terrific and painful adventure.

John Glass and the Grizzly

George Frederick Ruxton

Just why this story uses "John" instead of "Hugh" I cannot say. Perhaps by the time Ruxton heard this tale it had undergone considerable variation in the telling and retelling. An English soldier of fortune in the manner of Captain Mayne Reid, his contemporary, Ruxton traveled broadly in the Southwest, gathering material that he later published. His version of Glass's experience became one of the best known. It has been contended that the youth with Glass that Ruxton mentions was Jim Bridger, on his first trip to the mountains. But nowhere have I read of Bridger saying he was that same boy. In any event, we are fortunate to have this old trapper's tale so well preserved.

SOME YEARS AGO, a trapping party was on its way to the mountains, led, we believe, by old Sublette, a well-known captain of the West. Among the band was John Glass, a trapper who had been all his life among the mountains, and had seen probably more exciting adventures and had more wonderful and hairbreadth escapes than any of the rough and hardy fellows who make the Far West their home, and whose lives are spent in a succession of perils and privations. On one of the streams running from the Black Hills, a range of mountains northward of the Platte, Glass and a companion were one day setting their traps, when on passing through a cherry thicket, which skirted the stream, the former, who was in advance, described a large grizzly bear quietly turning up the turf with its nose, searching for pig-

From George Ruxton, *Life in the Far West* (New York: Harper & Brothers, 1849).

nuts. Glass immediately called his companion, and, both proceeding cautiously, crept to the skirt of the thicket, and taking steady aim at the animal, discharged their rifles at the same instant, both balls taking effect but not inflicting a mortal wound. The bear, giving a groan of agony, jumped with all four legs from the ground, and charged at once upon the enemy, snorting with pain and fury.

"Hurrah, Bill!" roared out Glass, as he saw the animal rushing toward them. "We'll be made meat of, sure as shootin'!"

He then bolted through the thicket, followed closely by his companion. The brush was so thick that they could scarcely make their way through, while the weight and strength of the bear carried him through all obstructions, and he was soon close upon them.

About a hundred yards from the thicket was a steep bluff; Glass shouted to his companion to make this bluff as the only chance. They flew across the intervening open and level space like lightning. When nearly across, Glass tripped over a stone and fell, and just as he rose, the bear, rising on his hind feet, confronted him. As he closed, Glass, never losing his presence of mind, cried to his companion to close up quickly, and discharged his pistol full into the body of the animal at the same moment that the bear, with blood streaming from his nose and mouth, knocked the pistol from his hand with one blow of its paw and, fixing its claws deep into his flesh, rolled with him to the ground. The hunter, notwithstanding his hopeless situation, struggled manfully, drawing his knife and plunging it several times into the body of the beast, which, ferocious with pain, tore with tooth and claw the body of the wretched victim, actually baring the ribs of flesh and exposing the very bones. Weak from loss of blood, and blinded with blood which streamed from his lacerated head, Glass dropped his knife and sank down insensible and apparently dead.

His companion, who up to this moment had watched the conflict, which, however, lasted but a few seconds, thinking that his turn would come next and not having even presence of mind to load his rifle, fled back to camp and narrated the miserable fate of poor Glass. The captain of the band of trappers, however, dispatched the man with a companion back to the spot. On reaching the place, which was red with blood, they found Glass still breathing, and the bear dead and stiff, actually lying upon his body. Poor Glass presented a horrible spectacle; the flesh torn in strips from his bones and limbs, and large flaps strewed the ground; his scalp hung bleeding over his face, which was also lacerated in a shocking manner. The bear, besides the three bullets in his body, bore the marks of about twenty gaping wounds in the breast and belly, testifying to the desperate defense of the mountaineer. Imagining that if not already dead, the poor fellow could not possibly survive more than a few moments, the men collected his arms, stripped him of even his hunting shirt and moccasins, and, merely pulling the dead bear off from the body, they returned to their party, reporting that Glass was dead, and that they had buried him. In a few days the gloom which pervaded the trapper's camp, at his loss, disappeared, and the incident, although frequently mentioned over the campfire, at length was almost entirely forgotten in the excitement of the hunt and the Indian perils which surrounded them.

Months elapsed, the hunt was over, and the party of trappers were on their way to the trading post with their packs of beaver. It was nearly sundown, and the round adobe bastions of the mud-built fort were just in sight, when a horseman was seen slowly approaching them along the banks of the river. When near enough to discern his figure, they saw a lank cadaverous form, with a face so scarred and disfigured that scarcely a feature was discernible. Approaching the leading horsemen, one of whom happened to be the companion of the defunct Glass in his memorable bear scrape, the stranger, in a hollow voice, reining his horse before them, exclaimed: "Hurrah, Bill, my boy! You thought I was gone under that time, did you? But hand me over my horse and gun, my lad; I ain't dead yet, by a long shot!" What was the astonishment of the whole party, and the genuine horror of Bill and his worthy campanion on the burial story, to hear the well-known but now altered voice of John Glass, who had been killed by a grizzly bear months before and comfortably interred, as the two men had reported and all had believed!

There he was, however, and no mistake; all crowded around to hear from his lips how, after the lapse of he knew not how long, he gradually recovered, and being without arms or even a butcher knife, he had fed upon the almost putrid carcass of the bear for several days, until he had regained sufficient strength to crawl, when tearing off as much of the bear's meat as he could carry in his enfeebled state, he crept down the river; and suffering excessive torture from his wounds and hunger and cold, he made the rest of his way to the fort, which was some eighty or ninety miles distant; and living mainly upon roots and berries, he, after many, many days, arrived in a pitiable state, from which he had now recovered and was, to use his own expression, "as slick as a peeled onion."

Farnham's Fare

Thomas Farnham

In 1839 Thomas Farnham's travels through what is now Colorado, Wyoming, and Utah resulted in a singular adventure that occurred in the desolate plateaus of northwestern Colorado, near the banks of the Little Bear River. His party ran out of food and found no game to shoot. Their plight was desperate. This story illustrates how bears were sometimes killed not for sport or punishment but out of dire need. It is interesting that the mother bear acted from her first instinct, self-preservation. One can never predict how a bear will behave.

AUGUST 6. Eighteen miles today over the barren intervals of the river. The wild wormwood and prickly pear were almost the only evidences of vegetative powers which the soil presented. A rugged desolation of loam and sand bluffs, barren vales of red earth, and an occasional solitary boulder of granite; no mountains, even, to relieve the dreary monotony of the sickening sight. About twelve o'clock it was pleasant to see a small band of antelopes show themselves on the brink of a bluff.

We halted and attempted to approach them; but they had been hunted a few days before by the French trappers, whom we had met, and by no means relished our companionship. Away they ran like the wind. Our hopes of finding game were at an end; the French trappers had seen, on all their way out, no other game

From *Travels in the Great Western Prairies, the Anahuac and Rocky Mountains, and in the Oregon Country*, Part II (London: Richard Bentley, 1843). Reprinted in *Early Western Travels, 1748–1846*, vol. 28, edited by Reuben Gold Thwaites (Cleveland: A. H. Clark Co., 1904–07).

than this band of antelopes. Our faithful greyhound could be eaten as a last resource, and we traveled on. Our excellent guide insisted upon walking nearly all the way, that I might ride. This was inestimably kind of him. The act flowed from his own goodness; for, during our long journey together, he had never failed to take every opportunity to make me comfortable. We arranged our camp tonight with unusual care. The Sioux were among the hills on the right, and every preparation was therefore made to receive an attack from them. But like many other expectations of the kind, this vanished as the beautiful mountain morn dawned upon the silent desert.

7th. Today we traveled across a great southward bend in the river. The face of the country was a desert — neither tree nor shrub, nor grass, nor water in sight. During the afternoon we fell in with an old grisly bear and two cubs. It was a dangerous business, but starvation knows no fear.

Kelly and Smith, having horses that could run, determined to give chase and shoot one cub, while the greyhound should have the honor of a battle with the other. Under this arrangement the chase commenced. The old bear, unfaithful to her young, ran ahead of them in her fright, and showed no other affection for them than to stop occasionally, raise herself on her hind feet, and utter a most piteous scream. The horses soon ran down one cub, and the greyhound the other, so that in half an hour we were on the route again with the certain prospect of a supper when we should encamp. Had we found water and wood where we killed our meat, we should have believed it impossible to have proceeded further without food; but as necessity seldom deals in mercy, she compelled us in this case, to travel till dark, before we found wood enough to cook our food, and water enough to quench our parching thirst. At last, turning from our track and following down a deep ravine that ran toward the river, we came upon a filthy, oozing sulphurous puddle, which our horses, though they had had no water the entire day, refused to drink. There was no alternative, however, between drinking this and thirsting still, and we submitted to the lesser of two evils. We drank it; and with the aid of dry wormwood for fuel, boiled our meat in it. These cubs were each of about twelve pounds weight. The livers, hearts, heads, and the forequarters of one of them, made us a filthy supper. It, however, served the purpose of better food as it prevented starvation. We had traveled eighteen miles.

8th. The morning being clear and excessively warm, we thought it prudent to seek the river again, that we might obtain water for ourselves and our animals. They had had no grass for the last twenty-four hours; and the prospect of finding some for the poor animals upon the intervales was an additional inducement to adopt this course. We accordingly wound down the ravine two or three miles, struck the river at a point where its banks were protective, and unpacked to feed them and treat ourselves to a breakfast of cub meat. Boiled or roasted, it was miserable food. To eat it, however, or not to eat at all, was the alternative. Furthermore, in a region where lizards grow poor and wolves lean against sand banks to howl, cub soup, without salt, pepper, etc., must be acknowledged to be quite in style.

Having become somewhat comfortable by feasting thus, we traveled on down this river of deserts twenty miles, and encamped again on its banks. At this encampment we ate the last of our meat; and broke the bones with our hatchet for the oily marrow in them. The prospect of suffering from hunger before we could arrive at Brown's Hole became every hour more and more certain. The country between us and that point was known to be sterile, so that not even a grisly bear was to be hoped for in it. It was a desert of black flint, sand and marl, rendered barren by perpetual drought.

9th. Traveled twenty-three miles along the river — nothing to eat, not even a thistle stalk. At night we tried to take some fish; the stream proved as ungenerous as the soil on its banks.

10th. Made fifteen miles today; country covered with wild wormwood; at intervals a little bunch grass — dry and dead; face of the country formerly a plain, now washed into hills. Our dog was frantic with hunger; and although he had treated us to a cub and served us with all the fidelity of his race, we determined in full council tonight, if our hooks took no fish, to breakfast on his faithful heart in the morning. A horrid night we passed: forty-eight hours without a morsel of food! Our camp was eight miles above the junction of Little Bear and Little Snake rivers.

11th. This morning we tried our utmost skill at fishing. Patience often cried "hold" but the appearance of our poor dog would admonish us to continue our efforts to obtain a breakfast from the stream. Thus we fished and fasted till eight o'clock. A small fish or two were caught — three or four ounces of food for seven starving men! Our guide declared the noble dog must die! He was accordingly shot, his hair burnt off, and his forequarters boiled and eaten! Some of the men declared that dogs made excellent mutton; but on this point, there existed among us what politicians term an honest difference of opinion. To me, it tasted like *the flesh of a dog, a singed dog;* and appetite, keen though it was, and edged by a fast of fifty hours, could not but be sensibly alive to the fact that, whether cooked or barking, a dog is still a dog, everywhere. After our repast was finished, we saddled and rode over the plains in a northerly direction for Brown's Hole. We had been traveling the last five days in a westerly course; and as the river continued in that direction, we left it to see it no more, I would humbly hope, till the dews of Heaven shall cause its deserts to blossom and ripen into something more nutritive than wild wormwood and gravel.

A Grizzly vs. California Bulls

Major Horace Bell

One of the sports of older boys a century ago was to persuade younger boys to fight each other. If there was a disparity in size, they would tie one hand behind the larger boy and then turn the boys loose to fight it out; and with plenty of urging the boys would usually put on a good exhibition. Early Californians extended this idea to include the wild animals of their region, so plentiful were they, and used them for similar entertainment, in the Roman style. Major Horace Bell, at that time a newspaperman of southern California, preserved an extraordinary account of this pastime, as practiced in the 1850s — the same rough sport witnessed by Zenos Leonard in Monterey in the 1830s.

Bearbaiting was considered fine sport. For this purpose, range bulls were formidable opponents and were most frequently used. The bear was handicapped with a short, stout chain, thus leveling the odds. The contest was sometimes less one-sided than one would suppose, since both animals had exceptional strength and tenacity. But Major Bell reports he knew of several fiestas where burros were put into the ring with bears and fought to the death. If the bear was a grizzly, he always won, chain or no; but the burro would worry him desperately for a long time. The bear would suffer terrific jolts on the jaw from the burro's heels, hard enough to send him staggering back again and again. When the grizzly fi-

First published under the title "That Grand Californian, the Grizzly Bear," from *On the Old West Coast, Being Further Reminiscences of a Ranger, Major Horace Bell*, edited by Lanier Bartlett (New York: William Morrow & Co., 1930). Copyright 1930 by William Morrow and Company, Inc., renewed 1958 by Lanier Bartlett. By permission of the publisher.

nally got hold of his lowly but far-from-humble antagonist, the burro would bite and hang on to the death, like a bulldog. Major Bell considered the bull-and-bear fight fair sport but always felt the match with the burro was unfair, brutal, and barbarous. The more tenderhearted might consider both to be on par with the Roman sports that took pleasure in cruelty.

IN THE GREAT FIESTAS of times past at the missions and presidios there was always a bull and bear fight for the entertainment of the crowd. The last one on record that I know of took place at Pala, a branch or *asistencia* of the once great Mission of San Luis Rey, in the mountains of San Diego County, nearly fifty years ago. One of the American newspapers in California published an account of it written by a correspondent who was present. I have the clipping of that and as it is a better-written description than I could produce myself, I give it herewith:

"The bear was an ugly grizzly that for years had roamed the pineclad region of Palomar Mountain, rising six thousand feet above the little mission. Tied to a huge post in the center of the old adobe-walled quadrangle he stood almost as high as a horse, a picture of fury such as painter never conceived. His hind feet were tethered with several turns of a strong rawhide riata, but were left about a yard apart to give full play. To the center of this rawhide, between the two feet, was fastened another heavy riata, doubled and secured to a big loop made of double riatas thrown over the center post. The services of a man on horseback with a long pole were constantly needed to keep the raging monster from chewing through the rawhide ropes.

"By the time the bear had stormed around long enough to get well limbered up after being tied all night, the signal was given, the horseman affected his disappearance, and in dashed a bull through an open gate. He was of the old longhorn breed but of great weight and power. He had been roaming the hills all summer, living like a deer in the chaparral of the rough mountains and was quick and wild as any deer. He, too, like old Bruin, had been captured with the noosed lasso in a sudden dash of horsemen on a little flat he had to cross to go to a spring at daylight, and felt no more in love with mankind than did the bear. As he dashed across the arena it looked as if the fight was going to be an unequal one, but the bear gave a glance that intimated that no one need waste sympathy on *him*.

"No creature is so ready for immediate business than is the bull turned loose in an amphitheater of human faces. He seems to know they are there to see him fight and he wants them to get their money's worth. So, as soon as the gate admits him, he goes for everything in sight with the dash of a cyclone. Things that outside he would fly from or not notice, he darts at as eagerly as a terrier for a rat the instant he sees them in the ring.

"This bull came from the same mountains as the bear and they were old acquaintances, though the acquaintance had been cultivated on the run as the bull tore with thundering hoofs through the tough manzanita and went plunging down the steep hillside as the evening breeze wafted the strong scent of the bear to his keen nose. But now, in the arena, he spent no time looking for a way of escape but, at a pace that seemed impossible for even the great weight of the bear to resist, he rushed across the ring directly at the enemy as if he had been looking for him all his life.

"With wonderful quickness for so large an animal the bear rose on his legs and coolly waited until the long sharp horns were within a yard of his breast. Then up went the great paws, one on each side of the bull's head, and the sharp points of the horns whirled up from horizontal to perpendicular, then almost to horizontal again as bull and bear went rolling over together. In a twinkling the bear was on his feet again, but the bull lay limp as a rag, his neck broken.

"In rode four horsemen and threw riatas around the feet of the dead bull, while the grizzly did his ferocious best to get at them. As they dragged the body of the vanquished victim out one gate, the runway to the bullpen was opened once more and a second bull, a big black one with tail up, as if to switch the moon, charged into the arena. On his head glistened horns so long and sharp that it seemed impossible for the bear ever to reach the head with his death-dealing paws before being impaled.

"But this problem did not seem to worry the grizzly. He had not been living on cattle for so many years without knowing a lot about their movements. When this new antagonist came at him he dodged as easily as a trained human bullfighter, and as the bull shot past him, down came one big paw on the bovine's neck, with a whack that sounded all over the adobe corral. A chorus of shouts went up from the rows of swarthy faces, with here and there a white face, as the victim, turning partly over, went down with a plunge that made one of his horns plow up the dirt, then break sharp off under the terrific pressure of his weight and momentum.

"The bull was not done for; he tried to rise and Bruin made a dash for him, but his tethers held him short of his goal. In a second the bull got to his feet and wheeled around with one of those short twists that makes him so dangerous an antagonist. But once he's wheeled around, his course is generally straight ahead, and a quick dodger can avoid him; however, he is lightninglike in his charge, and something or somebody is likely to be overhauled in short order. So it was this time, and before the bear could recover from the confusion into which he had been thrown by being brought up short by his tether, the bull caught him in the shoulder with his remaining horn.

"Few things in nature are tougher than the shoulder of a grizzly bear, and a mere sideswing without the full weight of a running bull behind it was insufficient to make even this sharp horn penetrate. The bear staggered, but the horn glanced from the ponderous bone, leaving a long gash in the shaggy hide. This only angered Bruin the more. He made a grab for the head of the bull but again was foreshorted by the riatas, which allowed him only a limited scope of action.

"The bull returned to the charge as soon as he could turn himself around and aimed the long horn full at his enemy's breast. But just as the horn seemed reaching its mark the grizzly grabbed the bull's head with both paws and twisted it half round with nose inward. The nose he seized with his great white teeth, and over both went in a swirl of dust, while the crowd roared and cheered.

"Now one could see exactly why cattle found killed by bears always have their necks broken. Bears do not go through the slow process of strangling or bleeding their victims, but do business on scientific principles.

"This time the grizzly rose more slowly than before; nevertheless he rose, while the bull lay still in death.

"The owners of the bear now wanted to stop the show, but from all sides rose a roar of 'Otro! Otro! Otro! Otro toro!' — 'Another! Another! Another! Another bull!' The owners protested that the bear was disabled and was too valuable to sacrifice needlessly; that a dead bull was worth as much as a live one, and more, but that the same arithmetic did not hold good for a bear. The clamor of the crowd grew minute by minute, for the sight of blood gushing from the bear's shoulder was too much for the equilibrium of an audience like this one.

"Soon another bull shot toward the center of the arena. Larger than the rest but thinner, more rangy, he opened negotiations with even more vigor, more speed. With thundering thump of great hoofs, his head wagging from side to side, eyes flashing green fire, he drove full at the bear with full force. The grizzly was a trifle clumsy this time and as he rose to his hind feet the bull gave a twist of his head that upset the calculations of the bear. Right into the base of the bear's neck went a long, sharp horn, at the same time that the two powerful paws closed down on the bull's neck from above. A distinct crack was heard. The bull sank forward carrying the bear over backward with a heavy thump against the big post to which he was tied.

"Again the horsemen rode in to drag out a dead bull. But the grizzly now looked weary and pained. Another powwow with his owners ensued, while the crowd yelled more loudly than ever for another bull. The owners protested that it was unfair, but the racket rose louder and louder, for the audience knew that there was one bull left, the biggest and wildest of the lot.

"The crowd won, but Bruin was given a little more room in which to fight. Vaqueros rode in, and while two lassoed his forepaws and spread him out in front, the other two loosened his ropes behind so as to give him more play. He now had about half the length of a riata. Allowing him a breathing spell, which he spent trying to bite off the riatas, the gate of the bullpen was again thrown open.

"Out dashed an old red rover of the hills, and the way he went for the bear seemed to prove him another old acquaintance. He seemed anxious to make up for the many times he had flown from the distant scent that had warned him that the bear was in the same mountains. With lowered head turned to one side so as to aim one horn at the enemy's breast, he cleared the distance in half a dozen leaps.

"The bear was still slower than before in getting to his hind feet, and his right paw slipped as he grabbed the bull's head. He failed to twist it over. The horn struck him near the base of the neck, and the bull and bear went rolling over together.

"Loud cheers for the bull rose as the bear scrambled to his feet, showed blood coming from a hole in his neck almost beside the first wound. Still louder roared the applause as the bull regained his feet. Lashing his sides with his tail and bounding high in fury he wheeled and returned to the fray. The bear rolled himself over like a ball and would have been on his feet safely had not one foot caught in the riata which tied him to the post. Unable to meet the bull's charge with both hind feet solid on the ground, he fell forward against his antagonist and received one horn full in the breast, up to the hilt.

"But a grizzly keeps on fighting even after a thrust to the heart. Again he struggled to his feet, the blood gushing from the new wound. With stunning quickness in so large an animal, the bull had withdrawn his horn, gathered himself together, and returned to the charge. The bear could not turn in time to meet him, and with a heavy smash the horn struck him squarely in the shoulder forward of the protecting bone. Those who have seen the longest horns driven full to the hilt through the shoulder of a horse — a common sight in the bullfights of Mexico — can understand why the bear rolled over backwards to rise no more."

A Soldier and a
Wounded Grizzly

Lewis F. Crawford

*This story was told by the colorful Ben Arnold, who was sixty
years an Indian fighter, gold miner, cowboy, hunter, and army
scout — all the trades available to fearless and footloose men on
the western frontier. This tale supports the belief that such is the
vitality of a grizzly that he can only be killed by a bullet in the
brain. The unstoppability of a grizzly is recorded often enough to
give even the skeptic pause. The fury of the wounded animal described in this story no doubt gave strength when none could
reasonably be expected. The outcome was surprisingly fortunate,
considering the rashness of the man and his companions.*

DURING THE WESTERN MIGRATION and army movements in
the mountains, it was necessary to turn the teams loose to graze
wherever they could find forage each night of encampment.
Sometimes the horses and mules wandered far during the night
and much time was lost hunting them. Not infrequently they
were driven off by the Indians.

This story is typical of the many experiences army men had in
the days of the early West. It could well have occurred above old
Fort Laramie on the Platte or Fort Pierre on the Missouri. It illustrates what happened sometimes while the men were hunting the
mules. Similar experiences came to emigrants along the trail but

From Lewis Crawford, *Rekindling Campfires: The Exploits of Ben Arnold* (Bismarck,
N. Dak.: Capital Book Co., 1926).

were never recorded. Ben Arnold, who experienced much as an army scout, is the narrator:

"While keeping a close lookout on the bare chance of seeing the mules, we discovered a dark object in the distance, and on approaching we found it to be a grizzly bear — the largest, I think, I ever saw in all my travels. On noticing us, the bear stood up on his hind feet and took a good look. Kerns said, 'Ben, you're the best shot; you shoot first,' and I fired, aiming as nearly as I could for the vital spot behind his foreleg. As soon as I fired the bear pressed a paw to its heart, dropped down on its four feet and started to run for a thick clump of high sagebrush, following a broken buffalo trail. He secreted himself there and after a short time in which we saw and heard nothing of him, we concluded he was dead. We dismounted and began to throw stones into the gnarled and matted sagebrush. When this brought no immediate results, we scattered out in order to comb the brush patch. Shortly a shot from Kerns, followed by a shout, 'I've got him,' rang out. We ran to him and were just in time to see the bear lurch to its feet, lunge for him, and knock the gun out of his hands. We retreated as fast as the brush would permit and held a consultation. It would not do to go back to the post and report that one of our party had been disarmed by a bear, so we again made a cautious sweep into the brush patch, trying as best we could to protect Kerns, who carried only a six-shooter, which I had loaned him. We had gone but a short distance when Kerns with a shriek threw both hands in front of him in an involuntary effort to protect himself from the sudden onslaught of the grizzly. The bear swept both of Kerns's arms into its mouth, the impact carrying him to the ground with the bear on top.

"Kerns, as he was borne to the ground by the beast, cried out frantically, 'Don't leave me, boys!' But in the meantime we had not been idle. Thomas was firing into the bear's head with a six-shooter, while I was shooting into his side. We were both firing as rapidly as possible and at such close quarters that the powder singed his hair at each shot.

"In spite of the noise of our shooting, we heard Kerns gasp, 'Roll him off, he's mashing me.' The bear now lay quiet across his body and it was all we could do to lift the immense, limp form enough to pull Kerns out, choking and exhausted.

"Later, on recovering from the excitement, we examined the

grizzly and found he had been pierced by thirteen bullets, several of which passed through his heart. I know of no other animal which is not instantaneously killed by a shot in the heart. I believe, however, that a bullet through the brain kills a grizzly instantly, just as it does any other animal.

"We tried to lift Kerns to his feet, but he was groggy and faint from loss of blood, which flowed freely from his mangled arms and a large wound across his abdomen, the result of a sideswipe of the bear's claws. From a nearby pool we bathed his wounds as best we could, using a part of his shredded shirt as a washcloth. Fortunately, no bones were broken and after the first feeling of exhaustion and faintness had passed he made bold to assert that he was not as badly hurt as we thought. Even so, however, he was too badly torn to be able to ride and it would be necessary to bring out a wagon from camp to haul him in. Thomas volunteered to ride to camp after help while I waited on Kerns and skinned the bear. I had a loaded rifle at hand for fear another bear would make his appearance, and kept a close watch.

"As camp was some miles away, about three hours elapsed before Thomas returned with a wagon and help. By this time Kerns's wounds and clothes were matted with blood, and he began to suffer much pain from his lacerations, which were becoming swollen and feverish.

"When the wagon came the mules objected to being driven up close to the carcass of the bear, which lay on its spread-out pelt; but after much mule talk and the spirited use of the 'mule skinner,' the rig was brought alongside and the man and the bear loaded up. It was getting dark by the time we reached the post, but the whole camp turned out to see us, with mixed motives of curiosity and sympathy. While such expressions as 'Ain't he a whopper,' and 'As big as an ox' were being passed, we took Kerns out as gently as possible and turned him over to the women who were laundresses for our company. Kerns's wounds, while painful, proved to be superficial and he was up and around in a short while, much to our surprise and satisfaction.

"The bear was an old fellow and too tough for eating. We did not even prepare the skin for bedding, as to cure it properly required much work in scraping off surplus flesh and tanning the hide. All we kept as relics of our fierce encounter were the claws, which we distributed among a few of our friends.

Combat Between a Grizzly and a Wild Bull

J. Ross Browne

On a "dangerous journey" from San Francisco to San Luis Obispo in the summer of 1849, the journalist J. Ross Browne, who left us many lively accounts of early California, had occasion to observe an extraordinary fight between a wild bull and a grizzly. Spanish cattle were tough and mean, as Browne had come to know. Although this struggle seemed remarkable to the unfortunate traveler clinging to the sanctuary of his tree, it was in fact not uncommon for cattle and grizzlies to fight. The grizzly naturally preyed upon the herd, and their protection was the bull's responsibility. These fine animals were evenly matched — horn and hoof versus tooth and claw — in the wild. Yet when men matched these animals for sport, in the ring, the grizzly always lost; if not to the first bull then to the second or third, whose energies would be fresh while those of the bear, staked and chained all the while, would be exhausted by continuous combat. Browne's opportunity to behold these goliaths of nature contending in their own way, on their own ground, and by their own choosing provides a stirring narrative.

ABOUT AN HOUR before sunset, as I was riding slowly along enjoying the approaching shades of evening, I discovered for the first time that my mule was lame. I had traveled very leisurely on account of the heat, making not over thirty miles. The nearest

From "A Dangerous Journey," *Harper's New Monthly Magazine*, vol. 24 (May 1862).

water, as the young Spaniard, Sobranis, had informed me, was at a point yet distant about five miles. I saw that it was necessary to hurry, and began to spur my mule in the hope of being able to reach this camping place; but I soon perceived that the poor animal was not only lame but badly foundered. At least it seemed so then, though my convictions on that point were somewhat shaken by what subsequently occurred. I had succeeded, after considerable spurring, in getting him into a lope, when he suddenly stumbled and threw me over his head. The shock of the fall stunned me for a few moments; but fortunately I was not hurt. I must have turned a complete somersault. As soon as consciousness returned I found that I was lying on my back in the middle of the road, the mule quietly grazing within ten feet. I got up a little bewildered, shook off some of the dust, and started to regain the bridle; but to my great surprise the mule put back his ears, kicked up his heels, and ran off at a rate of speed that I deemed a foundered animal entirely incapable of achieving. There was not the slightest symptom of lameness in his gait. He loped as freely as if he had just begun his journey. In vain I shouted and ran after him. Sometimes he seemed absolutely to enjoy my helpless condition, and would permit me to approach within two or three feet, but never to get hold of the bridle. Every attempt of that kind he resented by whirling suddenly and kicking at me with both heels, so that once or twice it was a miracle how I escaped. For the first time since morning, notwithstanding the heat of the day, my skin became moist. A profuse sweat broke out all over me, and I was parched with a burning thirst. It was thirty miles from Soledad, the nearest inhabited place that I knew of, and even if I felt disposed to turn back it would have been at great risk and inconvenience. My blankets, coat, pistol, and papers — the whole of incalculable importance to me — were firmly strapped behind the saddle, and there was no way of getting at them without securing the mule. Upon reflection it seemed best to follow him to the watering place. He must be pretty thirsty after his hard day's journey in the sun, and would not be likely to pass that. I therefore walked on as fast as possible, keeping the mule as near in the trail as his stubborn nature would permit. It was not without difficulty, however, that I could discern the right trail, for it was frequently intersected by others, and occasionally became lost in patches of sand and sagebrush.

In this way, with considerable toil, I had advanced about two miles when I discovered that a large band of Spanish cattle, which had been visible for some time in the distance, began to close in toward the line of my route, evidently with the intention of cutting me off. Their gestures were quite hostile enough to inspire a solitary and unarmed footman with uneasiness. A fierce-looking bull led the way, followed by a lowing regiment of stags, steers, and cows, crowding one upon the other in their furious charge. As they advanced, the leader occasionally stopped to tear up the earth and shake his horns; but the mass kept crowding on, their tails switching high in the air, and uttering the most fearful bellowing, while they tossed their horns and stared wildly, as if in mingled rage and astonishment. I had heard too much of the wild cattle of California, and their hostility toward men on foot at this season of the year, not to become at once sensible of my dangerous position.

The nearest tree was half a mile to the left, on the margin of a dry creek. There was a grove of small oaks winding for some distance near the banks of the creek; but between the spot where I stood and this place of security scattering bands of cattle were grazing. However, there was no time to hesitate upon a choice of difficulties. Two or three hundred wild cattle rushing furiously toward one in an open plain assist him in coming to a very rapid conclusion. I know of no position in which human strength is of so little avail — the tremendous aggregation of brute force opposed to one feeble pair of arms seems so utterly irresistible. I confess instinct lent me a helping hand in this emergency. Scarcely conscious of the act, I ran with all my might for the nearest tree. The thundering of heavy hoofs after me, and the furious bellowing that resounded over the plain, spread a contagion among the grazing herds on the way, and with one accord they joined in the chase. It is in no spirit of boastfulness that I assert the fact, but I certainly made that half mile in as few minutes as ever the same distance was made by mortal man. When I reached the tree I looked back. The advance body of the cattle were within a hundred yards, bearing down in a whirlwind of dust. I lost no time in making my retreat secure. As the enemy rushed in, tearing up the earth and glaring at me with their fierce, wild eyes, I had gained the fork of the tree, about six feet from the ground, and felt very thankful that I was beyond their reach. Still there was something fearful in being blockaded in such a place for the night. An intolerable thirst parched my throat. The effects of the exertion were scarcely perceptible at first, but as I regained my breath it seemed impossible to exist an hour longer without water. In this valley the climate is so intensely dry during the summer heats that the juices of the system are quickly absorbed, and the skin becomes like a sheet of parchment. My head felt as if compressed in a band of iron; my tongue was dry and swollen. I would have given all I possessed, or ever hope to possess, for a single glass of water.

While in this position, with the prospect of a dreary night before me, and suffering the keenest physical anguish, a very singular cirumstance occurred to relieve me of further apprehension respecting the cattle, though it suggested a new danger for which I was equally unprepared. A fine young bull had descended the bed of the creek in search of a water hole. While pushing his way through the bushes he was suddenly attacked by a grizzly bear. The struggle was terrific. I could see the tops of the bushes sway violently to and fro, and hear the heavy crash of driftwood as the two powerful animals writhed in their fierce embrace. A cloud of dust rose from the spot. It was not distant over a hundred yards from the tree in which I had taken refuge. Scarcely two minutes elapsed before the bull broke through the bushes. His head was covered with blood, and great flakes of flesh hung from his foreshoulders; but instead of manifesting signs of defeat, he seemed literally to glow with defiant rage. Instinct had taught him to seek an open space. A more splendid specimen of an animal I never saw; lithe and wiry, yet wonderfully massive about the shoulders, combining the rarest qualities of strength and symmetry. For a moment he stood glaring at the bushes, his head erect, his eyes flashing, his nostrils distended, and his whole form fixed and rigid. But scarcely had I time to glance at him when a huge bear, the largest and most formidable I ever saw in a wild state, broke through the opening.

A trial of brute force that baffles description now ensued. Badly as I had been treated by the cattle, my sympathies were greatly in favor of the bull, which seemed to me to be much the nobler animal of the two. He did not wait to meet the charge, but lowering his head, boldly rushed upon his savage adversary. The grizzly was active and wary. He no sooner got within reach of the bull's horns than he seized them in his powerful grasp, keeping the head to the ground by main strength and the tremendous weight of his body, while he bit at the nose with his teeth, and raked strips of flesh from the shoulders with his hind paws. The two animals must have been of very nearly equal weight. On the one side there was the advantage of superior agility and two sets of weapons — the teeth and claws; but on the other, greater powers of endurance and more inflexible courage. The position thus assumed was maintained for some time — the bull struggling desperately to free his head, while the blood streamed from his nostrils; the bear straining every muscle to drag him to the ground. No advantage seemed to be gained on either side. The result of the battle evidently depended on the merest accident.

As if by mutual consent, each gradually ceased struggling, to regain breath, and as much as five minutes must have elapsed while they were locked in this motionless but terrible embrace. Suddenly the bull, by one desperate effort, wrenched his head from the grasp of his adversary, and retreated a few steps. The bear stood up to receive him. I now watched with breathless interest, for it was evident that each animal had staked his life upon the issue of the conflict. The cattle from the surrounding plains had crowded in, and stood moaning and bellowing around the combatants; but as if withheld by terror, none seemed disposed to interfere. Rendered furious by his wounds, the bull now gathered up all his energies, and charged with such impetuous force and ferocity that the bear, despite the most terrific blows with his paws, rolled over in the dust, vainly struggling to defend himself. The lunges and thrusts of the former were perfectly furious. At length, by a sudden and well-directed motion of his head, he got one of his horns under the bear's belly, and gave it a rip that brought out a clotted mass of entrails. It was apparent the battle must soon end. Both were grievously wounded, and neither could last much longer. The ground was torn up and covered with blood for some distance around, and the panting of the struggling animals became each moment heavier and quicker. Maimed and gory, they fought with the desperate certainty of death — the bear rolling over and over, vainly striking out to avoid the fatal horns of his adversary; the bull ripping, thrusting, and tearing with irresistible ferocity.

At length, as if determined to end the conflict, the bull drew back, lowered his head, and made one tremendous charge; but blinded by the blood that trickled down his forehead, he missed his mark, and rolled headlong on the ground. In an instant the bear whirled and was upon him. Thoroughly invigorated by the prospect of a speedy victory, he tore the flesh in huge masses from the ribs of his prostrate foe. The two rolled over and over in the terrible death struggle; nothing was now to be seen save a heaving, gory mass, dimly perceptible through the dust. A few minutes would certainly have terminated the bloody strife, so far as my favorite was concerned, when, to my astonishment, I saw the bear relax in his efforts, roll over from the body of his prostrate foe, and drag himself feebly a few yards from the spot. His entrails had burst entirely through the wound in his belly, and now lay in long strings over the ground. The next moment the bull was on his legs, erect and fierce as ever. Shaking the blood from his eyes, he looked around, and seeing the reeking mass before him, lowered his head for the final and most desperate charge. In the death struggle that ensued both animals seemed animated by supernatural strength. The grizzly struck out wildly, but with such destructive energy that the bull, upon drawing back his head, presented a horrible and ghastly spectacle; his tongue, a mangled mass of shreds, hanging from his mouth, his eyes torn completely from their sockets, and his whole face stripped to the bone. On the other hand, the bear was ripped completely open and writhing in his last agonies. Here it was that indomitable courage prevailed; for blinded and maimed as he was, the bull, after a momentary pause to regain his wind, dashed wildly at his adversary again, determined to be victorious even in death. A terrific roar escaped from the dying grizzly. With a last frantic effort he sought to make his escape, scrambling over and over in the dust. But his strength was gone. A few more thrusts from the savage victor and he lay stretched upon the sand, his muscles quivering convulsively, his huge body a resistless mass. A clutching motion of the claws — a groan — a gurgle of the throat, and he was dead.

The bull now raised his bloody crest, uttered a deep bellowing sound, shook his horns triumphantly, and slowly walked off, not, however, without turning every few steps to renew the struggle if necessary. But his last battle was fought. As the blood streamed from his wounds a death chill came over him. He stood for some time, unyielding to the last, bracing himself up, his legs apart, his head gradually drooping; then dropped on his fore-knees and lay down; soon his head rested upon the ground; his body became motionless; a groan, a few convulsive respirations, and he too, the nobler victor, was dead.

During this strange and sanguinary struggle, the cattle, as I stated before, had gathered in around the combatants. The most daring, as if drawn toward the spot by the smell of blood or some irresistible fascination, formed a circle within twenty or thirty yards, and gazed at the murderous work that was going on with startled and terror-stricken eyes; but none dared to join in the defense of their champion. No sooner was the battle ended, and the victor and the vanquished stretched dead upon the ground, than a panic seized upon the excited multitude, and by one accord they set up a wild bellowing, switched their tails in the air, and started off full speed for the plains.

A Canadian Soldier's Encounter with a Bear

from *Chamber's Edinburgh Journal of Popular Literature*

This story is an account of a Canadian soldier's experience in 1856. While vacationing on leave, he became separated and lost from his Indian guide. During his attempt to find his way out of the woods he welcomed a cave as a refuge from the cold.

Some writers and acknowledged authorities on grizzly bears say that the grizzly does not "hug" his antagonist. I am glad to present this account in support of the old and widely accepted notion of the bear hug.

SOME YEARS SINCE, when serving with my regiment in Canada, I obtained two months' leave of absence for the sake of enjoying some of the wild sports of the Far West. While out hunting one day, without my Indian guide, I became lost and w⌐ndered several days in search of our camp.

One evening I esteemed myself fortunate in finding a cave, which a mass of brushwood at the entrance had kept free from snow; the air inside was so warm that it was positively luxurious; and while busy making a fire, I resolved on remaining there a day or two to recruit.

The very idea was refreshing; and in unusual spirits I skinned a hare I had shot during the day and placed it, hunter fashion, on

This account appeared in *Chamber's Edinburgh Journal of Popular Literature*, no. 257 (December 4, 1858).

two sticks before the fire. Scarcely was it placed in this torrid zone, when something between a grunt and a groan seemed to intimate its dislike to its new position. I started; and in horrible doubt whether I had not committed the barbarity of flaying and impaling a living animal, I stretched out my hand to draw it from the fire, when another grunt, unmistakably behind my back, caused me to look around. But nothing was visible in the deep dim cavern save the carpet of dried leaves, which the autumn winds had swept into it. Concluding there was some cranny in my new domicile through which the wind came grumbling down, I addressed myself to my roast.

The next moment a growl, so deep and fierce that it echoed through the cave, startled me to my feet; and I turned to find myself closely confronted by an enormous grizzly bear, the most fearful animal of the American wilds. How ferociously his eyes glared on me from under his shaggy brows, as he opened them from the new-fallen sleep, which the warm beams of my fire had dispelled, and how convulsively his huge jaws worked and quivered in eager longing to devour me! Ere I had time to snatch the revolver from my belt the gigantic beast rose toweringly above me, and opening his enormous paws, pressed me to him in close embrace — so close that my arms were pinned to my sides, and my very bones seemed to crack in that viselike hug. I believe I screamed with the sudden agony, but the sound was lost in the deep-mouthed growls, like muttering thunder, that filled the cave.

Weak and exhausted as I was, I felt myself unequal to cope with the powerful beast in whose grasp I was; but even if life were of little worth, to a solitary such as I, this mode of death was so horrible, that it nerved me to efforts beyond my ordinary strength, and somehow my hand managed to creep up towards my belt. But ere I could reach the weapon I sought, a movement of the bear had loosened it, and firing a single barrel, it fell to the ground among our feet. The report echoing through the cave alarmed my adversary; and with a more threatening growl, he clasped me closer, and for the first time his claws penetrated my clothes, inflicting terrible wounds.

But my hand had met an unexpected friend in my knife, which I had unwittingly thrust into my belt, and with it I inflicted several random stabs on my antagonist. This, however, seemed only to add to my own sufferings; for, maddened by the pain, the bear threw himself upon the ground and rolled over with me in his agony, while his huge teeth munched and tore at the blanket which a fortunate fit of toothache had made me wrap round my head. Not that, nor any other earthly matter seemed likely to concern me long, for the strength of excitement was already passing, a strange murmur was mingling in my ears with the fierce growls of my enemy; and the pain of his claws changed into a vague yet universal agony as unconsciousness and life were being pressed out in that terrible hug.

Suddenly a sound echoed through the cave, so sharp that it reached even my failing faculties, and appeared to thrill likewise on the nerves of my foe, to judge by the increased emphasis of his embrace; but the next instant he relaxed his hold, and sank helpless on the ground beside me, his almost insensible victim.

My first sensations as I revived were of burning pains all over my body, and exceeding cold in my hands and face; I opened my eyes to find a young Indian bending over me, and rubbing me with snow.

Passing near the cave, he had seen my fire, and heard the report of my revolver and had hastened to see what was the matter, just in time to save me from a miserable death and a revolting sepulchre.

All night long this Good Samaritan sat beside me, tending the gaping wounds through which life threatened momentarily to escape; and when morning broke, he left me for a short while to go to his village — which was scarcely a mile distant — for help. In one of the lodges of that Indian hamlet I passed the remainder of the winter, prized and tended as if I had indeed been the brother that in their stately yet kindly courtesy they styled me. Thanks for their skill in forest simples, my wounds healed marvelously; and when the sweet breath of spring broke the ice-fetters of the lakes and rivers, I was sufficiently recovered to embark in my preserver's canoe, the skin of my defunct foe forming a luxurious couch.

My return to the land of civilization somehow resembled that of a spirit to the land of the living. I will not say my place had forgotten me; for I had no longer a place, since my lieutenancy, my quarters and my uniform had other occupants and very loath the tenants were, especially that of the first, to admit the fact of my resurrection.

A Mortal Combat

A. J. Alexander

Old plainsmen and trappers often debated which was more powerful, the buffalo or the grizzly bear. Both were fearless titans. There are more accounts of grizzlies killing buffalo — perhaps the expected outcome, in view of the weapons and tactics employed by both animals. This story, then, should be of special interest. It concerns a bull buffalo that stood his ground against the most feared animal of the plains and mountains. The fight was fair; there was no one to interfere. The bear was the aggressor, for he was trespassing on the home ground of the buffalo.

Both animals entered the contest determined to win and gave no quarter. The fortunate witnesses were thrilled by the mighty combat, yet the white hunter, though stirred, would have shot the victor. But the Indian, in admiration, acclaimed the buffalo and turned aside the hunter's rifle. I would entitle this story "Big Brave."

SOME YEARS AGO I was one of a small party hunting in the Rocky Mountains. So far our hunt had been very successful, and we had made an ideal hunters' camp on a southeastern slope of the mountains near the crest, in a scrub-oak thicket which afforded us the best fuel in abundance. The dense timber protected both men and animals and from the cold winds, and plenty of bunch grass made our animals comfortable. As the huge campfire lit up the surrounding trees, there came into view carcasses of

From *The Life and Services of Brevet Brigadier-General Andrew Jonathan Alexander, United States Army; A Sketch,* by James Harrison Wilson (New York, 1887).

white- and black-tailed deer, bears, and mountain sheep hanging on convenient limbs. Our supper had been a beautiful one consisting of such choice parts of the different varieties of game as each one desired. Then came one of those happy periods which only a hunter knows, when fresh logs were piled on the fire, and the delicious aroma of the after-dinner pipe floated lazily on the air. Each one disposed of his tired frame in the most agreeable attitude, and the events of the day, and the prospects for the morrow, were pleasantly discussed.

Among our party was a mountaineer who had spent many years on the mountains, and had undergone all the vicissitudes of fortune incident to that wild life. The question came up as to which of the savage animals was the most powerful. This elicited the following story from the old mountaineer. I wish I could narrate it in his own words, and give his powerful picture of the scene he described, which would add much to the effect.

He said he was hunting once in the Rockies with an Indian as his companion. They saw at a distance a buffalo on one of the foothills, and at once commenced stalking him. As anyone knows who has visited the Rocky Mountains, they break off gradually to the eastward in ridges divided by deep and rugged ravines or canyons. The hunters approached under shelter of the ridge next to the one on which they had perceived the buffalo, and when opposite him, and within easy rifleshot, crawled slowly to the crest, carrying bushes in their hands to conceal their heads. Upon reaching the crest of the ridge they had a full view of the buffalo, which proved to be a bull of the largest size, in full flesh and vigor.

Their attention was at once attracted to the curious conduct of the magnificent animal. His head was turned partially from them, looking toward the ravine on the opposite side. He was emitting the low bellowing roar peculiar to the buffalo when excited, throwing up the dirt and raising his tail as they do when enraged. The hunters thought he was challenging another buffalo, and waited to see the result. In a few moments they saw an enormous grizzly bear moving slowly up to the knoll where the buffalo awaited his coming.

The bear approached cautiously, stopping every few yards to observe his antagonist, whose excitement and rage seemed to increase and whose continuous muffled roar drowned all the other sounds.

Finally, when the bear had arrived within a few rods of his noble enemy, on the narrow bench of nearly level ground, the buffalo brought matters to a crisis by lowering his gigantic head and charging with all his strength. The bear immediately raised himself on his hind legs, and skillfully avoiding the buffalo's horns, caught him around the head with his left arm, seizing him at the same time by the back of his neck with his powerful jaws. Then came a grand exhibition of strength, the buffalo using all his tremendous power to get his horns under the bear and free himself from the close embrace of his adversary, while the latter, clinging with his teeth and one arm, used the other in an attempt to cripple the buffalo by the most terrific blows on his left shoulder and side. In this tremendous struggle, they turned in a circle several times, until finally the buffalo accomplished his object and threw the bear from him.

For a few moments they remained gazing at one another, evidently recovering their breath, somewhat exhausted by their previous efforts. The buffalo was bleeding from several wounds in the neck, and the bear from wounds on his side. They both exhibited the extreme of savage anger, the buffalo bellowing, tearing the earth, and shaking his great shaggy head, while the bear returned his challenge by continuous roars, showing his great teeth and swinging his massive head from side to side. The buffalo brought the truce to a close by a rapid charge, which the bear eluded, striking his adversary a tremendous blow as he passed, which again brought blood. The buffalo turned with the rapidity peculiar to the animal, and repeated the charge several times, without effecting his object. At last they closed in the final struggle, the bear clinging to the buffalo's head and shoulders, while the latter maneuvered to get his horns under his formidable antagonist. Round and round they went, tearing up rocks and bushes, until the buffalo succeeded in his efforts, forced the bear over the edge of the little plateau, and, in the impetuosity of his charge, fell on the bear with all his enormous weight, and turned a complete somersault down the steep decline.

For an instant both lay still, but the buffalo soon recovered himself, and staggering slowly to his feet, again faced his antagonist with undiminished resolution. The bear, however, lay quiet, breathing heavily and evidently *hors de combat*.

After waiting a few moments for a renewal of the attack the buffalo slowly approached his fallen enemy, and applying his great strength, rolled him over. Finding him dead, he slowly ascended to the scene of the battle and proclaimed his victory by triumphant bellowing.

The white hunter raised his rifle to shoot him, but the Indian sprang forward and put his hand on the rifle, and turning it away said, "No shoot! Big brave!" and allowed the victor to march slowly away to seek his comrades.

The Capture of Ben Franklin

James Capen Adams

We are indebted to James Capen Adams for his great contribution to our knowledge of the nature and character of the grizzly. Adams hunted and trapped big game from 1849 to 1859 in California and along the Pacific coast. He captured numerous grizzlies, both old and young, and domesticated them. Among these were Martha Washington, who was taken as a cub in Oregon and domesticated, and his huge grizzly, Sampson, who reportedly tipped the beam of a hay scale at 1500 pounds. Adams also raised Ben Franklin, the cub captured in this story, along with the greyhound pup, Rambler. The two nursed from Rambler's mother, and they grew up as brothers.

As Ben matured, Adams trained him to carry a pack, and frequently Ben would carry a deer to camp, on his back. On one occasion, Adams came suddenly upon a large grizzly; he shot and only wounded the beast, and it charged him. Ben, still not fully grown, but sensing his master's danger, engaged the wounded animal and fought him off until Adams could reload his gun and shoot to kill. Adams and Ben were constant companions. When the old hunter retired from the mountains he rented a room on Market Street in San Francisco and kept a few wild animals. He charged a small admission fee, and for a dime children could ride the big grizzly bear, Ben Franklin.

This colorful account is thought to be by Adams himself. He is

From *Life of J. C. Adams, Known as Old Adams, Old Grizzly Adams, containing a truthful account of his bear hunts, fights with grizzly bears, hairbreath escapes, in the Rocky and Nevada Mountains, and the wilds of the Pacific Coast*, New York, 1860. (Privately printed.)

not as skillful a narrator as his biographer, Theodore Hittell, but the tale is told with the freshness of firsthand experience.

———————

WHILE HUNTING one day, I thought I detected what might be the den of a grizzly bear. I scrutinized the vicinity, and by the disturbed ground and the character of the tracks, I felt confident I could not be mistaken. I judged, too, that it was a bear with cubs that inhabited the den. I posted to the camp, and acquainted Saxey with my suspicions, asking him to assist in killing the mother and procuring the cubs; he revolved the matter over in his mind and then begged to be excused. He was not partial to encountering a grizzly bear in presence of her family, and within her own castle. He was decidedly of opinion that the speculation would not "pay." His ideas on the subject of bears led him to think that he had seen one as closely as it was wholesome to approach such an animal, and he felt no wish to put my rifle aim to another test as a guarantee of his safety. He preferred to go hunting for other animals, and to leave me all the glory to be gained in grizzly-bear experiments. I was satisfied. As I said once before, I prefer on such occasions to have none to look out for except myself; Saxey, therefore, departed his road on a hunt, and I on mine. First I collected provisions enough for myself to last three or four days; for I had come to the conclusion not to return without the cubs, and it was possible that I might be called upon to exercise a great deal of patience before I could get possession of them.

I proceeded directly to the bear's den, and after viewing it cautiously all round, at once laid my plans. It is the custom of grizzly bears, when they have young, to remain in close concealment with the cubs nearly all day, and just before sunset to commence ranging the wilderness for food. In this business they are usually engaged the whole night, returning a little in advance of sunrise. Taking advantage of this habit, I acted accordingly. I sought out a position for myself, in which I could command a full view of the mouth of the den, and yet be hidden from the eyes of its emerging occupant. This position, after much delay, I was able to secure, and making myself as comfortable as I could in it, there I sat, and patiently watched all that night. But no bear came in sight. Perhaps she was in, I thought; or perhaps one of her cubs was. At any rate it was not probable that she would remain housed for two nights in succession; so I prepared to maintain my vigilance. The second night, to my great satisfaction, I observed her make her appearance at the mouth of the cave — for I omitted to say that the den was a cave, which evidently penetrated the earth to a considerable distance, and thus made a capital retreat for the bear. Mrs. Bruin had a keen pair of nostrils. I was perhaps a hundred yards distant, and concealed above her in the brushwood, when she advanced out into the open, and smelled my presence. My walks about the environs of the cave in reconnoitering had, no doubt, left the scent upon track, and she at once perceived that she was not alone — that her solitude had been invaded. I had a full view of her; but before I could get my rifle to bear upon her, she dodged back and retired.

As these disappointments only increased my resolution, and I was confident the animal could not go much longer without food, I continued to watch all that day and the third night. But I considered it prudent to change my position, lest she might be able to ascertain by her eyes, as well as by her nose, that she had my company. I shifted my ambush out of sight of the mouth of the cave, but in a good line with the track to it, and thus was fortunate; for, on that day, while the sun was yet half an hour high, the bear presented herself in full sight. She rose upon her feet when she got out, and snuffed the air diligently all round, as though still distrustful that something which meditated mischief was afloat. She twisted and twined in all directions in her doubt, and this gave me an admirable opportunity for a deadly shot. The moment I had a fair aim at her heart I discharged my piece. The ball passed in back of her foreshoulder, and, as I afterwards discovered, went directly through her heart. She fell, and taking it for granted that she must be dead, I drew my bowie knife and rushed upon her, in order to lose no time in seeking for the cubs. When I reached her she looked dead enough; but I thought I might just as well make sure of it, as an enemy in the rear, when I should get into the cave, would be exceedingly troublesome. I popped my knife, therefore, as a matter of form, into her throat. But, good heavens! Only fancy my astonishment when, as the cold steel penetrated her skin, she leaped up and grabbed me by the legs with her huge paws! This was a contingency I had by no means counted upon. It was a performance distinctly *not* "set down in the bills." A desperately wounded bear is about as unattractive an acquaintance as the wild forest can show, and one that stands as little on trifles. And yet I was in just such a party's grasp. It was an appalling thought! But I had not much time to think, for it was obviously a death struggle for one or both of us; and as her horrible teeth met in my flesh, the exquisite pain left me nothing but an instinctive sense of the necessity for prompt action. We were both down upon the ground together now. Her teeth and claws were both at work. I was desperately struggling to get my arms free for offensive measures, but, growing exhausted with my loss of blood, was not, at first, successful. At length I twisted myself around underneath her, and caught her, with my left hand, by the great goatee which hung under her mouth, while I plunged my knife into her heart with my right, and worked it briskly round to insure its fatal operation. Her jaws opened; her claws relaxed her hold; and after one or two more spasmodic endeavors to mutilate me, she rolled over and expired.

This time there was no mistake about her spirit's departure; and as I tried to rise upon my feet, I felt grateful to Providence that mine had not departed, also. I conceived that I had a right to congratulate myself on winning a great battle. I was mangled — in fact, I was partially crippled. I had lost a great deal of blood, and was proportionately weak; but I was worth twenty dead men yet, and the cubs, I was aware, must be in the cave, expecting my attentions.

I bound up my wounds, therefore, in the best manner I could under the circumstances, and then took a rest. This effected, I summoned my remaining strength and determination to my aid, grasped my bowie knife in my hand, and going down upon my hands and knees, began to grope my way in towards the den. I soon discovered that it was too dark in the cave to make any safe progress in that manner. I was not certain that the father of the cubs might not be within, anticipating my visit, and prepared to receive me with affectionate embraces; and as his eyes, in the dark, were nicely fitted to perceive and welcome his guest, long before mine would enable me to judge of his presence, I had additional reasons for circumspection. I beat a hasty retreat into the open air, and, getting up some fat pine-tree limbs, I converted them into torches. Thus provided, I reentered the cave with plenty of light. Knife in one hand, and a blazing flambeau in the other, I fairly dragged my lacerated legs and weary body along the floor of the cave, examining the spot cautiously, as well as attentively, in my slow progress. My heart panted quite as much with alarm as with interest. I will acknowledge it, I was really full of fear. It was a long distance underground. I had no assistance to expect. I was miles away from the camp, and intruding upon the premises of the enemy. I was creeping towards his very bed, and considering the nature of the locality, my ignorance of its openings, its nature, and extent — considering my weak and disabled condition, and the chance of encountering a disturbed grizzly fresh from repose in his own lair — it was not remarkable that I should entertain an overpowering sense of danger, and indulge in a few thrilling apprehensions as to the result. But I had gone entirely too far to recede, and creeping on — creeping stealthily on — when I had penetrated a distance of perhaps twenty or thirty yards, I beheld, to my intense delight, the bear's nest. It contained two dear little fellows fast alseep, and there was no appearance whatever of their indulgent papa. The cubs were no larger than wharf rats, and had not yet gotten their eyes open, but lay snuggled up together, all unconscious of what was going around them, and innocent of every thought of mischief. I put them into my bosom, and then looked around the den. It was, I should think, from four to six feet wide, and six to eight feet in height; but how far the subterranean chamber extended, I had no disposition to inquire. I had achieved my purpose. The cubs were in my power. I was in pain with my wounds, tired in my gallant struggle with the bear, and had enjoyed no sleep for two or three nights. My only wish at that moment was to hasten home, exhibit with exultation my little trophies of war, attend to my wounds, throw myself on my bed, and sleep till I had recovered my natural strength and energy. But, scrambling out of the cave, no king upon his throne could have felt prouder than I did. No millionaire could have contemplated his property with more secret joy than I did those little creatures in my bosom! For they were the youngest and handsomest infants of the kind I had ever seen. They had no teeth yet; had scarcely any hair on them; they were so helpless and so confiding! So away I went to camp feeling as large as any Gulliver, with the Brobdingnag cubs to my heart!

Arrived at the camp, I told the whole story to Saxey and the Indian boys, but they laughed at it as a gross invention. Saxey, in short, said I was a — well, no matter what; but he used a very strong expression not often met with in the good Christian's vocabulary, and implying a generous sense of my ability to manufacture an exciting tale without being too particular to put all the facts in it on their affidavit. However, there were the cubs. There was no getting over that little circumstance. The next day, too, when I escorted them to the spot, there was the bear, and there were all the evidences of the fearful struggle between us. When we lit pine torches and entered the cave, there was still the cubs' bed, and the marks of my depredation. This left no chance to doubt any longer, and they confessed that I had a right to feel elated. As Saxey and I were equal partners in these hunting expeditions, I gave him one of the cubs and retained the other myself, naming mine, at the same time, Ben Franklin.

Saved by a Tree

William Kelly

The gigantic size of the bear in Kelly's lively account may pro-voke a smile, as will his naive explanation as to why a grizzly usually does not climb a tree. Yet many a man who has found himself in Kelly's situation, in the near vicinity of an aggressive bear, has looked for a suitable tree sanctuary and speculated on the speed with which he can negotiate the distance from ground to safety. And we have several reports that grizzlies can be dan-gerous even to men in trees. I have yet to hear of an encounter with a grizzly of small stature.

I NOW TOOK a long farewell of the horses and turned north-ward, selecting a line close in by the base of the hills, going along at an improved pace, with a view of reaching the trading post the same night; but stopping in a gully to look for water, I found a little pool, evidently scratched out by a bear, as there were foot-prints and claw marks about it; and I was aware that instinct prompts that brute where water is nearest the surface, when he scratches until he comes to it. This was one of very large size, the footmark behind the toes being full nine inches; and although I had my misgivings about the prudence of a tête-à-tête with a great grizzly bear, still the "better part of valor" was overcome, as it often is, by the anticipated honor and glory of a single com-bat and conquest of such a ferocious beast. I was well armed, too, with my favorite rifle, a Colt's revolver that never disap-

From William Kelly, *An excursion to California over the prairie, Rocky Mountains, and great Sierra Nevada. With a stroll through the diggings and ranches of that country* (Lon-don: Chapman & Hall, 1851).

pointed me, and a nondescript weapon, a sort of cross betwixt a
claymore and a bowie knife; so, after capping afresh, hanging the
bridle on the horn of the saddle, and staking my mule, I followed
the trail up a gully, and much sooner than I expected came
within view and good shooting distance of Bruin, who was seated
erect, with his side toward me, in front of a manzanita bush,
making a repast on his favorite berry.

The sharp click of the cock, causing him to turn quickly round,
left little time for deliberation; so, taking a ready good aim at the
region of the heart, I let drive, the ball (as I subsequently found)
glancing along the ribs, entering the armpit, and shattering
smartly some of the shoulder bones. I exulted as I saw him stag-
ger and come to his side; the next glance, however, revealed him,
to my dismay, on all fours, in direct pursuit but going lame; so I
bolted for the mule, sadly encumbered with a huge pair of Mexican spurs, the nervous noise of the crushing brush close in my
rear convincing me he was fast gaining on me; I therefore
dropped my rifle, putting on fresh steam, and, reaching the rope,
pulled up the picket pin, and, springing into the saddle with
merely a hold of the lariat, plunged the spurs into the mule,
which, much to my affright, produced a kick and retrograde
movement. But in the exertion having got a glimpse of my pursuer, uttering a snort of terror, he went off at a pace I did not
think him capable of, soon widening the distance betwixt us and
the bear; but having no means of guiding his motions, he brought
me violently in contact with the arm of a tree, which unhorsed
and stunned me exceedingly. Scrambling to my feet as well as I
could, I saw my relentless enemy close at hand, leaving me the
only alternative of ascending a tree; but in my hurried and nervous efforts, I had scarcely my feet above his reach, when he was
right under, evidently enfeebled by the loss of blood, as the exertion made it well out copiously. After a moment's pause, and a
fierce glare upward from his bloodshot eyes, he clasped the
trunk; but I saw his endeavors to climb were crippled by the
wounded shoulder. However, by the aid of his jaws, he just succeeded in reaching the first branch with his sound arm and was
working convulsively to bring up the body, when, with a well-
directed blow from my cutlass, I completely severed the tendons
of the foot, and he instantly fell with a dreadful plunge and hor-

rific growl, the blood spouting up as if impelled from a jet; he rose again somewhat tardily, and, limping round the tree with upturned eyes, kept tearing off the bark with his tusks. However, watching my opportunity, and leaning downward, I sent a ball from my revolver with such good effect, immediately behind the head, that he dropped; and my nerves being now rather more composed, I leisurely distributed the remaining five balls in the most vulnerable parts of his carcass.

By this time I saw the muscular system totally relaxed, so I descended with confidence and found him quite dead, and myself not a little enervated with the excitement and the effects of my wound, which bled profusely from the temple; so much so, that I thought an artery was ruptured. I bound up my head as well as I could, loaded my revolver anew, and returned for my rifle; but as evening was approaching, and my mule gone, I had little time to survey the dimensions of my fallen foe, and no means of packing much of his flesh. I therefore hastily hacked off a few steaks from his thigh, and, hewing off one of his hind feet as a sure trophy of victory, I set out toward the trading post, which I reached about midnight, my friend and my truant mule being there before me, but no horses.

I exhibited the foot of my fallen foe in great triumph, and described the conflict with due emphasis and effect to the company, who arose to listen; after which I made a transfer of the flesh to the traders, on condition that there was not to be any charge for the hotel or the use of the mule. There was an old experienced French trapper of the party who, judging from the size of the foot, set down the weight of the bear at 1500 pounds, which, he said, they frequently overrun — he himself, as well as Colonel Fremont's exploring party, having killed several that came to 2000 pounds. He advised me, should I again be pursued by a bear and have no other means of escape, to ascend a small-girthed tree, which they cannot get up, for, not having any central joint in the forelegs, they cannot climb any with a branchless stem that does not fully fill their embrace; and in the event of not being able to accomplish the ascent before my pursuer overtook me, to place my back against it; when, if it and I did not constitute a bulk capable of filling his hug, I might have time to rip out his entrails before he could kill me, being in a most favorable posture for the operation. They do not generally use their mouth in the destruction of their victims, but, hugging them closely, lift one of the hind feet, which are armed with tremendous claws, and tear out the bowels. The Frenchman's advice reads rationally enough, and is a feasible theory on the art of evading unbearable compression; but, unfortunately, in the haunts of that animal those slim juvenile saplings are rarely met with, and a person closely confronted with such a grizzly vis-à-vis is not exactly in a tone of nerve for surgical operations.

IV

HARD TIMES

The Grizzly Bear
of California

from *Harper's New Monthly Magazine*

At one time California had an immense bear population, proba-
bly the largest anywhere, encouraged by mild climate and plen-
tiful vegetation. Since time out of mind the Indians had called the
great central valley "the home of the bear." The native Spanish
population sought the bears primarily for sport, to pit them
against bulls in the arena. Not until Americans took possession
of the "Golden Land" was hunting the grizzly made a mere pas-
time and pursued for the amusement it might afford. The cool
courage that the hunter in the story, Colin Preston, displays was
a requirement of this dangerous sport. When California became a
state the bear was chosen to be the official emblem. By 1900 it
was rare to see a grizzly anywhere in California, except on the
flag.

MY HOST was an Arkansas man — a bear hunter, graduated in
the school of the forest, with his diploma marked upon his body,
in shape of ghastly scars. He was master of a cattle ranch, and of
a company of vaqueros, or native herdsmen. The fame of the
grizzly bear of California, and not of the gold diggings, had
drawn him to these remote regions. He made the voyage of the
Cape in 1845, and built a cabin of cedar logs in the wild oats
country, near San Luis Obispo. Preston had been a scholar and a

From "The Grizzly Bear of California," *Harper's New Monthly Magazine*, vol. 15
(November 1857).

lawyer, and his talk was a mixture of the rude and polished. Cool, grave, imperturbable, with eyes so still and fierce they burned into the very soul, he might have been the lord of some barbarous primeval tribe.

Such men exist only on the borders of the New World; incapable of folly and careless of wealth; the Knights Paladin of the wilderness, for whom modern society has no name, no poem, and no place.

"They talk of bears," said Preston, fixing upon mine, with still regard, his large gray eyes; "of bears in Arkansas. I was bred to the bear as well as to the *bar,* and through ten seasons hunted on the Red River with men of the woods, 'bar' hunters of the border, who have all the forest wisdom. I have read, too, what has been written by the great hunters, but none of them knew the bear of California. He is the sovereign of beasts; in strength, weight, endurance, and sagacity superior to the lion, and I doubt not has formerly destroyed some great and powerful tribe of lions on this continent."

"Last April," he continued, "I rode out, with my rifle and telescope, alone. Antonio, who should always go with me — and he is a good hunter, but a coward — Antonio was sick or indolent, so I went alone. From the summit of the low hill on the left of yonder mountain I swept the view with my glass. In the midst of a plain covered with the wild clover, which is deep and close at that season (you can pluck the clover heads with your hand without bending from the saddle), I perceived a movement, and saw that it was a grizzly of enormous size rolling in the clover, with his paws playing stupidly in the air. The cattle on a hillside not far distant were watching this movement, and a bull advanced toward it, drawn, it seemed to me, by curiosity. The wind carried away the sent of the bear."

"Do cattle distinguish all animals by the scent?"

"Men and the larger animals, when the wind is in their favor. But not as well as the deer.

"The bull drew gradually nearer to the bear, and the herd followed him, grazing as they went. He forced his way through the tall clover until he came within fifty yards, and bellowed, tearing up the earth. The bear moved less, only now and then rolling a little to stir the field. The curiosity of the bull now changed into anger; he came slowly up, snorting and bellowing, and at length stepped suddenly forward, and plunged at the bear, who caught him in his powerful arms and held him down.

"There was fifteen minutes of struggling and roaring, and the two immense beasts rolled over and over, crushing flat a wide area of the field. The herd gathered around, rushed upon them, and bellowed with rage and terror; but the bear never slackened his hold until the bull, exhausted, ceased to strive. Then up rose Bruin, light as a cat, and, striking out as a cat strikes, broke at one blow the shoulder of the bull. He fell as if dead, and the herd ran to the hills, groaning."

"I have been told that the bear is not a flesh eater."

"You shall hear. He stood over the carcass, and tore out the bowels, tasting with his tongue, and champing; but he did not bolt or gorge the flesh as tigers do. It was now the time to ride up and dispatch him. His eyes were smeared with blood, and his nostrils dulled with the strong odor of flesh. Leaving my horse, I crept through the clover, and planted a ball behind the shoulder. A bear shot through the heart falls dead."

"And if you had missed?"

"I seldom miss."

"You said 'seldom.' You should have said 'never' to be secure. That 'seldom' will one day interrupt you."

"Let us not fret ourselves about the 'one day.' To hunt bears you must hunt them."

"It is a passion."

"An ambition, rather. This region pleases me. There are bears larger, stronger, and more difficult to kill than the lions of Algiers. One of these will sometimes overtake a horse at speed. They are long-limbed, active, and full of cunning. As for their courage, they are seldom disheartened except by fatal wounds. The bear of this country resembles the man who hunts him, and it is this resemblance of character that gives interest to the chase."

"I heard Antonio telling you, yesterday, that a bear was made drunk?"

"Yes; you understood, then, Antonio's bad Spanish?"

"A little."

"We make large and dangerous bears drunk, when they have

cubs in February, and are too savage. The bear goes to and from his den or cover — usually a hollow among rocks — by certain paths, called 'beats.' A bear will use the same beat for years, going by night on one beat, and in the day taking another, more circuitous. You will often find a tree fallen across a beat, or you fell one, and wait till the savage has examined the new barricade, and finding that it is not a trap is willing to climb over it. Then you make a hole in it with an axe, large enough to contain a gallon of rum and molasses. Bears are greedy of sweets. In countries where there is wild honey they will overturn all obstacles to get at it. Of sugar and molasses, and sweet fruits, strawberries, mulberries, and the like, they are passionately fond. The bear reaches the log; he pauses over the hole full of sweet liquor; examines it, tastes of it, drinks all at a draught, and is drunk. And what a drunkenness is that! The brute rolls and staggers, rises and even bounds from the earth, exhausts his enormous strength in immense gambols, and falls at last, stupefied and helpless, an easy prey to the hunter. We have killed many in this way, but it is treacherous, and I do not like it."

"How many bears have you killed in California in one season?"

"Seventy large bears, and twice the number of smaller ones. The cubs and young bear of the season are excellent eating, but a man must be hungry to eat the sinewy flesh of a full-grown grizzly."

"Two hundred and ten in ten years!"

"Yes, but they are scarcer now. When I came here first we saw them every day. Now we ride sometimes fifty miles to find a bear."

"I would like to join you by and by on one of these hunts."

"Be dissuaded from it. To shoot well with a heavy rifle, to have presence of mind, quickness of aim, good legs to carry you far and fast out of danger, a seat on horseback as if you had grown to the saddle, and, above all, knowledge of the grizzly, his habits and temper, all are necessary. Bear hunting is sport only for those who set little value upon life."

"Is it true that they are taken with the lasso?"

"Antonio took a drunken bear with a lasso, and we tied and dragged him home; but the next morning he broke away, killed two horses, and escaped to the woods. We never venture upon them in that way unless they are drunk. I sometimes fancy the grizzly possesses a degree of human intelligence; for when he has resolved to kill a beef he selects the best of the herd. A bear of large size will meet the rush of a bull, move aside, and kill him, as does the matador in the arena, with a passing blow."

"I have read somewhere that the bear is emblematic of the savage state."

"The grizzly is emblematic of the backwoodsman. He has a rough surgery of his own, his claws are large and efficient, like the axe and rifle. He has the least fear of man among the greater animals; his motions, seemingly slow, are really rapid; he is the contemptuous enemy of the Indian — the human wolf — and is generally more than a match for him. He loves rum and molasses, bread, fruits, and vegetables; pumpkins especially. In a pumpkin field he selects the largest, makes a hole in it, and sucks out the seeds and pith. Bears hunt singly, or in couples. Each fights on his own hook. Savages, on the contrary, run in crowds, place an ambush and rush all together, with outcries, like the wolf.

"Two men whom I know, one of them Dr. Clemens of this state — lately killed by a grizzly — were in this district bear hunting three years ago. The bears had been destroying the pumpkins, and these men erected a wooden stage with a platform eight or ten feet high, in the middle of a field, with a wall or wickerwork of brush for an ambuscade, and from this point they watched the bears. The platform stood near a heavy fence of stones and timber. While they watched by moonlight they saw a large bear enter the field and come toward the platform. Dr. Clemens fired upon the bear; who instantly ran to the staging and overthrew it, tumbling our two hunters upon the ground. They escaped over the fence a good deal bruised and not a little frightened."

"I have seen bears in confinement quite tame. From the character you give of the grizzly it should be rather difficult to tame him."

"Not more than the bull, whom it is impossible to make harmless, with all your taming. I have seen a bear weighing twelve hundred pounds harnessed to a truck by a fellow who enjoyed such things, and he drew like an ox. This bear was taken when a cub and kept tame. The draught force of the full-grown bear is equal to that of a yoke of steers; but, like the backwoodsman, he will not endure beating. He has his points of honor. He is not cringing and treacherous like the tiger. In diet, too, he is human, preferring cooked meat to raw, and enjoys all the savors of the kitchen. He is domestic in his tastes, stays much about home, is a good parent, and friendly toward kindred. He plows and tears up the earth for roots, using his powerful claws. When acorns are ripe the grizzly grows fat and heavy — his belly drags along the ground. At such times it is easy to kill him; but even then he has a taste for flesh meat. We hunt them at night by the drag."

"How is that?"

"Fasten the entrails of a calf, or deer, to the end of a lasso, tie the free end of the lasso to the saddle, and ride across the country several miles, drawing it after you. Ride over the bear's beats, or paths; bring the trail, finally, to the foot of an oak tree — such as you see on the hillside yonder — where there is an open space around, and you can see and hear the bear as he approaches from a distance. Fasten the offal to the lower branch, just within reach — perhaps five feet from the ground.

"Night before last, while you were lying in bed here, Antonio and I, after preparing such a bait as that — though it is not acorn time now — took our places in an oak, just over the lower branch. It was late when we climbed into the tree, and we waited till the moon rose — near twelve o'clock — and no sign of a bear. See, then, how patient you must be in this kind of hunting."

"But would he not climb the tree and attack you?"

"Not at all; bears are not savages; they seldom attack without provocation."

"Would the bear, finding a trail of offal, know which way to follow it?"

"Yes. He judges, I suppose, by the appearance of the trail.

"I was seated on a branch just over the offal, which offended my nose prodigiously. I found it difficult to keep awake, watching so long and straining sight in the distance.

"A dusky object appeared, moving toward us in the direction of the drag. The bear came up the hill slowly, scenting the drag through the wild oak.

" 'Ah, Señor, the bear is here!' whispered Antonio; and there he was, pressing to the foot of the tree.

"We had our rifles ready; Bruin was only thirty paces off when, to my utter amazement, over went Antonio, rifle and all, and, striking the earth with a bound, fled into the darkness. The incident was more unexpected and ludicrous than anything I had seen in hunting, and I sat upon the branch paralyzed and trembling with suppressed laughter.

"The bear paused a moment when he heard the fall and then rushed forward and rose on his hams to seize the offal. I placed my rifle at his ear, fired, and saw him go down; but what with the kicking of the heavy gun, and my own unsteadiness, I, too, rolled off the branch and fell heavily, striking my shoulder against the bear's head. Terrified now, in good earnest, I rolled myself off and ran — nor stopped till I was safely in the ranch. The bear was dead, or he would have followed me — I have known them to overtake men when a portion of their head had been shot off, and with balls in the body. My left shoulder is still stiff and sore with that fall."

"I suppose the bears of the Rocky Mountains are larger and more dangerous than the grizzly. Were you ever east of the Sierras?"

"The brown bear of the Rocky Mountains is a formidable brute, and at some seasons of the year as vicious and destructive as the bear of California; but you will never find the grizzly east of the Great Desert, nor any brown bears on the Pacific Coast."

The remainder of that season and the winter I passed in San Francisco, and the February succeeding rejoined Preston on the ranch. He was in fine health and spirits, and predicted good hunting.

Two weeks elapsed before we heard of a bear. One morning Antonio wakened us at daylight, and we rode fifteen miles to a cove or shingle, on the shore of the sea. The surf rolled in heavily; a cool, stiff breeze came from the northwest. We picketed our horses in a hollow among the sandhills, hidden from the beach; and then, Antonio leading the way almost on his hands and knees, we stole along to the edge of a sand ridge, and looking over saw two grizzlies: one very large, feeding on dead fish along the edge of a marshy inlet, the mouth of a mountain stream; the other, a small bear not more than two years old, sunning itself at full length, like a lazy cat, in the shelter of the hill, seeming to watch the motion of the other, whom Antonio pronounced to be a female with cub. Preston pushed the sand up with his hands, so as to form a breastwork upon which to rest our rifles, the distance to the small bear being not more than a hundred yards.

I found myself trembling violently when I tried to take aim. All shot together, and the balls took effect under the shoulder. The bear rose to his feet with a tremendous roar, bounded into the air, and fell dead. We did not move, however, not knowing what course might be taken by the large bear to avenge the fall of her companion. As soon as I had recovered presence of mind enough to take a view over the ridge, I saw her making off with long strides along the edge of the inlet toward the breakers. She pushed through the heavy surf, disappearing and reappearing as it rolled over her; and in a few minutes we saw her swimming straight out to sea, as if bound on a voyage to the Sandwich Islands.

Meanwhile Preston consulted with Antonio as to the proper mode of meeting her on return. It was determined that we should go down to the shore and give her a broadside as she came in; hoping by this plan to disable her, at least, by a broken shoulder or a wound in the foot. If she did not fall at the first fire, we were to run to our horses among the sandhills, and follow her cautiously, getting each an occasional shot, and leading her to the steep sides of the hills.

While we were standing about fifty yards apart, waiting for the return of the grizzly, who was now swimming slowly toward us, rising and sinking on the long waves, I began to be disturbed with a violent rumbling in the bowels, as though attacked with cholera. Subsequent inquiries satisfied me that this was a very ordinary symptom of inexperience among bear hunters, and was a moral much more than a physical phenomenon. Nature, like a kind and anxious mother, makes an effort to rearrange the interior of the body, so as to put it in the best condition to escape from danger. Not to run away is a question of will, like standing up to be shot at in a duel. And by the same token a man who can await the coming of a grizzly will receive the fire of an enemy without flinching.

The bear paused and floated on the sea awhile when she understood that we were waiting for her coming with hostile intent. She was old, cunning, and had doubtless many balls in her clumsy carcass, and understood the nature of a rifle. At length she began to strike out boldly, making straight for Preston, who was on my right. I had consequently to shoot to the right, which is difficult either with the pistol or rifle. She struck ground about one hundred yards from us, and I raised my gun; but Preston called to me not to fire till the bear was in the last breaker. I could but just hear his voice above the thunder and simmer of the sea. And now she came on with a rush, charging upon our center. I saw out of the corner of my right eye that Preston had raised his rifle, and I did the same. The sea drew back, and the huge mass of hair and muscle began working up the beach, ready for a charge as soon as it could overcome the undertow. The rifles cracked successively; the bear turned and looked at her flank, gave a great roaring cry and sprang forward. Antonio darted up the shore like a deer. I rushed toward the sandhills, and looking behind me an instant saw Preston lying at full length flat upon his face on the edge of the sea, and the bear coming after my blessed self with a limp in the left forepaw, but making excellent time. Fear lent wings to my feet, and, being a good runner, in five minutes I was lost among the sandhills. A craggy tree, jutting out from the side of a slope, presented the idea of security, and in less time than it takes to write this I was hidden close in the middle of its windworn branches. To breathe and reload the rifle were the first acts dictated by nature and the small remains of reason left by fear.

More than an hour I remained in the tree to look quietly around upon the face of nature in this desert and desolate wild. The tree stood in the center of an indentation of the mountains occupied by sandhills. Inland I recognized the bluff we had descended in approaching the shore. By the direction of the wind, which blew with even force from the northwest, I made out the points of the compass.

Descending from the tree and keeping the rifle cocked, with a sharp lookout, I moved slowly toward the shore, and looking northward saw my two companions mounted and riding away along the beach. Preston looked back and waved his sombrero, and in fifteen minutes' time we saluted each other; Antonio being now quite bold and secure, and ready to laugh at me for running away. Preston, on the contrary, gave me his warmest congratulations, and confessed that he had not expected to see me again. He said that the bear knocked him over with her broken paw and then pushed on in pursuit of myself. After skinning the small bear, on our way homeward we found the horse I had ridden lying dead, where he was picketed, with his bowels torn out, but saw nothing of the wounded grizzly.

This adventure gave me a distaste for bear hunting. Preston urged another trial — he praised my coolness and presence of mind. "You shoot well," said he; "you ride tolerably, and have a good pair of legs."

"Some men," I replied, "are born bear hunters; others have bear hunting thrust upon them. I am of the latter class."

He laughed. "You must take home with you a bear cub of your own catching. I know of an old she-bear who has had cubs every year in a cave about twenty miles from here; you can see the crest of the mountain where she ranges yonder toward the southeast. We will go there in a few days and bring away the cubs." Three days after, we selected good horses, and set out in search of the old bear and her cubs.

We entered a valley of sycamores, and selected a place of encampment for the night. Antonio built a fire of deadwood and brush, and we roasted pieces of jerked beef over the coals, using a stick for a toasting fork. It was now noon. Preston took his rifle and rode away. In about three hours he returned, dragging the entrails of a deer behind him, but stopped and fastened the drag to a tree about sixty yards from the encampment. He then informed us that he had crossed the beat of a large bear about two miles off, followed it to a ledge of rocks, and saw three cubs sunning themselves on a flat stone, but no sign of the old one.

"Why did you not bring away the cubs?" I asked, innocently.

My companions looked at each other, as much as to say, "What does *he* know of bears?"

"Had I taken the cubs," said the hunter, "the mother, who is never long absent, would have discovered her loss before nightfall. She would then be the attacking party instead of ourselves, and would kill one of us, or one of our horses — which is the same thing, as she could easily overtake a man on foot — or tire out the horses on the long ridge yonder, catching us on the other side. A man who steals bears' cubs is much surer to suffer than one who kills a traveler on the highway."

We resolved to remain quiet for the afternoon. The horses were picketed in a bushy meadow, where there was fresh grass. Preston and I lay down and slept, while Antonio kept watch. At sundown I was awakened by the howls of wild beasts. I opened my eyes and saw Antonio in the tree overhead, and Preston kicking me to wake up.

I sprang to my feet, took my rifle, and followed him across the meadow. The horses had broken away. An eighth of a mile farther on was a waterfall; and with the sounds of the torrent came mingled the growls of two wild beasts, alternate and furious. We moved cautiously along the channel, pushing aside willows and grapevines that embowered the sparkling waters, till we reached the fall and could look over. The torrent plunged foaming down a declivity of thirty feet into a ravine filled with a green, transparent pool of water, over which had fallen a large tree, making a bridge with its trunk.

On the right hand, squatted on one end of the bridge, was a small, male grizzly, and opposite to him, at the other end, a full-grown panther, who was tearing up the bark of the trunk and gathering and relaxing herself as if for a spring. The alternate roaring of these infuriated beasts filled the valley with horrible echoes.

We watched them a minute or more. The bear was wounded, a large flap of flesh torn over its left eye, and the blood dripping into the pool. My companion bade me shoot the tiger, while he took charge of the bear. We fired at the same instant; but instead of falling, these two forest warriors rushed together at the center of the bridge, the bear rising and opening to receive the tiger, who fixed her mighty jaws in the throat of her antagonist and began kicking at his bowels with the force of an engine. At that instant both rolled over, plunged, and disappeared. We could see them struggling in the depths of the pool; bubbles of air rose to the surface, and the water became dark with gore. It may have been five minutes or more before they floated up dead, and their bodies rolled slowly down the stream.

Antonio had some difficulty in catching the horses, which he found feeding in a little green valley a mile distant from our encampment. It was midnight before he returned and we could lie down to sleep. It was my turn to keep watch while my companions slept.

At the first streak of the morning I roused Antonio and lay down to sleep. When I awoke the sun was two hours high. Antonio had skinned the bear and panther. We then took breakfast in the manner of hunters, after which Preston meditated:

"The small bear yonder," said he, "at the falls, was mate of the old she-bear. It is well to have *him* out of the way. He was keeping guard against the panther, who is quite as fond of bear's cub as we are. We have next to kill the mother, for I see no possibility of escape if we carry off the cubs while she is alive."

"Take two of them," I suggested, "and leave the other to amuse her."

"Too cunning for that," replied the hunter. "Whatever be the talent of other animals, bears can count; they know each cub, and will always save the pet where there is a choice."

"It strikes me then, my friend, that we are under a necessity of killing this troublesome she-bear, who interferes so impertinently with our arrangements for the cubs, whom we intend to remove and bring up in civilized society. She is a civilizee, with injurious tendencies to isolation and familism."

"In regard to our necessity," replied Preston, "you have spoken wisely and like a true hunter. As for the words *civilizee* and *familism,* I do not know their meaning; but I foresee that the killing of this brute is to give us trouble, and we must go about it, reconciled to every possibility."

"She is in no humor for fresh meat," I observed. "Our drag has either not been discovered or she neglects to follow it."

"I explain that by the presence of the panther, who may have prowled about here several days, hoping to carry off a cub. To prevent this the mother keeps herself near home, and will not follow the trail," said Preston.

"In that case have we to begin the attack?"

"Of course. But let us first see that the rifles are clean and in good order."

He began unscrewing the lock of his rifle. In half an hour we had cleaned the guns; and at three hours after noon were ready for the march. We made our approaches up the hill in three lines, converging upon the den of the bear. I took the left and Antonio the right of Preston. We advanced on horseback, moving up a hill with gentle slope, through an open grove of larger oaks, and could now see the front of rock under which was the cave of the bear; when Preston gave the signal to halt.

"She is coming," he said, in low voice, and at the same moment I saw both my companions raise their rifles. The cave may have been one hundred and fifty yards distant; an interval of fifty yards between myself, Preston, and Antonio, placed the bear as she approached under a crossfire upon both flanks. I spurred my horse forward a few steps, and saw the huge beast coming slowly down the hill. We fired almost together. My horse trembled violently and snorted, but did not move until I had fired; but then wheeled suddenly and dashed off to the left, bringing my breast, after a run of sixty or seventy yards, in violent contact with the extreme branch of an oak, which brushed me from the saddle like a fly. At any other time the force of such a blow would have made me insensible; but so intense was my excitement, I cannot even remember how I rose to my feet. Glancing along through the oak openings, I saw Antonio swinging by his hands from a branch, up which he was deliberately climbing, his horse scouring away through the forest after mine. The bear, wounded in front and in both flanks, had fallen back upon her haunches not thirty paces from Preston, who had wheeled his powerful horse to the left flank, my own position, and was whirling the lasso, which the next moment flew over the head and shoulders of the bear, and in less time than it requires to read this was turned on the bole of an oak tree a dozen paces from the bear, and Preston's horse pulling at it with frantic energy.

When the hairy savage found herself encumbered by a noose, tightening sharply and powerfully around her body and forefeet, she rose upon her hind legs with a tremendous roar and made a dash at Preston; but held back by the radius of the lasso, rolled over and over almost touching the hind legs of his horse, who looked back at the hairy avalanche near his heels and made a terrified bound forward, drawing the bear of course nearer, perhaps within ten feet of the tree. Preston still, however, maintained the requisite control over his steed, and wheeling to the right rode around, making one turn of the lasso about the tree, turned the horse to a dead halt, and began reloading his piece. It was fortunately a breechloading gun, and could be charged in a few seconds.

Meanwhile a crash from the tree and another roar and bound of the hampered bear, who had lain quiet for a moment, to recover the strength which she was fast losing — the dark blood pouring from her mouth in torrents — showed that Antonio had not been idle. By this time, with some bungling, I had driven a charge home in the barrel of my own awkward, old-fashioned piece. Preston, in a sharp, clear voice, which even now rings in my ears, called out to me: "Shoot quick, and then take to a tree; the lasso is breaking." I ran to the left of the bear, came within ten feet of her, and aimed at the head. At the same instant she rose again, roaring; the lasso burst with a sharp sound; I fired wild, and turned to run, but the beast fell along dead upon the ground; by singular good fortune my chance shot had sent a ball through her heart. Not trusting to appearances, I rushed to the nearest tree and swung myself up by a depending branch with marvelous agility, climbing from branch to branch much higher than was necessary.

With the breaking of the lasso, Preston's horse bounded away; but he presently succeeded in turning him, and coming close to the bear made the event of the battle sure with another ball through the enemy.

When Antonio saw that the bear was dead, he gave a shout and dropped off his branch upon the ground like a ripe pear. Preston called to me to come down, which I did with some difficulty, because of the bruise on my chest. The pain of this bruise was severe, and followed me a long time after, but I did not feel it while ascending the tree.

As we stood looking at the dead bear, Preston attempted to dismount, but found it impossible to do so, his right thigh being severely bruised by the lasso, which pressed upon it with the entire force of the horse in his last desperate spring. We lifted our companion from the saddle, and laid him down fainting and helpless. Antonio then took his master's horse, and went in search of our runaway steeds. Meanwhile, leaving my friend somewhat relieved by a draught of rum and water from a hunting flask, I went up to the rock, and found the three cubs sleeping quietly in a heap like kittens.

Antonio came back in high spirits with the two horses, after an hour's search, and presently building a fire of dry sticks, we roasted some jerked beef, and, after a hearty meal, lay down to sleep about sundown, using our saddles for pillows. At daylight we awoke, and, after skinning the bear, secured the cubs and skin upon Antonio's horse, and helping Preston into the saddle went over to the old encampment. Here we packed the two other skins and made the best of our way to the ranch, Antonio leading his own horse by the bridle.

Hand-to-Hand Fight
with a Grizzly

from *Harper's New Monthly Magazine*

The California bear hunter Colin Preston told the following story about his friend from Missouri, Colonel William Butts, whose encounter with a bear turned from a routine slaying into a harrowing struggle for survival. His valor prompted Preston's salute: "In beasts the body fights, in man the soul."

HE SPOKE OFTEN of Colonel William Butts, of San Luis Obispo, who had been wounded in a hand-to-hand fight with a bear in the spring of 1853. Colonel Butts was educated in the office of Colonel Benton of Missouri; entered the army, and served with distinction under Scott, and then passed into the border service as a commander of mounted troops in the Indian territories. Growing weary of the half-idle life of the army, he removed to California, practiced law, owned a cattle ranch at San Luis Obispo, and a newspaper at Los Angeles; keeping up the old habit of seeking danger for its own sake by an occasional bear hunt. Preston was enthusiastic when he spoke of Butts, whom he regarded as a man, born soldier and hunter, with equal qualities of action and command. He described him as of medium height, rather slight in person, with an eye betokening great courage and self-control; he had had eight or ten years' experience of war in Mexico and on the plains, and knew the interior of the continent like a garden.

From "The Grizzly Bear of California," *Harper's New Monthly Magazine*, vol. 15 (November 1857).

On the twenty-ninth of March, 1853, Colonel Butts — then on his ranch at San Luis Obispo — was making preparations for a voyage to San Francisco, and thence to the eastward. An old man, named Pacheco, came into the house and said that he had wounded an old she-bear, who had been known for several years in the neighborhood. She had made a spring at Pacheco, and caught his hand. Fearing to miss the steamer, Colonel Butts at first refused to go; but on the assurance of the old hunter that the bear was close at hand and badly wounded, he took his knife and rifle, and started on horseback to make a finish of the hunt.

They rode together to the summit of a hill near the ranch, but finding that the bear had gone down a ravine on the other side, they followed the trail. The brushwood and briars were almost impassable in the ravine. About halfway down the bushes forced them to the edge of a deep gully, which the horses could not get over. Colonel Butts then tied his horse and crossed the ravine, Pacheco forcing his way down through the bushes on the opposite side. After they had gone on a hundred paces or so, the Colonel reached an open space on the edge of the steep side of the gorge, and fearing they might fall unawares upon the grizzly, he called out to Pacheco to stop.

He then went to the edge of the ravine, which was a waterway trenched in the soft earth, and while he was looking over, the bank caved in under his feet, and he fell into the gully. Fearing that the concealed enemy might choose that moment for attack, he rushed up the bank and, at the same instant looking back, saw the bear coming behind close upon his heels — man and bear reaching the height at the same instant. Pacheco, who sat upon his horse on the other bank and saw this movement, did not fire. He seemed to be paralyzed with fear.

Colonel Butts carried a gun with a hair trigger that required to be "set" — a bad instrument for a hunter. Unfortunately, he had forgotten to set the trigger. The bear, as he turned upon her, seized the gun in her jaws and bit it, bending the barrel like a leaden rod. He jerked away the gun, however, and broke it over the head of the bear, who, at the same instant, seized his left leg in her mouth. Colonel Butts fell forward upon her, and seizing her wool with a strong grasp, the two rolled over and over down the bank of earth to the bottom of the ravine.

The enormous weight of the animal drove the breath out of his lungs, and he became insensible; but as instantly was roused by the surgical aid of Bruin, who retained her hold upon the leg and now sat upon her haunches deliberately chewing and shaking it as a dog shakes a rat. Just as his senses began to return, the bear, who was suffering from the wound Pacheco had previously given her, let go the leg and walked slowly down the ravine.

Colonel Butts now called out to his terrified follower to fire, but he did not do this; and the wounded grizzly, exasperated afresh by the sound of a human voice, turned and came back. Raising himself and leaning upon his left hand, Colonel Butts drew a long hunting knife and awaited the second attack with sullen determination. The thought flashed over his mind that if he could cut out an eye of the grizzly, she would again retire; and Pacheco might by that time recover his aim and courage. The idea was a good one. As she advanced he struck at the right eye and cut it out. The enemy fell back, the eye hanging from the socket, and again turned and moved down the gully. A third time Colonel Butts called upon his follower to shoot, but without avail; and the bear, startled as before by the voice, wheeled and made another charge.

"It is all over with me," thought the hunter, "unless I can cut out the other eye." On came the bear, jaws open, and roaring. Again the knife smote sharply in the hunter's sinewy hand, but glancing upon the heavy brow of the beast sank deep into the right side of the neck, and severed the carotid artery. The wounded brute pushed over and again seized the broken leg and crunched it; the blood spouted from the artery over the head and eyes of the hunter, blinding him so that he could not see to strike another blow. He fell back as if dead, passing his left hand over his eyes to wipe off the blood, and when he again opened them the bear had retired a few steps, faint and bleeding from the mouth and throat.

His evil genius suggested to him to call again upon the cowardly Pacheco, commanding him to shoot; but the sound of the voice, as before, only animated the dying rage of the bear, who now made her final charge; but as she came on, her hindquarters fell, through weakness. She pushed forward, moaning with fury, and Colonel Butts, animated by a shadow of hope in the midst of despair, put out both hands and seized her by the thick wool on each side of the head. In this attitude she pushed him along over the ground two lengths or more, and staggered and crawled over him, when, with a long reach and vigorous repeated thrusts, he laid open her belly, striking in the knife to the handle, and drawing it forward until the bowels of the bear fell out and dragged along the ground. This was the last act of the bloody drama; the bear turned again, seized the back of his head in her mouth, biting away a portion of the scalp and the right ear, and then rolled over and died.

When the bear crawled over him the last time, Colonel Butts lost his sight with the torrents of gore that poured from the animal. Her huge weight, treading and dragging over him, exhausted his little remains of strength.

When Pacheco saw the bear fall and die, he got off his horse, came down into the ravine, took up the mangled and exhausted hunter, and, bearing him to a spring, washed the blood from his face, so that he could see. Pacheco wished to leave him and go home for a litter, but Colonel Butts had still force enough left to cling to the saddle, and actually rode home in that condition. Six months after, he was going about with a cane, but a wound from the bear's tooth had paralyzed the left side of his face; nor did the injured leg, so often broken, recover quite its natural solidity. Had not the bear been weakened with loss of blood, her last bite would have crushed the head of the hunter like an eggshell.

Pacheco said later that Butts did not seem larger than an infant beside his huge antagonist, and that, when the brute fell upon him, he disappeared; nothing was visible but a writhing mass of blood and hair, in the midst of which Pacheco could only see the rapid gleams of the knife.

If Pacheco had fired again and wounded the bear, his master would have had no chance for life; and Butts's determination to kill the bear, at all hazards, was the cause of his extreme suffering and danger. Pacheco said that each time the Colonel called to him to fire, his voice sounded clear and ringing, as if he were ordering a charge of cavalry. Of such stuff are hunters made.

The Old Trapper
of Grand Lake

F. M. Young

When I met Charles Hedrich, he was living quietly in Jackson Hole, Wyoming, having followed trap lines for fifty years in Colorado and Wyoming. As a boy in Colorado he had had several thrilling experiences with grizzlies, and he still bore the scars of one of these on his bearded face. He told me the following experience, which took place in 1894, when he was a young trapper in the mountains near Hot Sulphur Springs. The old trapper in the story owed his life to Hedrich's friendly and fortuitous visit. Charles Hedrich is the speaker.

WHEN I WAS NINETEEN I joined a young man named Smith, and we went to the Grand Lake and Grand River country to trap. While there, we ran onto an old German recluse who lived in a shack on the William's Fork. He hunted and trapped, but we soon observed that he was a poor shot and also an inexperienced trapper, one who lived in the mountains without knowing enough about them: the old man, August Bohm, however, felt quite satisfied with himself and his skills.

Our camp was upstream some little distance from Bohm's. It occurred to us that we hadn't seen the old man for some time, so one day we went down to his cabin to be sure everything was all right with him. We knocked on the door but received no answer, so we opened the door and found him lying on the bunk, from the looks of things nearly dead. He could utter only the feeblest whisper, and could not raise a hand to greet us. We soon noticed his blood-drenched clothes and torn arms and legs. We cut away his trousers and removed his matted shirt, in the meantime building a fire and heating water for bathing him. We tore up some flour sacks to bandage his wounds, which we found to be deep and serious. After we had cleaned and patched him up as much as we could, and had given him some nourishment, he gained enough strength to tell us his story.

A few days before, he couldn't say how many, he had been out hunting and had run onto an old she-grizzly with two cubs. He got off his horse and fired at the old bear but missed her. The second shot hit, but it was a body shot which seemed to do no serious damage. The third shot missed altogether. The grizzly charged, and August hastened to climb a tree. In his hurry to get up the tree he dropped his gun. The enraged bear gnawed at the tree, stood up and reached for him, and clawed at the branches; then she would lie down and roll around in pain. Every time he moved she would rush to the tree. This went on for quite a while.

August thought he could subdue her if he could only jab her with a spear. He cut a limb and found a string in his pocket with which he bound his knife to the stock, and with this improvised spear he slipped down within reaching distance of the bear as it stood growling and reaching for him. Bohm held on to a limb with one hand and gave a fierce lunge toward the grizzly's head with the spear. Suddenly the limb he was holding to broke, and he lurched straight into the bear's arms. The enraged brute grabbed a leg in her mouth and bit it, tearing the muscles and mutilating the limb terribly. She tore and bit at the man viciously, but she was sick from the shot and finally wandered off. August lay under the tree unconscious for a good part of the day. Eventually, he regained consciousness. He couldn't see the bear, so he dragged himself to the old horse which was standing nearby. Somehow he managed to get into the saddle and ride two miles to his cabin, and there he lay until we found him.

Smith and I made a litter and carried the old man to a ranch; from there he was taken by wagon to Hot Sulphur Springs. He eventually recovered entirely but was always lame. We later found the carcass of the bear not far from the scene of the encounter, but the cubs we never were able to find.

A Remarkable Adventure

Elmer Frank

This experience differs greatly from most meetings with grizzly bears. There must have been a good feeding ground nearby to account for five full-grown bears in one bunch. Of course, when the men began the fight, all the bears were ready to meet the common enemy. It is a marvel that the two men in the story came away alive and that Frank was able to struggle so long in the powerful arms of a large grizzly with tremendous jaws and teeth and long claws, and yet survive with so little damage done. Not all men are killed or seriously injured in close encounters with grizzlies, and some fortunate few have even succeeded in killing a grizzly with a knife. In this adventure the fact that the grizzlies vented their rage on nearby brush accounts for the men sustaining so few serious injuries.

MY FIRST SAVINGS in life were invested in the Seven-H-L horse ranch, located in the heart of the mountains of Wyoming, my brand numbering about eight hundred head. This was my outfitting point, and thither I would fly at the earliest approach of Indian summer, that indescribably dreamy, restful season, only experienced in its full glory along the base of the main range of the Rockies. On the occasion to which this narrative refers, I was accompanied by six guests, to wit: a United States judge, a captain now in the Philippines, two Omaha lawyers, an ex-sheriff, a British capitalist, and, to me the most important of all, a full-fledged

From *The Outing Magazine,* vol. 39 (November 1901).

Texas cowboy, without whose brave and timely assistance this story would never have been penned.

His name is Clark — Ed Clark. "Uncle Ned," the punchers call him, which would indicate age, although not yet forty — one of those unaccountable misnomers peculiar to the Far West. He is far from handsome, resembling in form one of his own gnarled, timberline scrub cedars, rather than the sturdier growth of the lower-altitude pine. His wicked little eyes are black and piercing, and when animated rival the rattler's in their scintillations of viciousness; and yet, God bless him, when, crawling from under a dying bear, bruised, wounded, and faint from loss of blood, I saw that rugged face through the willows not ten yards away, hailing me with words of cheer, it had a halo surrounding it.

It was a battle royal, covering a period of about twenty minutes, the details of which, as I saw them, will ever remain indelibly stamped on my memory.

Five grizzly bears, weighing not less than six hundred pounds each, surprised in their lair by two men, threw down the gage of the battle. The issue was promptly accepted, from necessity, as there was no escape, and the fight was on.

Our camp was pitched in Halleck Canyon, at the headwaters of several streams flowing in as many directions, through a broken and mountainous country. Game was in abundance and our party had bagged its quota of elk, deer, antelope, and mountain sheep. No bears as yet, although at our nightly campfire comparisons of the day's events, each party had wonderful tales to relate of encountering innumerable trails, fresh beds, mutilated carcasses of game, and other signs indicating that bears were banded together in bunches ranging as high as thirteen. We counted that many fresh trails crossing a mountain meadow, and on this particular morning all of our party, except Clark and myself, got an early start, bent on their destruction or a fight to the finish, if unearthed. I was not feeling well and Clark remained in camp to keep my company. About three o'clock in the afternoon he proposed that we ride out and kill a mess of blue grouse for our hungry companions, and prepare a smothered feast for them on their homecoming. We thereupon saddled up our horses and proceeded about two miles up the canyon of a little creek, where a small lake had formed by falling rocks turning the current of the stream. The lake was roiled and the banks were beaten down by the fresh tramping of bears. After a hurried examination Clark exclaimed: "They are here on this creek — the tracks are fresh; we flushed them when we rode up, and we're going to make a killing sure." Here it is necessary to state that the horse I rode that day was a natty, powerfully built cow horse, swift as an antelope and mettlesome as a Kentucky racer. He was the pick of eight hundred, and when he scented the bears he began to get troublesome. However, we forced him up the creek toward a patch of willows, about seventy-five feet in width, the direction which the bears had taken, Clark leading the way.

These mountain willows grow in bunches, their branches spreading and interlacing at the tops, thereby making an almost impenetrable thicket. Here our quarry had evidently retreated, and a royal stronghold it was. On the opposite side a perpendicular cliff arose several hundred feet in height, with a ledge about six feet in width paralleling it, and appearing about three feet above the tops of the willows. On our side of the creek the canyon broadened into a sagebrush flat of about two hundred yards in width, and abutted against the willows, forming an almost perpendicular embankment about twelve feet in height. We were forcing our horses up onto this flat when the above conversation occurred, and Clark finished by excitedly exclaiming: "And by thunder there they are."

The brush seemed to be alive with them as they growled and leaped about, and one big fellow stood on his hind legs, with his head and breast towering above the tops of the willows, deliberately surveying us and hailing us with inquisitive grunts.

Clark's horse was a gentle old pack animal and he had no trouble in quickly dismounting and withdrawing his Winchester from its saddle sling. He took deliberate aim and fired, old Bruin dropping dead in his tracks. During this short period I had succeeded in dismounting and was fighting my horse in a vain endeavor to get my Winchester from the saddle sling. He reared, plunged, and kicked viciously, but I held his bit with one hand and the gun with the other until Clark shot. Then my horse gave a mighty leap into space, broke my hold, sent me rolling into the sagebrush, and ran off with my gun, Clark's horse closely following. When I regained my feet the commotion was still going on in the brush and another bear got on a rock and stood erect. Clark began to get a little excited and exclaimed: "The woods is full of 'em — Great God! Look at 'em!" I told him to keep his head and blaze away, which he did, wounding this fellow, who dropped off his perch and began to bawl and kick up a great row generally. Immediately three other bears stood on their hind legs and the wounded one regained his feet; they came for us with growls of rage. This was too much for me, being armed with a knife only, and the bears not ten jumps away. I told Clark I was going to quit him and rustle my gun, which I proceeded to do. As soon as I turned tail I ran for the horses, about a hundred and fifty yards away, whose bridle reins had gotten entangled in the sagebrush, thus securely holding them. As I ran for dear life I heard the sagebrush cracking behind me, but no more shots. I did not dare look around, as I expected Clark was down, and that a bear would grab me at every jump, but was intensely relieved when he chirped: "They made it too hot for me — my cartridges ran out. I had to quit 'em." Although he had plenty in his belt, his gun was empty, and he was too closely pressed to reload. Thinking discretion the better part of valor, he had followed me immediately, hence neither of us knew whether the bears in this charge reached the top of the embankment on which we stood. We hastily secured our horses, removed my gun from the sling, filled the chambers with the full quota of cartridges and fixed the bits so that we could hold our horses while shooting, and returned to redeem ourselves from the stigma of so hasty and undignified a flight. We rode up and down the willow patch, hallooed and threw rocks into it, but no sign of life gave answer. Thinking that of course the bears had taken flight up the canyon (and they had to go either up or down to get away), we followed the creek up toward its extreme timberline, beating the brush and exploring every possible hiding place. A hasty examination failed to disclose any trail in that direction, and we at once returned to our battleground, about three miles down the creek, feeling sure we would rout them out below that point. On our arrival there we dismounted, went into the brush, dressed the dead bear, and dragged him out with our lariats attached to the horns of the saddles.

As before stated, the willows grew in bunches and interlaced at the tops, and I was compelled to walk in a crouching position and at times to crawl on my knees. I could not see three feet ahead of me, and was thereby greatly handicapped. I had not proceeded twenty yards from the point where Clark left me, when I was greeted with a terrible growling and the crackling rush of a heavy body. I fired, and was embraced, it seems to me, almost simultaneously. The bear's mouth was wide open and he towered way above me — I distinctly remember that — and instinctively I ducked my head, knowing that it would be crushed like an eggshell if exposed. For this reason, when we came together I found my head under his shoulder, and immediately clinched him around the body, holding on for dear life, and calling to Clark as I went down under him. Clark heard my call and began cautiously to work his way toward me. Of course I had no idea of time when in that position, but Clark estimates it to have been five or six minutes before he reached me and fired. He says he forthwith responded to my call, guided by the racket the old bear was making; that he moved slowly and cautiously and at a point not fifteen feet away caught the first glimpse of us. He crouched down and waited some time for the bear to expose a spot for a fatal shot, without danger of hitting me. He saw that I was alive and "staying with him." He could not shoot him in the heart, for my head was there, nor could he see Bruin's head, and dared not move further for fear of attracting the attention of and bringing the others down on him. Becoming desperate and unable longer to stand the suspense and the bear's back being now turned toward him, he took deliberate aim and fired, the bullet entering the bear's hip, plowing its way just outside the ribs and lodging in the neck. There was a terrific crashing of brush, growling and bawling all around me. Whichever way I looked I could see bears either dancing around on their hind legs or rushing to and fro. My bear would raise up with me, shake me like a rat, and chuck me down again, threatening to loosen every joint in my body, but I realized that my only hope was to hold on. Suddenly I felt his teeth tearing at my hip, the only spot of my anatomy he could reach with his mouth, which he severely wounded, and literally tore my trousers and part of my chaps (heavy calfskin overalls) from me. Had it not been for the latter he would have made short work of my leg then and there.

I was in desperate straits and had about given up hope, thinking Clark had deserted me. The infamy of this act seemed horrible to me, and a wild desire to live long enough to murder him overcame me. I took fresh heart, held on tighter, and thought of my knife in a scabbard at my left side. I let go my right grip, worked my hand between old grizzly and my body, and reached my knife, which, to my horror, was tied in the scabbard with a buckskin string, used to keep it from jolting out when I was in the saddle. I labored hard to untie — to break — it, but old Bruin did not propose to have it that way. He let go my hip and seized my hand, crunching through and through it. I never expected to see it again. In my dire distress I thought nothing of it — it was only a hand, did I not have another one still left me? Just then, to my indescribable joy, I heard the sharp report of a Winchester not twenty feet away. It was Clark. Clark, the heroic Texan, now my savior, whom but a moment ago I thought a cowardly cur, and for whom I had murder in my heart.

I quickly struggled to my feet and seized my gun, just in time to see poor Clark go down under the now doubly enraged and wounded bear, it striking wickedly at him with its paw, hitting his gun and sending it spinning in the air. True to the hunter's tradition, he played possum in an admirable manner. He saw me get on my feet, so he said, and thought I would kill the bear before it hurt him very badly, hence he lay perfectly still. But in this he was doomed to disappointment. My gun was full of sand; it refused to work. I threw down the lever and was working the sand out of it as rapidly as possible. I saw my task was useless, the magazine refused to give up its cartridge. It was an awful moment of suspense. I forgot myself and thought only of poor Clark. One wrench on the lever and it sprang back into place, but no cartridge came with it. I could work with my left hand only, and the third finger of my right, but I quickly snatched a cartridge from my belt, and was thrusting it into the barrel, when another bear leaped on top of me from God knows where, I am sure I don't. I went down all in a heap under the crushing weight, and poor Clark's heart almost ceased beating when he heard me call: "Here comes another one — I can't help you — he's got me again." I don't believe this bear hurt me in the least, unless it was my left arm, which had several tusk holes in it and was pinched until it was black from wrist to elbow the next morning, but I have no recollection when it was done. He had evidently been wounded by one of our shots, for he tore up the ground and chewed at the willows all the time he was over me, almost burying both of us in dirt and broken sticks. Presently there was another roar and crash and tophet broke loose again, which evidently attracted my bear away from me, as he left me as suddenly as he had attacked. I was nearly used up, but I had life enough left to regain a sitting position and get hold of my gun once more, when Clark's bear, seeing me move, left him and came for me. I verily believe I made the last effort I was capable of at that time, and just as he was coming down on me, I poked my Winchester blindly against him and pulled the trigger. He fell dead with his head on my breast, knocking the breath out of me, and I went to sleep. My nap must have been a short one, for I was awakened by Clark calling to me: "Stay with 'em, Elmer, I've got my gun; you hit that d——l; I saw him fall. Give him another." I opened my eyes, looking into those of the dead bear on top of me. He didn't look a bit dead, and it was a few moments before I could persuade myself to make an effort to move; and when I did so it was as gingerly as one would walk on eggs, fearing he would suddenly awaken and make up for lost time. With considerable pain and labor, however, I finally succeeded in extricating myself, and, bareheaded, barelegged, with blood and sand smeared and plastered over me from head to foot, torn, bleeding, and sore, I dragged myself toward Clark, who had retreated to and mounted the stone ledge on the outer side of the brush. I had nearly reached him. He was standing on the ledge waiting to help me up. He asked me if I were much hurt. I told him I thought I was all chewed to a sausage, but that I was indebted to him for my existence; that his was a brave, generous and manly act, and, in short, "You are every inch a man." He extended his hand to me, saying, "Put it there and the same right back at you." But I did not get close enough to "put it there," for here came the remaining three bears on another furious charge. We fought them off three or four times, blazing away as they would leap over the brush toward us, before I succeeded in reaching the ledge. The smoke of our guns seemed to bewilder them, for after a volley they would jump up into it, bite and spat at it with their paws, and then retreat to their den, which we discovered was within a few feet of where they had me "in chancery."

After the last charge they seemed content to lie quiet, so Clark walked up the ledge about fifteen yards to try and peer into the den. He called to me that he could see the entrance, and to look out, as he would throw a stone into it; and as he threw I fired. We were answered by a howl, and two bears came straight at me. Two lucky shots from my rifle finished them, and they died in each other's arms at my feet near the foot of the ledge. Clark was wild with delight. He was sure there was only one more, and that badly wounded, as he was making the canyon ring and echo to his wails of pain. So we procured our whiskey bottle (always carried in the Rocky Mountains for snakebites, you know) and washed my wounds, tearing our handkerchiefs and the tails of our shirts into bandages, to do the best piece of dressing possible under the circumstances. The balance of the whiskey, it is needless to state, was used to wash the dust from our throats and revive our drooping spirits. We then deliberately sat down for the first time since the battle began, discussing how we should dispose of the remaining bear, who was still as noisy as ever. Clark proposed to set fire to the brush and burn him out; but it would not do to thus destroy our precious pelts, and besides, my only hat within a hundred miles was under one of them. Dusk was on us and we must act quickly, whereupon we determined to assault the den. We arrived within twenty or thirty feet of our quarry, when a gust of wind blowing down the canyon parted the willows and disclosed the old fellow lying on his stomach with his head on his forepaws, as if resting. I sent a bullet quickly to his heart and quieted him forever. It was now almost dark, and after dressing our game we struck out for camp, which we reached about nine o'clock. Our companions had all returned and we, of course, were the heroes of that night's campfire, and of the smothered grouse, which was never smothered.

In all the encounter Clark was fortunate enough not to receive a scratch, and this fact should be explained, if susceptible of an explanation. Old hunters say that a badly wounded grizzly will seize and hold onto the first object within reach, and expend its remaining strength in a desperate endeavor to rend it to atoms. I have seen this fact verified in at least a half-dozen instances. When the bear, on being wounded, sprang off me in its leap for Clark, it grabbed a mouthful of willows, and was crunching at them while over him, and he quietly playing possum. This might explain why the second bear did not make mincemeat of me, as both of them died with their mouths full of brush.

I make this statement for what is worth, anticipating skeptical mental inquiries upon this part of my story, and for the additional reason that it is information of sufficient value for the hunter to remember.

Grizzly-bear hunting is unquestionably the grandest sport that our country can afford. Many sportsmen proclaim the superiority of their favorite pastime over all other kinds, and each has its charm; but no man ever felt his heart swell with pride, his nerves tingle with animation, at the bagging of a bird or any small animal, as the man who has bagged his first grizzly.

A Fierce Battle
with a Grizzly

from *Current Literature*

*In this story, the manner in which the unfortunate Kennedy is
killed points up to the fact that too many men approached a grizzly without adequate protection in the way of firepower or sufficient knowledge about the bear's behavior. Sometimes the
bounty offered for the taking of a notorious bear drew men into
the field whose enthusiasm for the hunt exceeded their powers. A
seasoned bear hunter, such as J. W. Anthony or Than Galloway,
usually succeeded because of planning, the help of trained dogs,
or use of traps, nerve, and skill with a gun.*

*This anonymous relation, told by a man from Wyoming, of an
adventure involving cowboys and a grizzly bear, points out that
although cowboys are the closest thing to mountain men that we
have these days, many of them, even with modern weapons, do
not know how to shoot a grizzly to stop him. There would have
been many more mangled or dead trappers and hunters in the
days of single-shot muzzleloading guns if those men had not
made every shot count. Of all the shots fired in the following
story only one counted. This narrative illustrates the remarkable
staying power of a wounded grizzly.*

———————

THE MOST REMARKABLE instance that ever came to my notice
of ursine vitality and the danger of attacking a grizzly, except

Reprinted in *Current Literature*, vol. 36 (February 1904), and attributed originally to
the *Washington Star*. I have been unable to establish the earlier publication.

under the most favorable circumstances, occurred recently in the Wind River country of my state, amid the foothills that lie at the base of the main range of the Rockies.

A bunch of eighteen head of beef steers that had been kept in pasture had broken the wire fence and strayed off into the hills, and a party of six, including myself, went out to round them up and bring them back.

We had gone about twelve miles and were on the track of the truants, when the trail turned toward the foothills, and we had every reason to believe that we would find the cattle on the other side of a tumbling stream that went locally by the name of Teapot Creek.

While we were fording the creek the broncos began to snort and rear and give evidences of their unwillingness to go farther. This was rather unexpected, as the water was not deep, and we looked about for some reason for their action. As we clattered across we could hear above the noise of the rushing water the snap and clash of teeth and the peculiar hoglike growl of a grizzly.

Standing on his hind legs and stripping the serviceberry bushes of their succulent fruit was a big silvertip. He did not seem to be disposed to dispute passage, although his objection to the interruption of his feast was quite apparent.

Upon reaching the other side of the creek we rode up the bank and over a level stretch of ground that lay at the base of the foothills.

Although we were fully two hundred yards from the bear it was evident that his anger over our appearance had not entirely cooled down. The same swinish growls were borne to our ears, and the grizzly, still standing on his hind legs and devouring the serviceberries, could be seen where his head towered above the bank of the stream.

One of the cowboys, Alf Kennedy, took exception to the silvertip's mood. With the remark, "I ain't goin' to have no silvertip growlin' an' snarlin' at me!" he took his rifle from his saddle sling and proceeded to look at the magazine.

Seeing that other members of the party were also examining their firearms, Kennedy spoke up threateningly, saying that he wanted help from no one and that if a shot was fired by another man in the crowd there would be trouble. Knowing Kennedy as well as we did, we complied with his wishes.

Kennedy rode down until he was about one hundred yards from the bear. There he dismounted and turned the head of his horse away from the game. As a brave cowpuncher, he scorned to attack the grizzly except on foot, for, in his code of ethics, he and men of his stripe disdained to do anything that would savor of the tactics of the tenderfoot.

He stood by the side of his horse and drew his bead on the grizzly. The barrel of the rifle steadied down for a moment. A second later our straining ears caught the impact of the bullet as it found the game. The head of the bear went back as though it had been struck with a sledgehammer.

The bear disappeared for an instant, and a second later was seen clambering up the bank. Kennedy fired again, but this did not stop the enraged grizzly. He started in a lumbering but surprisingly rapid lope straight for the cowboy.

Kennedy did not flinch when he saw what was before him. The barrel of his rifle looked as firm and rigid as a bar of iron, so little was it disturbed by the process of ejecting the shells and throwing the cartridges into place. The smoke curled upward from the muzzle in a steady stream, and the rifle's crack came with the regularity of clock ticks.

The grizzly presented an appearance calculated to inspire terror in the hearts of the bravest. He was covering the ground at high speed in spite of his apparent awkwardness. His lumbering gait rendered him the poorest of targets, for the reason that only a chance shot could strike a vital spot. At one moment he would be doubled up like a jackknife with only his hump showing; the next he would be stretched out at full length, like a greyhound.

In less time than it takes to tell it Kennedy had emptied his rifle, but still he scorned to take advantage of his opportunity and mount the waiting bronco and escape. He cast his rifle aside and drew six-shooters, a pair of shot-barreled "forty-fours." As he threw his rifle away, he struck his horse with it, and the animal, already nervous from the firing and probably scenting the bear, started forward a few feet and then stopped. The animal's bridled rein hung in front of him, and the well-trained cow pony seldom moves until the rein is thrown back over his neck.

The foreman of the ranch had seen the movement of the horse, which had been unnoticed by Kennedy, and shouted:

"Step back with your horse, Alf! Step back with your horse!"

But Kennedy was too busy with his six-shooters to heed the warning.

It took only a moment for him to empty his revolvers, but, so far as their effect on stopping the bear was concerned, they might as well have been loaded with blank cartridges. The great hulking brute whirled up within eight feet of the dauntless cowboy and reared on his hind legs. With an indescribable howl of rage he waddled with uncertain tread toward his foe. Kennedy fired the last shots from his six-shooters pointblank at the breast of the towering beast, rendered more terrifying by the blood which colored his hairy coat. Next instant he threw his brace of weapons at the bear and turned toward his horse.

It was then that we gathered the full meaning of the foreman's warning cry. Instead of grasping the saddle, as he thought to do, Kennedy merely struck the haunches of the bronco. With a snort of terror the animal bounded away and left the rider at the mercy of the grizzly. The cowboy paused, dazed, and then started to run. He had taken only one step when the bear seized him with his forepaws and enveloped him in an embrace as merciless as the coils of the python.

A fusilade immediately began from our party. We galloped down to where the bear still stood, swaying to and fro with the man still in his paws. At last the brute dropped, lying in a pool of blood. Kennedy, too, was dead; the brute had ripped open his chest with his paws.

When we skinned the bear, although his hide was worthless, we found that he had been hit fifty-four times. The shot which had brought him to the ground, the only one which struck a vital spot, was from the foreman's "forty-four," and was right behind the ear.

A Fracas with Grizzly Bears

William T. Hornaday

The photographer of the early West not only had to carry his cumbersome equipment laboriously to sites where the view or wildlife invited pictures, but on occasion had to deal with an additional hazard to his occupation — the grizzly bear or bears that might be attracted to his camp by the fresh carcasses he was photographing. Hornaday's story records such an experience as it happened to the veteran Montana photographer, L. A. Huffman. This story is also interesting because one of Huffman's companions on this foray was G. O. Shields, a notable bear hunter, whose quick action and steady nerves are shown to good effect.

ONE MORNING last spring, when out in Miles City, Montana, my attention was arrested by some very fine photographs of hunting scenes, which were displayed in the window of the local photographer. Knowing full well the hard work it costs to bring a camera to bear on dead game just where it falls, I went in to compliment the artist on his pluck and enterprise, and also to secure a full series of the views.

In truth, they were praiseworthy pictures. There were freshly killed elk in pine forests, high up on steep mountain sides; big, old mountain rams on the edge of frightful precipices; buffalo lying on the snowy prairie in a straggling line, reaching from the huge old bull in the foreground away back to a mere black speck

From *Cosmopolitan*, vol. 3 (1887).

in the distance; antelope and deer in a picturesque valley; and a huge old grizzly bear lying at the edge of a prairie. There were pictures of huts made of buffalo skins, of hunters skinning grand game, of pack ponies with their packs on, and all sorts of camp scenes.

Even to the naked eye the views were most inspiring; but when put in a powerful stereoscope — great guns! I could hardly sit still, or keep from shouting. My fingers tingled to their very tips, and ached to clutch a rifle. I could almost feel in my lungs the crisp, cold air of the mountains, and the glad exhilaration of the chase. But for my dignity, I could have fairly danced around as a well-trained setter does at the sight of his master getting out his gun.

Fired by my enthusiasm, my photographer brightened up also. His name was L. A. Huffman, and of course he proved to be the same Huffman who is spoken of so often and so highly by Mr. Shields in his exceedingly lively and entertaining book, *Rustling in the Rockies*. I was charmed at finding him as rigidly matter-of-fact as a census taker, and wholly free from the spirit of self glorification that so often spoils a good hunter.

In the course of our discussion of the views, Mr. Huffman handed me one I had not seen before, with the significant remark:

"When I went to take that view, I came mighty near losing my hair."

It was the picture of an immense bull elk, with huge, spreading antlers, lying dead in rather open pine woods on a very steep mountainside.

"Really?" said I. "Who to? Indians?"

"No; bears," said the artist, laconically.

"Well, well! Now this is getting interesting. People out here have a profound respect for grizzlies, haven't they?"

"I should say they have. In some of 'em it comes pretty near to being reverence. Why, when you begin to talk to a great many old hunters about going out to hunt bear, they'll say; 'Oh, no! I don't care about it. I ain't lost no bears.' By the way, d'ye ever hunt grizzlies?"

"No; but I mean to pretty soon."

"Well now, a grizzly's noble game, and no mistake. I'd

rather down one old grizzly than a dozen head of any other game. You know, with a grizzly, after the ball is once opened, it's kill or be killed. He's a holy terror, and no mistake. It takes him so long to die, and so much lead to kill him, that he never seems to know when he's got enough. And he's such an all-fired big brute, and so powerful, that if he gets in just one good lick at a man, it's good-bye, John! I tell you, many a good man's been laid low by one blow of a grizzly's paw. It's just like being hit with a sandbag, to say nothing of claws. And what's the worst of it, a grizzly is so tough he'll get up and come at you after he's *nominally dead!* And very often, you know, a grizzly takes it into his head to do some hunting on his own hook, just when you're not expecting it. They're mighty uncertain in that way. That was what happened after I took that picture."

As a prospector would say, I knew I had "located" a good story, and so determined to have it out then and there. The best way in the world to bring out a narrative is to fire off a whole broadside of leading questions, all in one breath, which nothing less than a complete and circumstantial account will answer. So I said:

"Where did that happen, anyhow, and when? Were you all alone? How did you get into such a scrape, and how on earth did you get out of it? Did you kill the bear?"

"Well, I'll tell you about it, since ye want to know," said the hunting photographer. And as nearly as I can remember them, these were his own words:

It happened up in the Clark's Fork range, near the head of Pat O'Hara creek. In that neck o'timber you had only to tackle a plum thicket or a chokecherry patch to start up from one to three or four grizzlies. We camped down by the creek, and went up the mountains to find elk. Mighty steep the peaks were generally, I tell you.

Well, one morning two of our fellows — Shields and Sawyer — struck a band of elk in a thick fog, up on the side of this peak [pointing to the picture of a snowclad mountain] and killed a cow and a yearling. I was keeping camp that day, so missed that much of the fun.

They were hunting on foot, and, being without packs, of course could not bring down the meat. What was more, they wanted me to take a view of the game; so Shields decided to stay by it that night, and keep the bears away from it until I could get up to him the next morning with my outfit.

He must have had a lonesome watch; for it certainly was a wild night, blowing and snowing hard. By the way, do you know Shields, G. O. Shields, of Chicago? No? Well, he is one of the pluckiest and most tireless hunters I ever camped with.

Well, about daylight next morning, as I was rounding up my horses, I heard the bark of his Sharp's rifle, away up the mountainside; and after snatching a quick breakfast, old Ed and I took two packs in tow, and started up. The view in the early morning certainly was grand. For a time everything was shut out by the snow and the driving fog, and then suddenly it would lift, and through the breaks we could see the rugged crags and peaks looming up, all covered with snow and ice.

When we got within earshot of Shields, he greeted us with a regular war whoop.

"Hooray, old pard!" sezzee. "We've got the chief this pull. He's a ripper, I tell you; big as a beef steer; and horns — oh, hush! Just wait till I take you up to him."

"Where is he?" says I.

"Up the mountain a ways. He came snortin' and blowin' his whistle around my camp just once too often this time; and I'll pack his head to camp if it takes all summer. I blazed the trail as I came down, and I guess we can find him without any trouble."

I made haste, and took a view of the cow and yearling — here it is — and then loaded up again, and put some of the meat on my old sorrel. Just then Mike Weise came up; he was a Michigan boy; so taking him along with us, and leaving old Ed to go down alone, we pulled for the prize. It was a long, hard climb, and took us until past noon to make it.

Well, it was a grand old elk, and no mistake. No wonder Shields was proud of it! The horns were simply immense. It lay amongst the pines, surrounded by quite an undergrowth of scrub pines and bushes. A few yards below it and a little to one side lay the top of a fallen tree; but, to tell the truth, I didn't notice that until a few minutes later.

As soon as we got there I smelt bear. Do you know you can *smell* a grizzly quite a little distance?

— No, I answered, at least not in the woods.

Well, you can. A horse can smell one, too, as quick as a man, if not quicker. I saw then that my old sorrel smelled bear as plain as I did; for he showed it. Sure enough, we found signs of bear on the elk. By Jove! they had pawed the moss and dead branches away from the carcass on all sides, and cleared up for a regular picnic. We could see clawmarks on the soft parts of the carcass, here and there; and everything looked as if we had put in an appearance just as the first course was about to be served up.

Well, sir, I could smell those bears then just as plainly as I can smell the collodion in that darkroom now; and so could old sorrel. He sniffed, and snorted, and peered all about into the scrub pine undergrowth, with his nostrils wide open and his eyes just fairly bulging out. He realized the danger more than any of us men. Finally, I had to take a turn around his nose with a rawhide lasso to keep him from bolting down the mountain. The other fellows didn't seem to feel that there was any danger; but I vow I never felt more skittish in my life.

As quick as I could I began to unpack my view outfit to take a view of the elk, when all of a sudden old Rony, my pet saddle horse, in whom I had all confidence, and who had never flinched before, began to get terror-stricken. I tied him, also, then hurriedly made this view of the elk. It ain't a very good one, I know; but you bet I didn't linger very long with my head under that focusing cloth.

As soon as I got my negative I said to the boys: "Now, fellers, if you want to get back to camp with whole hides, you'd better yank the head off that wapiti right lively, for even a bear's patience won't hold out forever. There's a whole snarl of 'em *right handy by,* and don't you forget it!"

Shields and Mike Weise fell to work right off to skin the elk's neck and cut off the head; and in a few minutes I had my outfit all packed up again. I was standing about fifty feet away from the carcass and rather below it, with a turn of the old sorrel's lariat around my hand. The boys were both bent down over the elk, skinning away, with their backs uphill, when all at once, from the scrub pines, at a point above us all and between us, out came what seemed to me to be *twenty* grizzlies instead of only three. They were not over forty feet from either of us, and came *straight toward me,* grunting and "woh, wohing," crowding and snarling, bristles up and mouths open. They meant business, I tell you; but my rifle was on the other side of the elk!

— What on earth did you do? I asked breathlessly.

Well, sir, there was only one thing I could do. I faced the old bear that was in front, threw up both hands, and bawled out at the top of my lungs, as if I would eat him up: "Hooy! you son of a gun!"

The next instant old sorrel took a flying leap down the hill, jerked me backward through the air as if I had been nothing at all, and we all landed pell-mell in that treetop, horse, man, elk meat, outfit and all, with one tremendous crash.

I was scratched and torn all over; but scrambled out double quick, you bet. The bears had pulled up short; but the boys had not seen them at all, and there they stood, knives in hand, looking at the circus old sorrel and I was making. I yelled out at them: "You blasted fools! get your guns, and give it to 'em quick, or they'll tear us all to pieces!"

Well, sir, those varmints were so kinder startled by the row, they turned about, "woh, wohing" and snarling, and deliberately walked back into the cover, and stopped not fifty feet from where the boys stood.

Weise caught up his gun, and Shields followed suit, while I waved my hat frantically, and pointed in the direction of the bears, urging the boys to "get up there and pump 'em full of lead before they make another sally on us."

I tell you, I was scared plenty. Did you ever see an old grizzly stick up his nose and say "Woosh!" to a dog? I had seen that before; but never until I looked up square into that old she's ugly mug had I ever seen or heard anything quite so ugly.

It was Mike's turn next. He made about a dozen or fifteen short, tiptoeing steps in the direction I had pointed, when he suddenly leaped to one side, partly raised his Winchester, and then, without firing, he cleared the distance back to Shields and I in about three of the highest and longest jumps I ever saw a man make. Right after him, lighting right in his tracks at each jump, came an old she-grizzly, crashing through the undergrowth, with blood in her eye.

By this time Shields had grasped the situation, and when Mike and the bear broke cover, he stood gun-in-hand, ready to receive the procession. But Mike showed good pluck. As he landed in the trail near us, he pulled up short, wheeled about, threw his piece to his shoulder, and planted a .45 bullet squarely under the bear's ear, smashing her brains to jelly and killing her instantly. Shields's gun then spoke, and laid another low within fifty feet of us; then, rushing a few yards up the hill in the wake of the third one, they sent him into the woods badly wounded.

And then there was such a handshaking as I never saw outside of a revival meeting, and a hurrah that could have been heard in camp, three miles away. We dragged the two bears down to the elk, and fifteen minutes after taking the first picture I made this one. We named it "Elk and Bears: Glory Enough for One Day." Then we packed our trophies, and soon landed in camp, where we had such a supper and such a war dance as I venture to say was never indulged in by palefaces on the Pat O'Hara before nor since.

Ropes and Silvertips

Roy Sharpe

Though many a hunter has pursued the grizzly bear under conditions that gave neither any particular advantage, thus making the outcome dependent on which adversary was superior in quickness and canniness, on other occasions bears have been hounded to death for mere wanton sport. A casual attitude toward wild game has developed over the years, traceable in large part to the great abundance of all species in our plains, forests, and mountains. This has contributed to wastefulness rather than conservation, and it invites casual if not indifferent or contemptuous attitudes toward animals.

The buffalo is only the most notable victim of this attitude. It is true that bears have created problems for stockmen, but not every grizzly bear becomes a cattle killer. This story is an example of reckless and unnecessary destruction. At least the cowboys involved here shot their victims at the conclusion of their sport. Dr. William Hornaday tells a story of some Montana cowboys who came upon a grizzly while riding rounds. Since there were three men and only one bear, the men decided to try their skill at lassoing the bear. One cowboy caught him by the hind leg, while the other two noosed the head. After a while they grew tired of joshing the animal and, fearful of its increasing anger, concluded it would be unwise to risk shooting the beast, since all three were on horseback at the ends of their short lariats. They decided the only thing for them to do was stretch their ropes and choke the bear to death. Fortunately the cowboys in the story reprinted here finally used their guns.

From *The Outing Magazine*, vol. 49 (February 1907).

THE "HUNDRED AND ONE" outfit was crossing the divide
from the head of the Little Missouri westerly onto the Little
Powder River, in northeastern Wyoming. The mess wagon and
beef herd had been sent on ahead in the afternoon, with instruc-
tions to encamp on Cottonwood Creek, near its confluence with
Little Powder River, while the other men were to make one more
roundup on Prairie Creek, a tributary of the Little Missouri,
before crossing. The roundup was held in sight of the D Ranch
and worked for about thirty head of beef cattle, with which the
men started on horses already tired after a forty-mile ride, for
Cottonwood Creek, following up Prairie Creek to its head and
intending to travel thence down the westerly slope.

Before reaching the divide, and with the D Ranch still in view,
two full-grown silvertip bears were started from a wild-plum
thicket, where they had been foraging for fruit, and set out up the
creek, in the direction of Mitchell Creek, five or six miles away
and nearly on the course the men were taking — an exceedingly
rough region, where bears had been frequently encountered and
where bear signs were always to be seen — on the Little Powder
River side of the ridge.

The bears were nearly half a mile away when the men discovered them, and looked like great shaggy dogs running up the long
hillside. Two men were detailed to follow with the thirty recently
gathered beef cattle, and the others started rapidly in pursuit,
each fingering his rope expectantly and yelling with excitement.

It was a lively race, starting in a moderately rolling country
that became gradually more broken as Mitchell Creek was approached. The best horses soon left the others, and in a few minutes the hurrying riders were scattered over a line a fourth of a
mile long. One mile, two miles, were covered, and the distance
between the leading horses and the bears was not perceptibly
diminished. The latter were loping along with slow, ungainly
strides, and the element of speed in even a moderate degree was
not suggested by a casual contemplation of their progress. Nevertheless, three miles were run before the best of the horses came
up with them, and at that the riders had to whip and spur
vigorously to maintain the distance.

Fully another mile was passed after the foremost riders caught
up with the bears before the latter began to show the effects of

the hard run. In the meantime the other cowboys had come up, several with ropes in their hands, and one after another tried long throws. Dick Foster fixed a loop over one of the animals so that one foreleg was thrust through it and the rope drawn tight across the shoulders. With the first strain the bear wheeled and in two bounds was so close that he was reaching for Foster's horse with claws four inches long, before the horse could win clear, and inflicted long gashes on the thigh. Foster dropped the end of the rope, and it was quickly severed in two places by the bear's teeth.

Amazed at the bulk and surprising agility of the bears, which weighed eight hundred pounds apiece and were as lively as squirrels, and owing partly to the fear and exhaustion exhibited by their horses, the men deferred putting their original plans into execution, in the hope that circumstances would eventually be more propitious.

At this juncture there broke upon the men a realization that they were absolutely unarmed; lacking as it was in confirmation of what is popularly attributed to cowpunchers, there was not a firearm of any description in the party. The bears, frothing and covered with foam, were by this time growing weary, and would occasionally stop to snap and growl at the pursuers, throwing the cow ponies into consternation and retreat, from which their riders restrained them with difficulty.

This was in favor of the bears, and, taking advantage of it, they would again press on in the direction of Mitchell Creek, where the men knew there could be no hope of capturing them. The chase was advancing through a country of rapidly increasing ruggedness, covered with sagebrush that nearly came up to the stirrups of the men, and furrowed by draws and gullies, not deep but sometimes with precipitous sides, over which the bears tumbled in somersaults, with a reckless absence of discrimination, always alighting on their feet and scrambling up the opposite bank with astonishing alacrity, while the men had to choose their crossing with greater care.

Attempts were made at times to divert the bears from the direction of Mitchell Creek and to get them out into more open ground, but they held stubbornly to their course, and would not tolerate any unusual pressure, one way or the other. Another summit was gained, and the breaks of the creek, bristling with cedar and scrub pines, could be seen, little more than a mile away, across the next wide creek basin. In the upper part of the basin the herd of six hundred beeves were grazing toward Little Powder River, which was in sight a few miles to the northwest.

The bears were not making headway so rapidly, and were displaying more temper, turning frequently and dashing at the horses, their muzzles bristling; and even the sinewy cow horses, the most active on their feet of any in the world when fresh, jaded as they were, displayed embarrassment in dodging about the sagebrush quickly enough to avoid the savage rushes. The men, learning more and more of bears and their ways, were keeping a respectful interval to the rear, and had almost entirely relinquished their endeavors to rope them.

Gradually the bears slowed to a shambling trot, until they were within a few hundred yards of the creek bed, when they again broke into a run. The men, wondering a little, whipped up and were in time to see them plunge headlong from an embankment fifteen feet high and disappear.

Some of the men rode to the left, others to the right, to find a better crossing, expecting momentarily to see the bears burst into view in a last desperate endeavor to reach the Mitchell Creek jungle. But the bears had abandoned the race for the time, and, separating, one of them had turned up the creek bed, where he encountered a party of the cowboys, whose horses, brought face to face with a charging fury, became frantic and involved a new peril by scaling embankments with their riders. The silvertip kept on at a leisurely gallop several rods to a small pool, containing little more than a tubful of water, into which he splashed and began rolling and wallowing with much evident satisfaction, apparently oblivious to his enemies. In a moment a shout from down the creek bed told that the other bear had also found a water hole and was disporting himself similarly.

Someone in the party then remembered that the horse wrangler had a six-shooter in his bed on the wagon. One man was dispatched to find camp and get the weapon, while the others watched the bears.

The main herd was approaching slowly, and the two men on herd duty soon took in the situation. One of them, Turner McKenzie, came on a run, taking his rope down and shaking its coils free. The first bear he reached was laving himself and grunting contentedly, while three or four men were stationed about him on their horses, from 75 to 150 feet away.

"Let me tie onto him," shouted McKenzie.

Wylie DeLashmette interposed. "Wait," he said. "His head is toward you and away from me. Let me try first, and if I get my rope on his neck I'll turn him end for end and keep him going, with a downhill run, so you can get your rope on his hind feet."

DeLashmette approached the bear cautiously from the rear, coaxing his horse, and when he thought he was within the length of his forty-foot rope, swung and tossed the noose. It fell short a foot and struck the bear across the back. The action of that silvertip was almost incredible. With a roar and a spray of mud and water he left the pool and made straight at McKenzie. The latter wheeled his horse, and his arms and legs worked like windmills in a gale, applying lash and spurs. At that the bear raked the horse's hindquarters savagely, followed perhaps fifty yards, stopped, looked sullenly after for an instant, and returned at his own pace to the pool. McKenzie's bear-lust subsided suddenly. He did not look around until he had gone two hundred yards, when he saw the bear again throwing the muddy water over his back and sides.

The wagon was only about two miles away, and the messenger soon returned with the revolver — a rusty, long-neglected .44, from which two inches of the barrel had been sawed without replacing the sight.

At the first shot the bear left his wallow like a rocket, steering for DeLashmette's horse. But the horse was alert, and a series of retreats and advances was inaugurated by DeLashmette and the bear, the other men keeping as far in the background as their excitement would admit of, recognizing an added danger in the partially dismantled six-shooter. DeLashmette would fire at every opening, empty the gun, and reload. Every time he fired the bear would drop to the ground, and the next instant would spring to his feet running, sometimes in DeLashmette's direction, sometimes up or down one of the numerous gullies, finally running into a deep washout, overgrown with ash, chokecherry, wild rose and buffalo-berry bushes and vines. It was a pit of the kind common to a gumbo country, fifteen or eighteen feet deep and almost sheer on all sides. DeLashmette rode around it several times, seeking another shot. The men shouted at him to "crawl in after." At last from an eminence he could see the bear, sitting up at the bottom and trying to observe things. He fired, and the bear dropped into a huddle.

Twenty minutes elapsed, and DeLashmette and the other men were waiting for further indications of life. There being no movements, the question was asked, "Who'll go down after the bear?"

DeLashmette volunteered, and one of the others let him down with a rope that was secured to the saddle horn, it being understood that he should be hauled back quickly in case of surprise.

As DeLashmette stopped over the animal an eddying current of air, or possibly a last convulsion, raised the long hair on the bear's neck and shoulders. DeLashmette sprang back, dropped the rope, tripped on a vine, and fell, creating a vast commotion. The horses at the top stampeded with loud snorting, and the rope was dragged into the sagebrush, two hundred yards away. Some of the men dismounted and ran back to rescue DeLashmette, and reached the brink to see him, breathless and hatless, scaling the side through the brush, his face scratched and bleeding from contact with the briars. He nearly reached the top before learning his mistake. The bear had been lifeless nearly half an hour, his hide punctured by fourteen bullets, some of which had passed entirely through the carcass.

"Doc" Long, the foreman, killed the other bear with five or six well-directed shots.

The men regarded their ropes with airs of disgust.

Trapping a Grizzly

Allan Kelly

As a journalistic stunt commissioned by William Randolph Hearst's San Francisco Examiner, *Allan Kelly was dispatched in 1889 to journey into the mountains and secure a splendid grizzly bear for the San Francisco zoological park, in order to "preserve a specimen" of the grizzly bear featured on the state flag and seal. In 1889 a hunter had to look hard to find a grizzly in California, but Kelly was a seasoned veteran and knew where to look. He wrote an account of that hunt, and his comment at its end is of particular interest. He was not alone in his sentiments, for in 1904, just four years after Enos Mills spoke an elegy for the California grizzly, Ernest Thompson Seton published a book that caught the popular imagination — Monarch the Bear, a poignant "portrait from life" of that same grizzly captured by Kelly.*

THE GRIZZLY BEAR of the California Coast Range, classified as *Ursus ferox* to distinguish him from *Ursus horribilis,* the silvertip of the Rocky Mountains, is rapidly disappearing and in a few years probably will be extinct. The rapid removal of the grizzly from the face of the earth is not being achieved by the unerring rifle of the daring hunter, notwithstanding hair-raising newspaper stories of terrific combats with the monarch of the mountains. The deadly work can be traced directly, in nine cases out of ten, to the surreptitious strychnine of the deplorably practical rancher and the gentle but vengeful sheep herder.

A grizzly wanders down from his mountain lair to a cattle

From *Cosmopolitan,* vol. 9 (July 1890).

range, kills a steer and eats a portion of the beef. The stockman finds the carcass, and, knowing that the bear will return for another meal, makes an incision in the flesh and introduces a heavy dose of strychnine. The next night the bear comes back to his prey, eats another hearty meal without noticing the seasoning, and shuffles off toward his lair in the chaparral. He stops at the first spring to drink and then a queer feeling comes over him. He is seized with convulsions that rack his tough frame from head to heel, but his marvelous vitality resists the action of the poison for a time, and after a brief struggle, in the course of which he tears up the ground and smashes dense thickets as a man tramples reeds, he recovers temporarily and rushes madly into some deep dark gorge, where the final fit stretches him out stiff and cold. An ignoble death for such a noble brute!

The proprietor of the *San Francisco Examiner,* desiring to preserve a specimen of the grizzly whose figure was borne by the original flag of the state of California and is represented on the seal of the state, entrusted to me, in May 1889, the task of capturing a bear, and in the fall of that year I returned to San Francisco with a splendid Coast Range grizzly, the only full-grown specimen now in captivity.

Information gathered on previous hunting trips led me to select as a field of operations that part of the Coast Range running through Ventura County and the northern part of Los Angeles County, and early in June the first permanent camp of the expedition was made in the heavy timber on Mount Pinos, about 7500 feet above sea level.

During the summer months about 12,000 sheep, driven up from the dry plains of Kern, graze on Mount Pinos and afford high living to all the bears in that part of the country. The grizzlies that live in the rugged ranges within a radius of thirty miles seem to know when the mutton season opens on the big mountain, and most of them go up there to spend the summer vacation and grow fat. They walk into the sheep camps, usually at night, select their mutton and eat their fill, and very seldom are they disturbed at their meals. They pay no attention to dogs, which usually have discretion enough to bark at a respectful distance, and the herders commonly climb trees, being paid to herd sheep and not to fight bears.

In one of the canyons on the south side of the mountain, where I had found the tracks of a huge bear that was raiding the sheep camps, I built a strong log-cabin trap twelve feet long, four feet wide, and five feet high, inside measurement. The side logs were eighteen inches and the roof logs twelve inches thick, all securely fastened with stout oak pins. The cabin rested upon a floor of heavy logs, and three of the corners were buttressed by standing trees which happened to grow in advantageous arrangement. In its general features this trap was a type of all the traps built on the expedition. The door was made of four-inch plank, weighed 200 pounds, and was held in place, when raised, by a rope running over a pulley and attached to a trigger projecting through the roof. A pole lever was substituted for the rope in the other traps.

Only three grizzlies came to Mount Pinos while we were there and they would not go near the trap, although it was baited temptingly with mutton, venison, and honey and the carcass of a sheep was dragged daily from the trap and back again by a circuitous route over the mountain. One of the bears called upon us one night in a sociable way and drove all our horses out of camp, but he ignored the comfortable cabin erected for his special accommodation. It was evident that the grizzlies preferred to select and kill their own mutton. Then the herders began putting out strychnine, and although none of the bears died they became sick and suspicious and retreated to the roughest gorges on the north side of the mountain, where the danger of following them was aggravated by the presence of spring guns set by an unsportsmanlike sheepman.

I soon discovered that my hired guide, fearing that I would break camp and go somewhere else to build traps, had concocted an ingenious scheme to encourage me to remain. He had whittled out of bark a very good model of the sole of a bear's foot, with which he made bogus tracks in the vicinity of the trap. As these tracks came from nowhere and led nowhither but seemed to have fallen from the sky, my suspicions were aroused; and when I found the model hidden in some brush, I discharged the ingenious hired man, left Mount Pinos and resumed the hunt for trappable grizzlies in other places, accompanied only by De Moss Bowers of Ventura, a young man who joined the expedition for the fun of it.

During the next three months we found the trails of many bears, saw some grizzlies face to face and built several traps in the mountains, leaving them in charge of mountain men as we moved along. We suffered many disappointments, most of them due to the cattleman's reprehensible habit of prowling about in the brush with his unerring bottle of strychnine. One trap baited with two live squealing pigs would have caught a large grizzly one dark night; but the inevitable poison was in his path, and he got such a big dose that he turned up his toes in the middle of the trail. It was with mitigated grief that we saw the poisoner's two dogs come down from the mountain the next day, drink at the spring, look greatly surprised for a moment, and tumble over as stiff as crowbars. They also had found the strychnine.

Two months were consumed in fruitless efforts to capture the big bear that had lived for many years on the Liebra peak and destroyed hundreds of cattle. The audacity of this bear and the extent of his depredations had established his reputation as "mucho diablo," and the Mexican who had charge of the Rancho Castac was inspired with such respect for the old grizzly that nothing could induce him to go a foot upon the mountain. The grizzly's den was a rocky hollow covered with manzanita brush, near the top of the highest and most rugged ridge of the mountain, and from this almost inaccessible retreat he made regular marauding raids down through the timber belt to the grazing lands. A green flat near Castac Lake was strewn with the whitened bones of cattle that had been killed by the bear, and in an hour's tramp over any part of the mountain one would be certain to find the remains of from two to half a dozen of his victims.

We hired axemen to chop down oak trees thirty inches in diameter and build enormously strong traps for that bear, and we used hundreds of pounds of honey to entice him into them. Day after day I went up into the chaparral and among the rocks to follow his trail and study his movements, and every day I could find the fresh imprints of his feet. Frequently the trail was so fresh that great caution was necessary to avoid coming upon the grizzly suddenly in the dense brush.

Sometimes in the middle of the night we heard a steer bellow in terror, and the next day found the carcass of the animal partly eaten by the bear. In every instance the animal's neck had been broken by a blow from the grizzly's paw. In his midnight forays the bear often passed the camp at no great distance, and twice he attacked and slightly wounded our horses, which were running at large. Had they been tethered he would have killed them.

One night the bear killed a steer within 150 yards of an unfinished trap, and the next day Bowers rode out to Gorman's store, ten miles away, to get some nails, while I worked on the trap. We expected to complete the work that night and drag the carcass down to the trap, knowing that the bear would soon return for another meal. Late in the afternoon, while I was sawing and hammering and making a great deal of noise, the grizzly came walking along a ridge within plain view and sat down by the carcass to eat his supper, not in the least disturbed by my presence or the noise of the hammer. The old fellow's calm assurance was amazing.

Presently Bowers returned, and as nothing more could be done that night we walked up the slope toward the grizzly until within forty or fifty yards, and sat down on a log to watch him. Although we knew that we could not afford to kill him, each of us confessed afterward that he had half a hope that the grizzly would resent the impertinence and compel us to shoot him full of holes. But he paid no attention to us beyond an occasional glance of curiosity, and in a few minutes he went away.

The next day Bowers returned to his home and I was left alone to drag bait, watch the traps and plan new schemes for the undoing of that bear. I had been nearly five months in the wilderness and had been ordered home by the editor half a dozen times; but, as I respectfully but firmly declined to return without a bear, the editor had grown tired of sending for me and adopted the equally futile expedient of stopping my salary. I had been conducting the hunt on my own resources for more than three months, and the longer I stuck to it the more I needed that bear.

I had devised some new schemes and was deriving some encouragement from the fact that the cattle were leaving the mountains for the winter, and from the accompanying reflection that the grizzly would soon be hungry enough to accept my bait, when I received word that a bear had got into one of the traps on Gleason Mountain which was watched by a Spaniard named Mateo Palma. I lost no time in making my way to Gleason Mountain and there found that a famous big grizzly had yielded to the temptations strewn in his way by the wily Mateo and had walked into the trap. He was a very angry bear when he found himself caught, and his efforts to break out of the trap were insanely furious. He bit and tore at the logs, hurled his great bulk against the sides and desperately tried to enlarge every chink that admitted light. He required unremitting attention with a sharpened stake to prevent him from breaking out.

For a full week the grizzly raged like a lunatic, refusing to touch food that was thrown to him. Then he became exhausted, ceased his mad struggles and began to eat. Assistance was procured and the task of securing him and removing him from the trap was undertaken. The first thing necessary was to make a chain fast to one of his forelegs. That job was begun at eight o'clock in the morning and finished at six o'clock in the afternoon. Much time was wasted in trying to work with the chain between two of the side logs. But whenever the bear stepped into the loop, as it lay upon the floor and the chain was drawn tight around his foreleg, just above the foot, he pulled it off easily with the other paw, letting the four men who held the chain fall over backward. The feat was finally accomplished by letting the looped chain down between the roof logs, so that when the bear stepped into it and it was drawn sharply upward, it caught him well up toward the shoulder.

Having one leg well anchored, it was comparatively easy to introduce chains and ropes between the side logs and secure his other legs. He fought furiously during the whole operation, and chewed the chains until he splintered his canine teeth to the stubs and spattered the floor of the trap with bloody froth. It was painful to see the plucky brute hurting himself uselessly, but it could not be helped, as he would not give up while he could move limb or jaw, and succumbed only when the superior intelligence directing the inferior strength of his foes had made it impossible for him to stir.

The next operation was gagging the bear so that he could not bite. The door of the trap was raised and a billet of wood was held where he could seize it, which he promptly did. A cord made fast to the stick was quickly wound about his jaws, with turns around the stick on each side, and passed back of his ears and around his neck like a bridle. By that means his jaws were firmly bound to the stick in such a manner that he could not move them, while his mouth was left open for breathing.

While one man held the bear's head down by pressing with his whole weight upon the ends of the gag, another went into the trap and put a chain collar around the grizzly's neck, securing it in place with a light chain attached to the collar at the back, passing down under his armpits and up to his throat, where it was again made fast. The collar passed through a ring attached by a swivel to the end of a heavy chain of Norwegian iron, every link of which had been tested by use aboard ship. A stout rope was fastened around the bear's loins also, and to this another strong chain was attached. This done, the gag was removed and the grizzly was ready for his journey down the mountain.

In the morning he was hauled out of the trap, growling and struggling, and bound down on a rough skeleton sled made from a forked limb very much like the contrivance called by lumbermen a "go-devil." Great difficulty was encountered in securing a team of horses that could be induced to haul the bear. The first two teams were so terrified that but little progress could be made, but the third team was tractable, and the trip down the mountain to the nearest wagon road was finished in four days.

The bear was released from the go-devil and chained to trees every night; and so long as the campfire burned brightly he would lie still and watch it attentively, but when the fire burned low he would get up and restlessly pace to and fro and tug at his chains, stopping now and then to seize in his arms the tree to which he was anchored and test its strength by fiercely shaking it. Every morning the same old fight had to be fought before he could be tied to his sled. He became very expert in dodging ropes and seizing them when the loops fell over his legs, and considerable strategic skill was required to lasso his paws and stretch him out. In the beginning of these contests the grizzly uttered angry growls, but soon became silent and fought with dogged persistency, watching every movement of his foes with alert attention and wasting no energy in aimless struggles. He soon learned to keep his hind feet well under him and his body close to the ground, which left only his head and forelegs to be defended from the ropes. So adroit and quick was the bear in the use of his paws that a dozen men could not get a rope on him while he remained in that posture of defense. But when two or three men grasped the chain that was around his body and suddenly threw him on his back, all four of his legs were in the air at once, the riatas flew from all directions, and he was vanquished. Then he roared in rage at his humiliation, and his eyes were green as emeralds. When he was not excited, the grizzly's eyes were dark brown and not unkindly in expression, and his countenance denoted much intelligence; but when he was angry his eyes glowed like green coals, and savage ferocity was expressed in every feature.

There was no trail down the mountain, and therefore the journey was very uncomfortable for the captive, although all care possible was observed in hauling him over the rough places. He was pretty well worn out when the wagon road was reached, and doubtless enjoyed the few days of rest and quiet that were allowed him while a cage was being built for his further transportation. He made the remainder of the journey to San Francisco by wagon and railroad, confined in a box constructed of inch-and-a-half Oregon pine, that had an iron grating in one end. The box was not strong enough to have held him for five minutes, had he attacked it as he attacked the trap and as he subsequently demolished an iron-lined den, but I relied upon the temporary subjugating effect of his experiences and put my trust in the moral influence of the chain around his neck. My confidence was not misplaced. The grizzly accepted the situation resignedly and behaved admirably during the whole trip.

He had one tantrum at Mojave, but it was perfectly justifiable. A crowd of depot loungers invaded his special car, and the inevitable fool in a crowd poked the big bear with a sharp stick to make him stand up. When I got to the car the grizzly's eyes were blazing with wrath, and in another minute there would have been a rush, a crash of broken planks, and in all probability a dead fool. I bundled the crowd out of the car and rode with the bear over the next division to pacify him and get his wrath cooled down. A watermelon sliced and handed to him between the bars produced a good effect in soothing his ruffled temper, and we became very good friends in a distant sort of way before we parted.

Close acquaintance with the grizzly inspired me with genuine respect for his character and admiration for his indomitable courage. He certainly was savage and belligerent but there was not a trace of treachery in his disposition. He maintained an attitude of uncompromising resistance, and no matter how many times he was defeated he was ready to resent promptly, and with all the strength and energy he possessed, every fresh assault upon his dignity or his liberty of action. He never submitted quietly to any indignity, and he would permit no stranger to lay a hand upon his chain. His strength was wonderful and his motions almost incredibly swift for such a massive creature — he stood four feet high at the shoulder and weighed a trifle less than a thousand pounds.

Our acquaintance reached this stage of intimacy: he would allow me to handle his chain and would take food from my hand. He would not strike at me when I was feeding him, but at other times his whole demeanor plainly said: "Let us understand each other. I recognize the fact that I am your prisoner and shall make no useless display of resentment; but neither will I pretend to bear you any love, and you had better keep at a reasonable distance from my claws." He knew my voice, and when I called him by his name, "Monarch," he would look up at me not unkindly, and if I had nothing for him, lay his head upon his paws and go to sleep; but if a stranger came near his cage he would assume a watchful attitude and utter low warning growls.

When finally caged he exhausted every means at his command to break out, and when convinced that he was beaten he spent one whole day in grievous lamentation and then ceased his futile efforts. Monarch is a brave old fellow and he ought to be free in his native mountains. If he still regrets that he was captured I sympathize with him, for I'm more than half sorry myself.

V

SUNDOWN

The Bull Moose
and the Kodiak Bear

F. M. Young

Many good big-game stories have been lost because when related they were not recorded. Africa is not the only big-game country in the world, as some hunters who have been in Canada and Alaska will tell you. The moose, the caribou, and the great Kodiak bear have been the answer to the prayers of American hunters. My friend Charles A. Bunch once told me of a fight between a Kodiak bear and a bull moose, a marathon combat he observed as a boy in the rugged Alaska territory.

We have heard and read many stories about how easily a grizzly can fell a buffalo or a steer by a swat with his powerful paw. This particular fight took eight hours to settle. Charlie Bunch never regretted that long day he and his father spent witnessing, spellbound, this extraordinary battle, and this is how he described it to me.

WHEN I WAS A BOY of twelve, living in Alaska in the early part of this century, my father decided to visit a gold-quartz-mining claim for which he had furnished the grubstake. He usually took one of us boys along with him on his trips, and this time he took me. We started from Seward, took Santa Anna Mail through Cook Inlet to Anchorage. From there we mushed over to the trading station of Matanuska, where we outfitted with saddle and packhorses. It is one hundred and ten miles from this station to the Mabel Mine. It was in May, and very pleasant riding. The country was a flat benchland, and we followed up Little White Horse Creek for quite a distance. The creek ran down a canyon, sloping to the rim on our side; a rocky, rugged wall made up the opposite side.

On the second morning of our journey, about nine o'clock, Father reined up his horse and examined some fresh tracks.

"Son," he said, "there is a large bear ahead of us and not far away, so we must be on the alert." I didn't need any urging to be "on the alert." From here on we rode near the rim so we could look down into the canyon. There were some trees, not many, in the bottom, but no underbrush. So we had a good view of hillside and creek bed. The canyon was about two or three hundred yards deep.

We had not gone far when Father said, "There is our bear down by that big tree in the bottom. He is a big Kodiak, and if I'm not mistaken, he is stalking game." We noted his apparent interest in something ahead. He would hurry for a few rods then stop, then walk slowly forward again. We eased along, keeping our eyes on this king of the forest. We hadn't long to wait, for not far ahead, near some trees by the ledge, we spied a large bull moose and two cows. So this was what Mr. Kodiak was after! There was no pouncing upon his prey unseen; it must be attack and kill. From all we had heard of Kodiak bears and their great strength, we figured it wouldn't take that bear long to procure his game. It was a natural conclusion to make, but as we got a better look at the bull moose, with his powerful build, those big horns with their wide-spread and sharp points and spike, that great head and muscular neck and shoulders, and those sharp hoofs, we concluded that even the Kodiak might have some killing to do.

The wind, what there was of it, blew down the canyon, so the bear had not noticed us, nor had the moose been aware of the Kodiak until he was rather close. Some of the bear's approach was made in the open, as the trees were in groups or patches. When the moose became aware of his enemy, he snorted a warning to the cows, and they moved quickly into the timber while the guardian stood his ground. He pawed the earth and tossed his huge antlers. The Kodiak immediately began a series of preliminary and threatening rushes and sideward advances, keeping his eyes constantly on his prey.

At this point the two giants of the North Country were not far apart, only two or three yards. The bear champed his jaws and made a whining half-whoof and rose upon his hind legs, a magnificent specimen of strength. But to our surprise and amazement, the moose took the challenge and sprang to the fray. As he came near to the bear he rose upon his hind feet for the charge, his great horns making a formidable spectacle. He was fully as tall as the Kodiak.

Then they both made the plunge to kill, simultaneously, but the bear's huge paw found its mark first and tore the moose's shoulder and side with such accuracy and force that it sent the animal whirling and slipping for thirty feet, and left a ragged, open cut a yard long in his flesh. Was this the end? Surely it would seem so, but it was not. To our surprise the moose gathered himself and with quick bounds was upon the furry beast with all his might, tearing into him with those terrible sharp antlers. When the bear shook loose, it took him some time to recover and strike the moose again.

They separated and sparred for an opening. Our pack animals had become excited at this point, so we took them back from the rim and made them fast to a tree. When we rode back to our vantage point, we found the monsters in a fierce struggle again. This was repeated many times. We believed the bear would soon finish the moose, but the anger and strength of the bull was a fair match for the Kodiak.

Dad said, "How long do you think this thing can last?" We had been so interested we forgot about the time, and the sun was far in the west. The beasts would hit and gore and struggle for advantage and occasionally separate and move apart to get their wind. Neither would give up. At any minute we expected to see one or the other admit he had had enough and leave the arena.

It was a battle of champions. Since that day I have seen some fights by men and animals and have read of many, but never have I seen or heard of such a vicious struggle as my father and I witnessed from a ringside seat on the rim of Little White Horse Creek. I thrill to think of it even now.

The combatants had moved away from each other, and it looked as though it might be a mutual agreement to postpone the decision. The moose stood off a few yards looking at the shaggy, torn Kodiak as he walked up the rocky slope toward the ledge.

When the bear turned, with his back to a massive block of stone, he looked at the moose as though to say, "If you want me, come up and get me!" The moose shook his stack of broad, sharp-pointed horns, struck the ground with a strong hoof, and accepted the challenge. With a spring over the rocks, and head down, he struck old Kodiak in the side with those two spikes and drove them home. He heaved the bear up against the wall. The bear had no doubt looked to the wall for protection; it now served as a backstop. The moose's legs stiffened and he bored in on the bear, which gave forth a bellowing howl unworthy of such a boastful fighter. The bear struggled to free himself. He bit and struck with his front paws and clawed with his hind feet, but the moose never for a moment relaxed his determination to put an end to the struggle. For three quarters of an hour, by my father's watch, this gripping round went on. It was getting late, and we wanted to be on our way, but could not pull ourselves from such a contest. We had to know its outcome.

The bear's moans and groans became fainter and died down. Then the moose withdrew those gory antlers, gave his head a shake, snorted to clear the blood from his nostrils and mouth, stepped aside, freeing the bear, and watched his vanquished enemy roll over three or four times to the level ground. The moose went to the carcass and looked at it a moment; then, being satisfied, proudly limped away up the canyon to the cows.

For eight hours we had been held spellbound. Now we rode down and examined the mutilated Kodiak. We measured him. Father said he was thirteen feet, six inches, from the tip of the nose to the end of the tail — and a bear's tail is not long. The skin was too much torn to be of any use, so we proceeded upon our journey.

Coming back a week later, we ran on to the carcass of a very large moose. His bones had been stripped by the wolves, but the antlers showed the effects of that gallant fight. Whether he had been attacked and killed by wolves or had died from the awful blows and bites of the bear we could not know. But his courage and tenacity had made him a worthy adversary against the great Kodiak. I wondered then how many such dramas are enacted in the wilderness when no man or even other animal is present to give testimony.

Besieged by Bears

Enos Mills

Few men have studied bears more carefully than the Colorado naturalist, Enos Mills, and he said the following was the best bear story he had ever heard. One wonders at the carelessness of two miners living all winter in the mountains without a suitable weapon at hand, at a time when bears and other big game might be encountered any minute.

Any man with an ordinary knowledge of bears would have been on the alert for these bears after observing their curiosity and interest in his pack. The prospectors had a lively time saving their hides because of their lack of precaution. We hardly know whether to sympathize with them or to laugh at their predicament.

TWO OLD PROSPECTORS, Sullivan and Jason, once took me in for the night, and after supper they related a number of interesting experiences. Among these tales was one of the best bear stories I have ever heard. The story was told in graphic, earnest, realistic style so often possessed by those who have lived strong, stirring lives among crags and pines. Although twenty years had gone by, these prospectors still had a vivid recollection of that lively night when they were besieged by three bears, and in recounting the experience they mingled many good word-pictures of bear behavior with their exciting and amusing story. "This happened to us," said Sullivan, "in spite of the fact that we were minding our own business and had never hunted bears."

The siege occurred at their log cabin during the spring of 1884. They were prospecting in Geneva Park, where they had been all winter, driving a tunnel. They were so nearly out of supplies that they could not wait for snowdrifts to melt out of the trail. Provisions must be had, and Sullivan thought that, by allowing twice the usual time, he could make his way down through the drifts and get back to the cabin with them. So one morning, after telling Jason that he would be back the next evening, he took their burro and set off down the mountain. On the way home next day Sullivan had much difficulty in getting the loaded burro through the snowdrifts, and when within a mile of the cabin, they stuck fast. Sullivan unpacked and rolled the burro out of the snow, and was busily repacking, when the animal's uneasiness made him look around.

In the edge of the woods, only a short distance away, were three bears, apparently a mother and her two well-grown children. They were sniffing the air eagerly and appeared somewhat excited. The old bear would rise up on her hind paws, sniff the air, then drop back to the ground. She kept her nose pointed toward Sullivan, but did not appear to look at him. The smaller bears moved restlessly about; they would walk a few steps in advance, stand erect, draw their forepaws close to their breasts, and sniff, sniff, sniff the air, upward and in all directions before them. Then they would slowly back up to the old bear. They all seemed very good-natured.

When Sullivan was unpacking the burro, the wrapping had come off two hams which were among the supplies, and the wind had carried the delicious aroma to the bears, who were just out of their winter dens after weeks of fasting. Of course, sugar-cured hams smelled good to them. Sullivan repacked the burro and went on. The bears quietly eyed him for some distance. At a turn in the trail he looked back and saw the bears clawing and smelling the snow on which the provisions had lain while he was getting the burro out of the snowdrift. He went on to the cabin, had supper, and forgot the bears.

The log cabin in which he and Jason lived was a small one; it had a door in the side and a small window in one end. The roof was made of a layer of poles thickly covered with earth. A large shepherd dog often shared the cabin with the prospectors. He was a playful fellow, and Sullivan often romped with him. Near their cabin were some vacant cabins of other prospectors, who had "gone out for the winter" and were not yet back for the summer prospecting.

The evening was mild, and as soon as supper was over Sullivan filled his pipe, opened the door, and sat down on the edge of the bed for a smoke, while Jason washed the dishes. He had taken only a few pulls at the pipe when there was a rattling at the window. Thinking the dog was outside, Sullivan called, "Why don't you go round to the door?" This invitation was followed by a momentary silence, then smash! A piece of sash and fragments of window glass flew past Sullivan and rattled on the floor. He jumped to his feet. In the dim candlelight he saw a bear's head coming in through the window. He threw his pipe of burning tobacco into the bear's face and eyes, and then grabbed for some steel drills which lay in the corner on the floor. The earth roof had leaked, and the drills were ice-covered and frozen fast to the floor.

While Sullivan was dislodging the drills, Jason began to bombard the bear vigorously with plates from the table. The bear backed out; she was looking for food, not clean plates. However, the instant she was outside, she accepted Sullivan's invitation and went round to the door! And she came for it with a rush! Both Sullivan and Jason jumped to close the door. They were not quick enough, and instead of one bear there were three! The entire family had accepted the invitation, and all were trying to come in at once!

When Sullivan and Jason threw their weight against the door it slammed against the big bear's nose — a very sensitive spot. She gave a savage growl. Apparently she blamed the two other bears either for hurting her nose or for being in the way. At any rate, a row started; halfway in the door the bears began to fight; for a few seconds it seemed as if all the bears would roll inside. Sullivan and Jason pushed against the door with all their might, trying to close it. During the struggle the bears rolled outside and the door went shut with a bang. The heavy securing crossbar was quickly put into place; but not a moment too soon, for an instant later the old bear gave a furious growl and flung herself against the door, making it fairly crack; it seemed as if the door would be broken in. Sullivan and Jason hurriedly knocked their slab bed to pieces and used the slats and heavy sides to prop and strengthen the door. The bears kept surging and clawing at the door, and while the prospectors were spiking the braces against it and giving their entire attention to it, they suddenly felt the cabin shake and heard the logs strain and give. They started back, to see the big bear struggling in the window. Only the smallness of the window had prevented the bear from getting in unnoticed, and surprising them while they were bracing the door. The window was so small that the bear in trying to get in had almost wedged fast. With hind paws on the ground, forepaws on the windowsill, and shoulders against the log over the window, the big bear was in a position to exert all her enormous strength. Her efforts to get in sprung the logs and gave the cabin the shake which warned.

Sullivan grabbed one of the steel drills and dealt the bear a terrible blow on the head. She gave a growl of mingled pain and fury as she freed herself from the window. Outside she backed off growling.

For a little while things were calmer. Sullivan and Jason, drills in hand, stood guard at the window. After some snarling in front of the window the bears went round to the door. They clawed the door a few times and then began to dig under it. "They are tunneling in for us," said Sullivan. "They want those hams; but they won't get them."

After a time the bears quit digging and started away, occasionally stopping to look hesitatingly back. It was almost eleven o'clock, and the full moon shone splendidly through the pines. The prospectors hoped that the bears were gone for good. There was an old rifle in the cabin, but there were no cartridges, for Sullivan and Jason never hunted and rarely had occasion to fire a gun. But, fearing that the animals might return, Sullivan concluded to go to one of the vacant cabins for a loaded Winchester which he knew to be there.

As soon as the bears disappeared, he crawled out of the window and looked cautiously around; then he made a run for the vacant cabin. The bears heard him running, and when he had nearly reached the cabin, they came round the corner of it to see what was the matter. He was up a pine tree in an instant. After a few growls the bears moved off and disappeared behind a vacant cabin. As they had gone behind the cabin which contained the loaded gun, Sullivan thought it would be dangerous to try to make the cabin, for if the door should be swelled fast, the bears would surely get him. Waiting until he thought it safe to return, he dropped to the ground and made a dash for his own cabin. The bears heard him and again gave chase with the evident intention of getting even for all their annoyances. It was only a short distance to his cabin, but the bears were at his heels when he dived in through the broken window.

A bundle of old newspapers was then set on fire and thrown among the bears, to scare them away. There was some snarling, until one of the young bears with a stroke of a forepaw scattered the blazing papers in all directions; then the bears walked round the cabin corner out of sight and remained quiet for several minutes.

Just as Jason was saying, "I hope they are gone for good," there came a thump on the roof which told the prospectors that the bears were still intent on the hams. The bears began to claw the earth off the roof. If they were allowed to continue, they would soon clear off the earth and would then have a chance to tear out the poles. With a few poles torn out, the bears would tumble into the cabin, or perhaps their combined weight might cause the roof to give way and drop them into the cabin. Something had to be done to stop their clawing and if possible get them off the roof. Bundles of hay were taken out of the bed mattress. From time to time Sullivan would set fire to one of the bundles, lean far out through the window, and throw the blazing hay upon the roof among the bears. So long as he kept the fireworks going, the bears did not dig; but they stayed on the roof and became furiously angry. The supply of hay did not last long, and as soon as the annoyance from the bundles of fire ceased, the bears attacked the roof again with renewed vigor.

Then it was decided to prod the bears with red-hot drills thrust up between the poles of the roof. As there was no firewood in the cabin, and as fuel was necessary in order to heat the drills, a part of the floor was torn up for that purpose.

The young bears soon found hot drills too warm for them and scrambled or fell off the roof. But the old one persisted. In a little while she had clawed off a large patch of earth and was tearing the poles with her teeth.

The hams had been hung up on the wall in the end of the cabin; the old bear was tearing just above them. Jason threw the hams on the floor and wanted to throw them out of the window. He thought that the bears would leave contented if they had them. Sullivan thought differently; he said that it would take six hams apiece to satisfy the bears, and that two hams would be only a taste which would make the bears more reckless than ever. The hams stayed in the cabin.

The old bear had torn some of the poles in two and was madly tearing and biting at others. Sullivan was short and so were the drills. To get within easier reach, he placed the table almost under the gnawing bear, sprang upon it, called to Jason for a red-hot drill. Jason was about to hand him one when he noticed a small bear climbing in at the window, and, taking the drill with him, he sprang over to beat the bear back. Sullivan jumped down to the fire for a drill, and in climbing back on the table he looked up at the gnawed hole and received a shower of dirt in his face and eyes. This made him flinch and he lost his balance and upset the table. He quickly straightened the table and sprang upon it, drill in hand. The old bear had a paw and arm thrust down through the hole between the poles. With a blind stroke she struck the drill and flung it and Sullivan from the table. He shouted to Jason for help, but Jason, with both young bears trying to get in at the window at once, was striking right and left. He had bears and troubles of his own and did not heed Sullivan's call. The old bear thrust her head down through the hole and seemed about to fall in, when Sullivan in desperation grabbed both hams and threw them out of the window.

The young bears at once set up a row over the hams, and the old bear, hearing the fight, jumped off the roof and soon had a ham in her mouth.

While the bears were fighting and eating, Sullivan and Jason tore up the remainder of the floor and barricaded the window. With both door and window closed, they could give their attention to the roof. All the drills were heated, and both stood ready to make it hot for the bears when they should again climb on the roof. But the bears did not return to the roof. After eating the last morsel of the hams they walked round to the cabin door, scratched it gently, and then became quiet. They had lain down by the door. It was two o'clock in the morning. The inside of the cabin was in utter confusion. The floor was strewn with wreckage; bedding, drills, broken board, broken plates, and hay were scattered about. Sullivan gazed at the chaos and remarked that it looked like poor housekeeping. But he was tired, and, asking Jason to keep watch for a while, he lay down on the blankets and was soon asleep.

Toward daylight the bears got up and walked a few times round the cabin. On each round they clawed at the door, as though to tell Sullivan that they were there, ready for his hospitality. They whined a little, half good-naturedly, but no one admitted them, and finally, just before sunrise, they took their departure and went leisurely smelling their way down the trail.

John N. and the Uintah Bears

F. M. Young

The Uintah Mountains in northeastern Utah were among the last regions of the West to be exploited by man. A few cattlemen from Ashley Valley, to the south of the range, ran some cattle there, but the Ute Indian reservation to the west kept white men out of the country. Not until sheepmen came into the Uintahs from the north, through Wyoming and across the Green River, in 1886, did the country really become known.

In 1888 I spent the summer on the Diamond, Taylor, and Wild Mountains and visited on the north slope of the Uintahs on the Green River. At this time bears were still plentiful and were frequently killed. The year previous several sheepmen from Utah had driven their herds into this region; among them were the Naylor brothers and my friend John N. Davis. Mr. Davis later gave me the story of his experiences as follows.

IT WAS IN THE SPRING of 1888 that we moved down on Pot Creek at the mouth of the Jackson Draw, although we had come to the Uintahs the year before. If ever there was a sheepman's paradise, we found it here. Cattlemen had been in sole possession of the range up to this time, and the country was really wild and an ideal place for the animals that made it their home. There were bears, cougars, wildcats and gray wolves, not to mention all the lesser predatory animals. The silvertips seemed to be even more numerous than the black bear. There were also elk, deer, antelope and mountain sheep; the latter were so friendly they mingled with the domestic herds. It was not unusual to see a hundred head of deer grazing in the meadow in the early evenings. I suppose there was no more primitive section in the West than the Uintahs at the time we moved into it. When several large herds of our sheep pulled onto the range that summer, the bears and lions and wolves must have thought Nature was mighty grand to them. The predators began doing what their instinct told them to. Some herds lost as many as forty sheep in a single night, just plain willful slaughter. It was not at all unusual for the men to see bears in broad daylight; they were used to having free range and had never been molested. The cattlemen had never taken the trouble to fight them. It was different with sheepmen, however. There would have to be a stop put to the slaughter of sheep, or else we would have to find a new range.

It was the first days in May, when the lambing season was on. We gave the ewes their freedom, herding only the outside so they wouldn't wander too far. I was alone, the boss, Mr. Naylor, having gone to Vernal for supplies. About ten o'clock one night I heard someone coming into camp in a hurry, lashing his mount on both sides and calling for a gun. It was Naylor, who returning had noticed the sheep were disturbed and bleating. When he rode over to the herd he found himself between a mother bear and her two cubs. The old bear rushed viciously toward him. Naylor laid on the whip and sped toward camp. Each of us armed with a gun, we returned to the scene of trouble at once, but the bears were gone. The next morning we found some dead lambs and saw where that mother bear had made a sixteen-foot leap when rushing Naylor. She had torn up the ground a-plenty, too. We knew we had a big bear to contend with.

Two nights later while I was cooking a late supper, I heard the sheep bleating. I took my double-barreled shotgun, the shells loaded with buckshot, and went out to investigate. I soon spied a dark object in the bushes, larger than sheep, and cocking both barrels I approached to about fifteen steps of the object. It was the bear, who rose up and gave a loud "hough-hough." I let go both barrels, and then ran until I had reloaded, not an easy thing to do in the dark. Then I turned, expecting to meet my bear. But she did not come, nor could I see her anywhere, but I heard a plaintive whining, and after a little search I found two cubs. I shot one, but the other escaped.

The next morning, I found, to my surprise, the bear. My shot, probably the luckiest of my life, had severed the old grizzly's jugular vein. After skinning the old bear and the cub I found the other little one on the hillside and shot it also.

In my experience with bears, and most of our bears were silvertips, I found that I could get them with two charges of buckshot much more effectively than with rifle balls, so I figured out a method of fighting them. My gun was the latest model, double-barreled, breechloaded, and when I loaded the shells with a good charge of powder and buckshot and walked up toward old Bruin, he would invariably rise on his hind legs to greet me; then I would let go both barrels at his upper breast and neck. I never failed to get my grizzly or any other animal. But it was a good thing for me that my gun was reliable and did not fail to fire.

Another time, I was running my sheep out on Wild Mountain in the Uintahs, and lambing my ewes down on the south slope that dips into Jones' Little Hole (so named by the early trappers). John Shelton, an old Welsh character well known in the mountains, was herding for me, and I put him in charge of the lambing herd. During lambing we usually give the sheep their freedom over a considerable range, just herding the outer fringe to keep them within bounds. A young fellow, Andy Jackson, who had run away from his home back East, was hired on to help John.

One day John found a dead ewe and lamb and saw plenty of big bear tracks around the carcasses. We had too many young lambs at stake, so we decided to get old Bruin and put a good sprinkling of strychnine in the liver and different parts of the flesh. The next day he went to look at his bait, but on the way, to his surprise, met old grizzly before he ever got to the "set." John was not in the habit of carrying his gun, and wishing for it didn't bring it. With pain from the poison wracking her system, the old bear made for John, in savage leaps, and John lost no time in finding a tree, a large cedar up the hill about thirty feet to the left, up which he shinnied like an agile squirrel. But he was not fast enough, and the bear's claws raked his ankle as he pulled himself up into the higher branches. Snarling with rage, the bear bit and tore at the limbs with all her might. The dogs which had followed John barked and nipped the bear and worried her until she left him and disappeared into the cedars. John hopped out of that tree and ran for camp as if his life depended on it.

He got the Marland rifle and some cartridges, told Andy to strap on his old horse pistol, and away they hurried to find the bear. They were not long in locating their quarry. John shot at her and she fell and rolled and bounced around, then disappeared down a steep cedar slope toward the canyon below. The men followed, tracing her easily from the splotches of blood on the ground and expecting at any moment to find her dead. Had she died then, this story would not have been written.

The men followed her down to the bottom of the wash which led to the canyon, anticipating every moment to run onto her carcass. As they came to a big rock, the bear suddenly reared up in front of them. John was so astonished he shot the gun into the air. The bear walloped him one with her paw and knocked the gun out of his hands; then she bore him to the ground. He put up his arm for protection and the bear crunched his hand and wrist between her powerful jaws, and bit him on the shoulder.

John was yelling to Andy to shoot her, for God's sake. The boy, pale and scared but remarkably nerveless, put the muzzle of his six-shooter to the bear's ear and snapped three times, but the hammer fell on empty shells. The noise he made, however, drew the bear from Shelton to him, and she knocked him down and sank her ugly teeth into his thigh in several places. Andy called desperately for John to shoot her. Hastily John recovered his gun but in his excitement failed to shoot, and used the rifle instead to club the bear, intending to strike her over the head. In his excitement, instead, he hit her on the back, whereupon the bear left the prostrate boy and turned upon Shelton again, knocking him down and chewing viciously on his arms and legs.

The boy, now free once more, again brought his pistol to the bear's ear and pulled the trigger, and this time it counted, the ball entering the bear's head with terrible effect. She relaxed her hold and moved away from her victims, and the two herders lost no time in clambering up on a ledge nearby. They watched the old grizzly she-bear grope around in a bewildered manner until she slumped to the ground, gave a few twitches, and was dead.

And what of those two wounded, lacerated herders? The strangest part of this tale is that those two fellows skinned that bear and carried its hide up that steep mountain to their camp. That evening a neighboring sheepman came along, and when he found the condition of John Shelton, he took him forty miles to the nearest town to a doctor, and there he remained in the hospital for a month. Andy stayed at camp. To him went the bearskin and the bounty — a gory trophy to take to his family back East.

A Story of the Sierra Madre

F. M. Young

My friend from Mexico, George Naegle, told me this story one cold winter's night, in a small room on the banks of the Rhine River, in the city of Mannheim, Germany, in 1894. We had met while both of us were doing missionary work for our church, and we were exchanging experiences about our homes, family, and friends, who were so far away, in terms of geography, and yet so close to our hearts. Despite the distance in time and space from the events he described that night, it was difficult for George to tell me about his brother.

OUR FAMILY HOME was in Pacheco, Colonia Juarez, Mexico. Father had a large family and a large cattle ranch there. He was seeking more pasture and ranch space for his growing business and family and had gone to Sonora with two of the older boys to negotiate for several thousand acres of new land. Always a careful and conscientious man, before leaving he had directed me and my brother Hyrum, two years my senior, to go to the "range house," about twenty miles up in the mountains, to take a look at the cattle and attend to their needs, seeing that there was salt properly distributed and taking notice of the condition of the range. We were glad to do so and set out at once, traveling lightly, for we knew there would be some flour and bacon at the cabin. We took our rifles along, as we customarily did when riding about the country. We had some expectations of a little grizzly hunting, because Father had received reports that the animals were killing some of our young cattle.

Hyrum was newly married, and as he left he bade his young

wife goodbye and told her not to worry, as he should be back in two or three days. We rode with good spirits over the hills and through the chaparral, observing the stock and their condition with satisfaction. We arrived at the cabin in the late afternoon. As we drew near we noticed many fresh bear tracks. Hyrum said that perhaps a bear had got wind of the bacon inside and had come to investigate. After scouting around we found a freshly killed calf and agreed that the morrow would bring a bear hunt. In the meantime we made ourselves comfortable. Toward evening Hyrum shot a deer, and we enjoyed a pan of good fried liver. Later we hung the dressed deer in a tree near camp. That night, as we relaxed around the fire, we planned a campaign to get Mr. Bruin, who would only become an increasing menace to the herd, with his appetite for fresh meat.

The next morning we found that a large bear had paid us a visit during the night but had not molested the deer hanging in the tree. After a hearty breakfast of venison we saddled our horses, took our rifles, and set out to find the bear. Tracks led up the right fork of the stream but soon took off into the benchland. We had not ridden far when we spied a huge grizzly in the chaparral. The bear, raising its head, sensed danger and disappeared into the brush. We soon overtook him, however, and each fired a shot. Both shots hit the beast, of this we were sure, but not fatally, and he continued to move away.

At this point I noticed that the shell had not been ejected from my rifle's breech, and I had to dismount to cut a stick of serviceberry bush to drive it out of the gun barrel, where it had stuck. Hyrum, in the meantime, followed the fleeing bear. While I was working at the shell I heard a shot but could see nothing when I looked around. I was delayed only two or three minutes when I mounted and hurried in the direction of the shot.

I had ridden a few hundred yards when I saw Hyrum's horse standing in the brush, but no rider. Approaching closer I heard the smothered growl and snarl of the beast. Suddenly I spied the animal, with his forefeet on Hyrum's breast, tearing at his head with those great white teeth. I urged my horse as close as he would get, then sprang off. The brute, seeing me, left my brother and rushed toward me. Fortunately my rifle was in working condition, and I was able to fire, dropping the bear in his tracks. I then gave him another slug to make sure he would not rise and fight again. This done I hurried to Hyrum, who lay on his back, one arm mangled and useless at his side, his head and face a mass of blood and shredded flesh. I could see his jaw was broken, and there were deep holes in his skull and face.

How had it all happened, and so swiftly? No doubt when my brother fired the shot I had heard, the bear had fallen and appeared to be dead. Then Hyrum must have dismounted and run up to administer the coup de grace, when the bear had roused, sprung up, and with powerful blow knocked Hyrum down and proceeded to tear and bite him with terrible fury. When I came on the scene the animal left one attacker for the other.

I did not know what to do. I could not leave my stricken brother to go for aid, but I knew I could do little for him there. I was in a quandary, for Hyrum was a large and heavy man, while I am of slight build. I will never know from whence I summoned strength to lift my inert brother, but somehow I did, managing to get him up on my horse and across the saddle, to which I lashed him securely, and got back to the cabin. There I stanched his wounds as best I could, filled the canteens with water, and set out, myself on Hyrum's horse, for the long ride home. Twenty miles seemed a distance without end. Worse, Hyrum was conscious most of the time and in great pain, trying to talk but not able. He seemed to want water often, and I stopped frequently to pour a little into his torn fragment of a mouth.

We arrived home about eleven o'clock at night. In answer to my calls, lights were lit and family members hurried in their nightdress to help us. Hyrum's bride fainted when she saw him. Loving hands carried him into the house and made him as comfortable as possible, and a rider was dispatched immediately for a doctor. In spite of the grievous hurts Hyrum lived two days, and then succumbed, as we feared, to the wounds and shock. My father, summoned from Sonora, hastened to be with him before he died.

I have had many hard experiences before and since this incident, but this was the most harrowing and left me feeling saddest.

Jim Parker's Fight

F. M. Young

I knew Jim Parker for a long time out in the Uintah country — a big, powerfully built man apparently well able to take care of himself, yet quiet in demeanor, not a talker. For several years he had herded sheep for my brother. A deep, ugly scar over his eyelid and right cheekbone made me curious, when as a young man I first knew him, as to what experience he had gone through that made him so scarred and nearly blinded. Rumors were that he had wrestled with a grizzly bear, something not many men could do and live. If they did, they usually told the tale. But Jim was a modest fellow. Finally, years later, when I was collecting material for this book, I asked him for his story.

———

BILL WALL had a bunch of cattle up the center hollow of Big Dry Fork. I had gone up there to round up some horses and made camp with Bill. In the early evening the horses came running down from the clearing where we had hobbled them, acting as though they wanted to get home, and right away.

Bill rode over to turn a bunch of steers, so I headed off the saddle horses and took them back to their pasture ground. Then, as a short cut back to camp, I cut over a little ridge and through a patch of fallen timber towards camp. When nearly through the timber I saw a short growth of pines swaying, and, not knowing what could be in there, I picked up a rock and threw where I thought the animal was, whatever it might be. And I soon found out. There was a growl and a rush through the pines, and suddenly a good-sized grizzly bear was hough-woofing into my face.

He rushed right at me, evidently to find whoever threw the rock which had struck him.

Well, we looked at each other for a few seconds, then I had an urge to be going, so I stepped lively to grab for a limb of a tree above me, but a jutting branch snagged my boot and threw me flat upon the ground, and then the bear was upon me. He struck me twice very rapidly and then turned me over like a rag doll so my face was up. I grabbed at his arms, but he shook me off and slashed his claws down over my face. I could feel the blood surge out of my wounds. He grabbed my shoulder with his great teeth and dragged me under a fallen tree. I felt a goner. Then to my surprise — for I surely expected him to finish me there — he ran away.

In a few minutes I managed to get to my feet and clambered over the rotting timber to the clearing. Just then Bill Wall came up on his horse, never more welcome. I suppose the bear had heard him and, not wanting to meet another man, left the area.

The presence of the grizzly explained why the horses had run from their feed. Bill didn't follow the bear but took me to town at once, where the doctor fixed me up, as best he could; but, as you can see, I still bear the scars of the encounter and always will. I was fortunate that it was only my face that took the beating, and that with claws rather than teeth. And lucky for me Bill scared the grizzly off before he had a chance to work me over more thoroughly, I guess. I don't mind the scars. They're better than what I expected from the bear at the time.

The Grizzly of the Idaho Woods

Claude T. Barnes

This adventure happened to my friend Claude T. Barnes during one of his many excursions into Yellowstone country. He was lured there not only by the consummate fishing and hunting opportunities but also by the rough, challenging beauty of those forest deeps. Though by profession a lawyer, he nonetheless had a naturalist's eye and inclinations and was well versed in botanical subjects. No doubt his concentration on classifying the delicately beautiful night-blooming plant distracted his mind from other details, causing him to fire his rifle when he sighted the cub, without giving thought to the almost certain presence of its mother. It is a moot point whether the mother bear would have attacked him without the extreme provocation of her cub being wounded. Anyone surviving such an encounter must publish its report, as Claude did.

EVEN NOW as I recall the dreadful experience that befell me during my sojourn in that thickly timbered district which lies immediately west of Yellowstone National Park, I shudder at the thought that only by the merest chance I survive to tell the story. To me nature presents an endless array of interesting detail; and I may as well state in the beginning that it was this eagerness for observation that led me into the woods alone and into an indifferent attitude toward all save the beauty of my environs.

Originally published in *The Outer's Book*, vol. 32, December 1916.

It was a cloudy afternoon in the latter part of July when I left my friends fishing in the placid waters of the upper Snake River, beside which we had made our camp, and struck off into the dense forests of lodgepole pines. Interspersed among the pines were balsams and other evergreens, and in the dry gulches that sloped imperceptibly towards the river there appeared frequently dense growths of quaking aspen, the latter being usually knurled, twisted or bent by the heavy snow blankets of many winters. One unaccustomed to lodgepole pines can scarcely appreciate their density. In places they appeared in patches a quarter of a mile across, each tree being about the thickness of one's wrist and actually but a few inches from its neighbor. I had great difficulty in penetrating such groves, for aside from the necessity of bending each tree from my path and the inconvenience of walking in a shower of pollen, my range of vision comprised a radius of a dozen yards or more and a delusive portion of the sky above. Soon I discovered that to facilitate my progress I had unconsciously sought bear trails through the timber, the occasional dry excrement that I chanced upon inciting little comment, as I knew that bears were numerous throughout all that region.

Not all of the pines were so thick, and frequently I issued forth upon charming, grassy meadows fringed with monarchs of the woods of various sizes. It was while sitting upon the dried trunk of some ancient conifer that had been prostrated across the green, that I enjoyed to the fullest the aroma, the beauty and the awesome silence of the woods.

I seemed to be resting in a bed of flowers. Purple lupines, crimson Indian paint brushes, varicolored columbines, deep blue fringed gentians, and striking sulphur flowers appeared as if placed there for my sole delight, while lungworts, violets and balsams gave a delightful redolence to the air.

Frequently I stopped to place some plant or blossom in a little book which I carried in my hunting coat; and I noted at such times that the silence of the woods was not complete. Indeed various voices and sounds came through the apparent stillness. Richardson red squirrels scolded at me persistently; several times Rocky Mountain flying squirrels noisily sounded their alarm at my presence; and once I heard the loud clear whistles of a pair of yellow woodchucks (*M. flaviventer*). Frequently I listened to the

pleasing "chivee, chivee-chivee-ah, chivee" of the Audubon war-
bler, once discovering a nest in a pine tree beside which the tame
songster gave rare opportunity for me to observe with the glasses
its newly acquired black breast patches. The strident notes of the
Rocky Mountain jay and the sharp call of the red-shafted flicker
likewise emphasized the "silence" of the woods. Rubbing pines
squeaked with every breeze, and even when there was no audible
sound my fancy caught that distant, indescribable moan, the
rather ominous fairy-whisper or "voice" of the woods.

I carried a Springfield rifle, and, the evening being chill, I wore
a thick chamois vest of the Guitterman type, in addition to a
heavy Gem hunting coat. I must have walked several miles before
my heavy clothing became comfortable; and it was due to this
that I suddenly appreciated that I must be quite a distance from
camp, that evening was approaching, and that I would better return. Twice before, in different years, I had ventured into these
perplexing woods alone, and had become so engrossed with the
multitudinous attractions of nature that I had been for a time
lost, once not reaching camp until long after darkness had fallen.
Though many hunters have lost their way and frozen to death
while hunting elk in the very woods of which I speak, this knowledge did not startle me, as in summer there is more inconvenience
and annoyance than danger in being compelled to spend the
night alone beneath some whispering conifer. I had not seen the
sun at all that afternoon, and as my meanderings had taken a
desultory course I was annoyed, upon surveying the monotonous
timber and equally confusing sky, to discover that I was not exactly sure which direction to proceed. I carefully observed the lay
of the ground and had no little difficulty in determining the direction of water flow of the now grassy little hollow I was in. Satis-
fying myself, however, I proceeded in the hopes that whatever led
me towards the river must eventually take me towards camp.

I at last came upon a rather bare spot in the midst of which
was a very thick patch of young balsams, intermingled with pine
trees about a foot in diameter. I could not see through the balsams, and in going around them I stopped for a moment to examine a thistlelike plant which I recognized as the night-blooming mentzelia. I was pleased that its gleaming white flowers were
already beginning to open, for twilight was nearly upon me. I
stopped to get a whiff of its delightful, heavy perfume.

Upon looking up again I was startled to see a bear cub about twenty-five yards away walking around the balsams directly across my path. It did not see me, so, aiming rather low, as I habitually did when shooting close with the Springfield, I fired. It had not occurred to me for the moment that the she-bear would likely not be far off; but I had no sooner shot than the little fellow bit at his side and set up a squealing that could have been heard for a quarter of a mile. Simultaneously there came a "woof" from behind it, and I scarcely had time to throw in a second cartridge before there loomed up before me what then appeared to be the largest monster I had ever seen loose. It looked as big as a cow; and its size, its head and its color, quickly told me that it was a she-grizzly. For a second I was aghast, and when she stood up her great claws looked longer than the fingers of a man. I know somewhat of the marvelous tenacity of the grizzly, and as it suddenly dawned upon me that at this short distance it would be almost impossible to stop the brute no matter where I hit her, a horrible sense of my extreme peril went all over me. Strange to say, my first flush was succeeded by a calmness which I believe comes to most men when actually confronted with the jaws of death.

I shot at her heart while she yet stood towering before me; but almost instantly thereafter she came at me on all fours, with short, quick bounds and grunts, and with her great white teeth gleaming with hideous anger. I reloaded as quickly as I could and fired into her face. She was right on me; and as I turned and stopped to avoid the swipe of her great claws she grabbed the gun barrel with her teeth, knocked me down with her body, and rushed right over me before she could stop. In a flash thoughts of home went through me, and I was certain my end had come. I knew it was not only useless but also foolhardly to attempt either escape or defense, as I had no knife. Instinctively I felt that the more I struggled the less were my chances of survival.

I was prostrated on my side on the ground, with my face towards the cub. I expected to be torn to pieces; but determined that so long as I could endure I would lie perfectly still. The huge body turned on me almost as soon as I was down, and her great jaws sunk into my side just below my right shoulder. The pain was excruciating, but my thick coat and chamois vest offered considerable resistance before they tore away. A huge foot was placed on my shoulders and I could smell the hot breath of the tremendous brute above me. I surmised with despair that next bite would tear my ribs out; and though I lay quiet I wondered why there was an apparent delay in the sickening process. The bear put most of her weight on my shoulder, if I may judge by the feeling, and then silently peered toward the cub, which all the time had been bawling frantically, and getting further away up into the conifers. Its crying and bawling seemed to worry the big bear standing over me, for the next I knew she sniffed at my ear, breathing a bloody, frothy spray before my eyes, walked over me, came back and sniffed again and then made off toward the noisy cub, the crying of which she apparently attributed to a new enemy.

Lying as I was with my face toward her, I could, of course, observe everything, though I hardly dared to wink. She got about forty yards away, when she stopped, swung her head from side to side looking first toward me then toward the cub. Then she bounded toward me again and when a few yards away slowly approached me snuffing and smelling. Frothy blood appeared at her mouth; and she looked more wicked and vengeful than words can describe. Seeing no movement she again walked towards the bawling cub now over a hundred yards away. She went directly to it this time, and for a moment the thick pines concealed her. I did not know where my gun was but a pine tree about a foot in diameter was only three yards away.

I quietly, quickly arose, ran for it, and proceeded to climb, climb, climb, as I had never climbed before. Again I heard a "woof," and before I was out of danger the great bear came bounding back towards me. She rose with her great claws beneath me, grabbed my foot with her jaws, and tore heel and sole completely off. She hesitated just long enough to give the leather a bite and a flip, and when she came after me again I must have been beyond her teeth, for her ugly claws tore the side of my trousers and cut gashes in my leg. One more effort and I was out of reach!

I continued to climb, and it seemed ages before I could reach a branch of sufficient size to permit a rest. I could hear the bear biting and breathing below me; but even though I knew that a grizzly cannot climb a tree, I knew not what the fearful monster might be capable of. Upon looking down I concluded that I was reasonably safe for a time at least, and I grew calmer. It was fast growing dark but I still could see the angry animal tearing at the tree below. I even thought that she might eat it in two, so frantic she seemed; but at last she again walked away toward the cub, whose cries were still constant but weaker. My leg and side were bleeding but I knew no ribs were broken, thanks to my heavy clothes.

For a long time I could hear the whimpering of the little cub and the responsive sounds of the "tender" old grizzly. It grew pitch dark, and then at last the cries of the little one grew fainter and fainter, finally dying away; and I knew it had expired. I heard loud sniffing in about five minutes, then the sweep of bushes, and the big she-grizzly again stood beneath me tearing at my tree. After a time the sounds ceased; and the silence I could not understand. I dared not descend — I simply had to sit and wait. The night was cold; the robins had long ceased to chatter in neighboring trees, and I feared I might fall. I thought surely the bear must have gone; but after what seemed hours, I heard her expel her breath with what sounded like a guttural, spasmodic effort. Whether she was lurking for me or dying I could not tell; so all night long I sat in the greatest of suspense, my side and my bones aching from my cramped position and the cold. My hands were sore from holding to the rough bark of the tree; and once, to relieve them, I attempted to fasten my belt around the trunk, but it would not reach. I had had too narrow an escape to think of sleep; and as I had not the slightest impression concerning the status of the vicious brute below me, I of course dared not go down. It was an awful night!

How thankful I was when the first signs of dawn approached, and how I peered into the semidarkness below to ascertain if the bear was still there! Finally the darkness began to gray, and I could make out the form of the monster below me, dead or alive I could not tell. When light came, I could see that the bear was sprawled out, apparently dead.

I waited for quite a while, watching for any movement — for many a hunter has met death by taking it for granted that a grizzly that did not move was dead — and then at last I slowly let myself down, threw cartridges at the bear and shouted to see if it would move; but it did not. Even then I hesitated to go down further; but upon looking closely and observing no breathing movement, I concluded she was surely dead. Cautiously I descended and more cautiously approached. She was dead, my first bullet having gone through her lungs and my second having glanced off from her skull behind her eye. I searched for my gun, finding it in the bushes nearby. The wood was bitten clear through to the barrel; but otherwise it was in good condition. I found the cub dead in the pines from which its last sounds had come; the bullet had gone clear through its body.

How I trudged back to camp with my one bare foot hurting me and my mind troubled over my wounds can well be imagined; and the boys were horrified at my condition. They had been searching for me, shouting and firing guns all night long, they said. A doctor was quickly brought from a clubhouse down the stream, and I was exceedingly relieved when he assured me that having received proper treatment so soon after my terrible experience, I need have little fear of blood poisoning or other complications. It turned out that he was right.

In coming back from the scene of my adventure I had broken off pine limbs every fifty yards or so and left them on the ground, for I valued my prize too highly to run the risk of never finding it in those impenetrable woods. I was provided with a saddle horse, and the boys walked. It took a long time to do the skinning, as most of us were novices in this science, but at last it was accomplished. We had to blindfold the horse before he would let us place the hides on him, but finally we succeeded. As I sit now in my library and look at that pelt, which is as big as a carpet, I sometimes shudder over again. Can you blame me?

The Chalk Creek Grizzly

F. M. Young

In the early eighties my brother George was running sheep in the Chalk Creek country near the Weber River. He had a good herder, a big burly Swede who called himself George Carpenter. That was not his real name, which he never told anyone, saying only that he was in fact a Swede. There was a certain mystery about him. He claimed to have been a member of Jesse James's gang. He claimed that in Kansas, one night, the boys were surprised by a posse, and he received a shot in the foot as he scampered for cover in the bush. That injury prevented him from actively participating as a raider, so he drifted out west, eventually winding up as a sheep herder. A very strong fellow, in spite of his limp, who could pick up a hundred-pound sack of salt and throw it upon a packhorse with one hand, he worked dependably for brother George for several years. In addition, he was a crack pistol shot, perhaps because of his earlier training, and frequently brought grouse and prairie chickens to camp, having shot their heads off. Fortunately he was not a quarrelsome man, because he seemed better able to take care of himself than most and would have been formidable in a fight, even with a grizzly bear.

IN THE YEAR OF 1882, brother George was expecting a friend to visit him and celebrate the Fourth of July, and he thought that while he had an extra man handy it would be a good time to move the camp downstream a couple of miles. Accordingly, after the friend arrived, George directed Carpenter to remain with the sheep and feed them down to the new campsite. In the meantime George and his companion would move the horses, have the new camp set up and supper ready by the time Carpenter came in with the sheep.

Evening came on. George and his friend talked idly over the campfire. Sheep bells could be heard approaching as the men began preparations for supper, then several pistol shots sounded up the creek, which George took little notice of at the time. He commented to his friend pleasantly, "Well, I guess the herder is killing some grouse, and we shall have them for breakfast."

The potatoes had browned, and the fresh corn, which the friend had brought with him from home, boiled in the pot. It began getting late, nearly dark, and still no sheep in sight and no herder. George decided they should investigate. They scouted the vicinity where they thought they had heard the shots and found the sheep feeding, but nothing else. By that time it was too dark to seek further, so they returned to camp.

Early next morning, my brother was feeling puzzled and anxious about the herder's failure to appear, so the two men set out to search. It suddenly struck George that the dogs had not come into camp during the night, and he began calling them. Finally old Gyp, Carpenter's special dog, came to them and led the men, with beseeching little barks, into a thicket of quaking aspens not far off. There they found Carpenter, on his back, with the side of his head bashed in and an ugly wound on his thigh. His wide-brimmed hat had fallen off to one side; on the other was his pistol. Gyp ran up to the body, snuggled close to it — he had apparently spent the night there — and snarled and snapped at the men when they drew near. Tracks in the soft ground near the body indicated that one old bear and some smaller bears had been there. George concluded that the herder must have surprised a mother bear with her cubs. Sadly they rode down to the nearest town to fetch the coroner — an uncongenial conclusion to the Fourth of July.

A year or two later a large grizzly was killed in that same neighborhood. When it was skinned, several slugs were found in the carcass, which my brother agreed were no doubt from Carpenter's pistol. He mused that the pistol which Carpenter had carried with him to Utah from his private past on the wrong side of the law, and which he had taken pride in using, to demonstrate his prowess, had proved to be of no more effect than a popgun, when drawn against this wrathful brute of a mother. Such are the turns of Fate.

"Bear-Face" Dodge

F. M. Young

Of all the states, Wyoming has probably been the prime big-game territory, its vast high plateaus and mountain ranges providing an ideal habitat for elk, deer, antelope, and bears. Today Wyoming is one of perhaps only two states where the grizzly can yet be found in the wild (the other state is Montana). Of course, during the latter part of the nineteenth century there were many more bears in greater Wyoming than there are today, and they attracted many hunters. The man in this story was one of those men who made a business of hunting. Such a man would be out of work today. Professional hunting was a risky business; but hunters, like soldiers at war, take their risks lightly, though they never know what the next bend in the trail will bring. For this man it brought a surprise encounter with a ferocious mother grizzly.

Hand-to-hand combat with the grizzly is the most awesome experience in the wild, as the legends of Hugh Glass and similar savaged comrades clearly dramatize. Records of the early West contain more accounts of this sort of adventure than we today can imagine.

The appellation of "Bear-Face" was not given to Mr. Dodge because of any resemblance to a bear but was the result of terrible facial disfigurement that resulted from a chance encounter with a grizzly. His eyes, cheekbones, and nose were so disfigured from lacerations and broken bones that his face could scarcely be called human. But only his face was disfigured. His voice and demeanor were most pleasant, and he lived a full, long life in the Green River country of western Wyoming, an object of considerable respect to his neighbors.

How COULD a man have such an experience and live to tell about it? Mr. Dodge wondered about that himself. Dodge remembered a part of the story; those who found him and nursed him back to life supplied the remainder of it. Though he bore marks ever afterward, his experience was, in the long run, fortunate — he survived.

Dodge was a mountain man, a hunter from choice and instinct, and western Wyoming furnished the setting he liked. He had hunted and killed bears, grizzly and black, and he always brought home his share of elk, antelope, and deer for the table. Experienced and careful, he knew the ranges of all the game animals and was familiar with the trails and haunts of the grizzly.

At the time this story took place, he was camped in a valley in the upper Green River country, near a cattleman's cabin. Bears had been killing some of the younger stock, and Dodge "scented grizzly." That morning as he started on the hunt he felt he might meet up with one of the marauders. He had not traveled far when he decided to go up a side hollow, where the timber was less dense. He had followed the trail but a short distance when suddenly out of the timber came three grizzlies, head-on — a mother and two well-developed cubs, from the looks of them. Their coughing and woofing startled him somewhat, but he soon began firing at them, shooting the old she-bear first; she dropped with the first shot. Then he took care of the two-year-olds. But the old bear was not really done for. She scrambled onto her feet and came after him with a roar, eyes looking fierce and blood staining her big white teeth. Dodge gave her one shot as she closed in, then threw away his gun and drew his hunting knife. He plunged it to the hilt in her breast, and the life-and-death struggle began. The huge bear struck him. He felt his head going numb from the impact. Raking claws lacerated his head; blood filled his eyes and covered his face. Feeling the heavy jaws close on his shoulder, he braced himself for the savage tearing they would inflict. Loss of consciousness relieved him of knowing how much he was mauled before the vicious old animal dropped dead from loss of blood. With one hasty shot, Dodge had saved his own life.

Fortunately for Dodge, a cowboy happened along the trail in the afternoon and, to his amazement, found three dead grizzlies.

More amazing still, he found the largest bear lying across a dead man's legs — or was he dead? Upon close examination he discovered that the man, though seemingly dead, still breathed.

The cowboy hastened for help, and the battered and torn body of the hunter was taken to the nearest doctor and later to a hospital. His wounds were dressed, and the lacerations were patched up as well as was possible in those days. Fortunately Dodge had an iron constitution and recovered, after months of careful nursing. He lived many years after the encounter, but, like other men who have tangled with the bear face to face, found he had lost his desire to hunt grizzlies.

At Close Quarters

William H. Wright

*One of the foremost authorities on bears of the Rocky Moun-
tains recounted this adventure, which owes much of its success to
the bravery of his dogs. Horses may be spooked by bears, but not
dogs.*

*Feisty little Davids to lumbering grizzly Goliaths, dogs have
been known to act, out of courage or foolhardiness, as though
they are equals to grizzlies. More than one sheep herder or hunter
has owed his life to the intervention of his dog, as the story of
Old Ephraim, to mention but one other, proves.*

———

LATE IN THE FALL of 1891, I took Dr. C. S. Penfield and James
H. Adams of Spokane into the Bitter Root region after big game.
I had just returned from a bear hunt in which our party had
killed thirteen grizzlies, and, as neither of these gentlemen had at
that time killed a bear, this made them particularly anxious to get
some. We took my two bear dogs, the bull and the Indian mongrel, with us, and, entering the mountains from the west, we followed the old Lolo Trail that keeps to the crest of the main ridge,
from four to five thousand feet above the valleys on either side. It
was late in the season, and, the bear having sought lower alti-
tudes, we did not find any along the trail, nor, though we camped
beside it for a couple of days and hunted elk and moose, did we
have any success. We therefore followed the Lolo for two days
more, meeting several parties of Indians returning, heavily loaded
with elk and bear meat, from their annual hunt, and then we

From William Wright, *The Grizzly Bear* (New York: Charles Scribner's Sons, 1910).

turned to the right, descended some five thousand feet, and camped on the banks of the middle fork of the Clearwater River.

This stream is about one hundred yards wide, and is, at this season, quite shallow and, like all the streams in this country, very rapid and very cold. Its banks and bed are lined with large boulders, and the water makes a tremendous noise in running over them. Our camp was on a narrow strip of flat land that paralleled the river for half a mile, and ran back two or three hundred yards to the foot of the mountain. Just above us the Clearwater made a turn almost at right angles, and in the bend, on a little patch of open ground, with two large trees in the center, the Indians for years had made their camp, and the place was marked by piles of refuse and by their racks or scaffolds for drying meat.

After unpacking our horses, I sauntered up to this opening to see if the Indians had left any elk antlers — they hardly ever carry them away — and the bulldog trotted after me. As I emerged from the bush I saw, behind a bunch of bushes and near the drying racks, what at first I took to be a black stump. Remembering, however, that I had camped at this place many times, and had never seen a stump there, I took a closer look and saw that it was an old bear gnawing the discarded bones. The animal was so dark in color that I supposed it was a black bear, and determined to tree it for the doctor or Adams to shoot. I had no weapon of any sort with me, as I had taken off my belt in unpacking the horses and had thrown it, with my hatchet, on the ground, and had left my rifle standing against a tree. I had, however, no idea of killing the bear, and even had I had my gun, would not have robbed the others of their opportunity.

The bear was near the two trees, and I thought there would be no trouble in putting him up one of them, so, calling to Jim, the dog, to "sic 'em," I started toward him. But the dog had not yet seen the bear and, dog-fashion, simply ran back and forth looking for he knew not what, so that I was soon within fifty feet of the bear and, not caring to quite jump on him, I gave a yell; whereupon he stood up to see what had broken loose, and Jim got sight of him and made for his hind legs.

I now began calling at the top of my voice for the doctor and Adams, while the bear moved off toward the trees. But as he had to pay attention to the assaults of the dog, he could not run very fast, and I easily kept up with the procession, yelling the while for reinforcements. But the bear did not seem to have the least intention of climbing. He stopped under one of the trees and made a few passes at the dog (I, meanwhile, getting in a few more yells), and then he moved on toward the river, the bank of which was some thirty feet above the water, and while not straight down, was so steep that it was quite difficult to negotiate either way.

We came out about two hundred yards above the bend and just where, along the bottom of the bank, there grew a few old cottonwood trees. Here Jim grabbed the bear from behind, and the latter, in turning to strike him, lost his footing, and bear and dog both disappeared down the bank. I ran to the edge and, seeing them bring up against the old cottonwoods, thought the bear, who must by now have had enough of fighting, would surely climb. But instead he plunged into the river, and as soon as he got to where the water was deep, turned and faced the dog. This, as the bear seemed to know, put Jim, who had to swim, at a disadvantage. But the current was swift, and swept them both downstream to where, at the head of a riffle, several large boulders stood out of the water. Jim crawled out on one of these and the bear sat down just above it, and every time the bear started to move Jim made a rush for the edge of rock and the bear turned back.

On the opposite side of the river there was some heavy timber, and I thought that if the bear got into this he would surely tree. So I determined to drive him across, as, once in a tree, I could watch him until the men at camp hunted me up. I figured that if I did not return before night they would start a search, and if my voice did not give out, they would soon find me.

In fording a swift stream where there is danger of being swept off one's feet, a stout pole, used as a brace downstream, will often make easy a passage that would be impossible without such aid; and I now, therefore, looked about for a pole and, finding one, started to drive the bear across the river. When he saw me coming he started for the other shore, and Jim, leaving his boulder, followed close behind him. My own crossing was a more difficult matter. The water was swift, the boulders were slippery as glass, and it was all that I could do to make headway. By the time I got across, the bear and the dog had both disappeared in the brush, but an occasional bawl told me that Jim was still on the job; and hearing a bark behind me, and seeing old Pete, the mongrel, just entering the water, I felt sure the hunters were coming and started contentedly ahead.

I soon came up with Jim and the bear, and whenever I saw an opportunity to do so without getting cuffed, brought my pole down on Bruin's back. The brush, however, was so thick that it was hard to do the bear any harm, or indeed to produce any effect beyond a snort and a more than usually vicious stroke at the dog; and my pole soon became so shortened by constant breaking that only a small club remained.

We now came to a little stream that drained a spring fifty yards back from the river. Across it there was a fallen tree about eighteen inches thick, and across this tree, and parallel with the creek bank, another tree had fallen, forming a sort of pen ten or twelve feet square. Pete now came up, the bear and the dog stumbled against these logs and fell into the pen, and as they tumbled over I happened to notice the bear's paw; and for the first time, and to my utter astonishment, realized that it was a grizzly, instead of a black bear, we were trying to tree.

I now saw that I was probably in a scrape if those hunters did not show up, and I tried to yell louder than ever, but I had done so much of that already that my voice was nearly gone. However, I stood outside the log pen and did the best I could, and now and then, when I thought the bear was not looking, I whacked him over the head with my club, but of course did him no harm. Jim, the bulldog, was on the side next the creek, while Pete, the mongrel, was over next to the log. When the bear came Pete's way he slid under the tree out of reach. Jim, on the other hand, was not so lucky, as he had to jump the two-foot bank, and I cannot to this day see why the grizzly did not kill him.

I saw that if I had a good two-handed, heavy club that would not break I could likely smash the bear's head, and regretted taking off my belt, on which a small hatchet was slung. I never carried a hunting knife, but did all my skinning with a pocket-knife containing one three-inch blade and one smaller one, and as this was the only resource at hand I got it out. I was looking around for the sort of club I needed when I heard a snort, and looking back saw that the bear had decided to turn his attention to me. I sprang back, caught my foot in a root, and fell flat on my back in the creek, with my head about a foot lower than my heels. "Now," thought I, "you are in for a good chewing," and being unable to take any other precaution, I grasped a bush in my left hand, got a good grip on the knife, and determined to run it into the bear's belly and open him up. But when the bear got his front paws over the log, with his nose just at my feet, both dogs grabbed him by the flanks, and bear and dogs were all tumbled back into the pen.

As they fell I made a thrust and drove the knife in behind the bear's right foreleg, and the blade slipped in so easily that it gave me an idea. I got up and, placing one knee against the log and the other foot against the root that had tripped me, I waited my chance and made another thrust. Had I a long-bladed hunting knife, the fight would have ended then and there, but the knife was short and the bear fat. So that the stab was only incidental.

Up to this time I had, in a desultory sort of way, kept on yelling; the bear, when he got an unusually hard nip, had given an occasional bawl; and now one dog and now the other had given a yelp when he feared the bear was about to get him. But now these sounds were hushed. Each of us had his work cut out and we got right down to business. I kept my place by the log, and when the bear turned to attack Jim, it was my turn to stab. When the bear went for Pete I let him most severely alone, but this was Jim's opportunity and he never missed it. After the bear had been stuck by the knife a number of times he became foxy. He would feint for Jim and, as I started to make my thrust, would turn like lightning and make a pass at me. Several times he came so near me that I thought I could hear the swish of his nails, and I was soon compelled to be more cautious and to wait until Jim became actually entangled with the brute, when Pete and I would join forces and make the most of our opportunity, till we drew the fight back to our quarter.

Jim was now becoming winded; he could no longer retreat as quickly as at first, and I myself was beginning to miss the breath I had spent in yelling. Pete was the only one of the attacking force that was in first-class shape, while the bear seemed to have more wind than he knew what to do with. Under these circumstances it was not long before he made a pass at me and caught me through the ball of the hand. The wound was rather a nasty one, and the blow knocked the knife from my grasp; but after striking a bush it dropped nearby, so that I was able to recover it without losing my next turn, and we continued the fight. Little by little the bear himself weakened. At first this was only noticeable in that it required more biting and punching than formerly to make him turn from one to the other. Then bloody froth began flying from his mouth. But he held on so amazingly that I about lost hope of killing him and saving the dogs. Still, I had got them into the scrape. I knew that they would fight to the death, and I made up my mind to stay with them.

Finally I saw a change come over the bear — the change that marks the transition from doggedness to desperation — and I knew that it would likely go hard with the next one he grasped. This proved to be Jim, and, wrapping his forelegs round him, the bear dropped on his side and began trying to rip the dog up with his hind claws. Pete dove to the attack from under his log, but the bear paid scant attention, and, hearing Jim's smothered cries, and the bear lying with his head and back toward me, I grasped the knife handle by the extreme end, laid my left hand on the bear's head, and, in a last, desperate effort to reach a vital spot, drove blade and shaft both into the bear's side. Then I leaped away, and I was not a second too soon. The stroke — as though it had released a spring — brought the bear convulsively to his feet, and I barely missed the mighty stroke he aimed at me. But this time my thrust had gone home, and, the force of his own blow carrying him off his feet, the grizzly fell prone across the logs and the fight was over.

I had received no hurts other than the one in the hand, and although I was covered with blood, little of it was my own. Pete escaped without a scratch, but Jim, as far as appearances went, was worse off than the bear. One of his legs was so chewed up that he could not use it; his neck was lacerated until it seemed as if his head was cut half off, and there were several other severe cuts about his body; but he was not subdued by a good deal.

For a few moments, bloody and panting, I sat on the fallen tree and watched the dogs worry the dead bear. Then I rolled the carcass over and out of the arena and, the way being a little downhill, and finding that by reaching back and grasping a side of the head with each hand I could just drag the body along, I started with it for the river. Several times in the short distance I was brought to a sudden stop, and, on looking around, found Jim, the bear's hind paw in his mouth and his own three legs braced, pulling back for all he was worth. Arriving at the bank, I rolled the body in and succeeded in towing it across, but being unable to lift it out of the water, I drew it in behind a ledge of rock, left it there, and went on to camp.

There, very much at their ease, sat the two hunters who were so anxious to kill a bear. When they saw me, wet and covered with blood, they became excusably excited and wanted to know what was the matter. I told them that I had been killing a grizzly. "But what did you kill him with?" they said. "Your gun is here in camp." "Well," I answered, "as you fellows did not come when I yelled for help, I had to kill him with my pocketknife." But it took the body of the bear and a post-mortem to boot to satisfy their doubts.

It seemed that, as soon as I had left camp, they had gone down to the river to get a drink, and the noise made by the stream prevented them from hearing me. Once, they said, they thought they heard a dog barking, but as the sound was not repeated, they thought no more about it. When we came to skin the bear — he was a handsome animal, his pelage a deep black, scantily touched with white — we found seventeen knife wounds back of the right shoulder. Three of his ribs were completely severed, and the last stab had pierced his heart. Jim and myself were considerably knocked up. The doctor sewed up our wounds. Jim had to make the rest of the trip on three legs, while my right hand was out of commission for a while and I had to talk in whispers. As it turned out, this was the only bear we saw.

The next day it began to snow and rain, and kept it up for a week, and when we climbed the five thousand feet back to the trail we found the snow so deep that we came near having to abandon the horses, and of the six we had with us only got three home.

Nat Straw, the Last of the Grizzly Hunters

J. Frank Dobie

*With an uncanny ear for a good story, J. Frank Dobie has pio-
neered in collecting and preserving the folklore and history of the
Southwest. This story records an adventure of Nat Straw, one
of the best of the grizzly hunters, a tough and colorful breed
now all but extinct. The story is written as if Nat himself were
speaking.*

LIKE THE BAD MAN, the grizzly was always looking for trouble.
Both found it. Both are virtually gone now. The grizzly was the
only animal of America that did look for trouble. He was the
king and the bully of the animal world. Whoever says he would
not attack man unless bothered don't know. Grizzlies, like other
wild animals, tend to fear men; human beings tend to be decent,
but nobody who knows either kind of these two animals has to
go far to find exceptions. I hesitate to tell what I have experienced, for fear of not being believed, but a man can't deny sixty
years of his life.

My narrowest escape, I guess, was from an enormous grizzly I
had trapped. You don't fasten those gigantic steel traps to a tree,
but to a log, or a piece of log, that drags. If the trap is fixed, the

Reprinted from *The Saturday Evening Post,* © 1934, The Curtis Publishing Company,
with their kind permission and that of the author.

animal is liable to gnaw or pull his foot off. With a drag he will move slowly, leaving a distinct trail.

Well, I found my trap gone, and signs along the trail told me the grizzly was a giant. I followed, slowly and cautiously, for a trapped bear is always in a great rage, and it is apt to show up and charge a man at any minute. The trail went down into a narrow zigzag canyon cut through solid sandstone with many sharp corners. Turning any of them I might step into the jaws of the bear. Common sense told me I had better not follow, but I was like a hunting dog hot on the trail. I would not turn back. The sandstone walls had in them many crevices, some just about wide enough for a coon to squeeze into, some high enough to admit a man, and some wide and deep. I was walking softly, and I was halting at every bend and taking a good look ahead before I went on.

At a very sharp corner I halted and stuck my head around to look. I almost stuck it into the grizzly's face. Perhaps he had smelled me. Anyway he seemed to be expecting somebody. Before I could move he lunged at me on all fours, steel trap and pain forgotten. I can't swear that his mouth was open, but I think it was. His head and foreparts were covered with blood and red foam. He had broken out all his teeth biting the trap, and the steel had cut deep into his gums.

When he charged I darted into the first of those cuts in the canyon wall at hand. I don't know if I had seen it before. It was right at me. It was just wide enough to admit my body, and it was not more than three feet deep into the sandstone. By the time I was flattened against the back wall, the bear was standing now on his hind legs, was pawing into the opening. The trap was on his right foot, leaving his south paw free. His bloody jaws, under beady bloodshot eyes, were so close to me that when he tossed and breathed, the red foam covered my own face. His great paw raked within four or five inches of my face and breast, but the opening was too small for his breast to squeeze through. I kept my long rifle held perpendicular against my body, and I sucked in my stomach until it was against my backbone. There was no room for me to raise the muzzle of the rifle to shoot; if any part of the gun came within the grasp of the bear's paw, he would, I knew, tear it from me and probably break it. I have never heard a bear growl, although I have read many times about their growl. A bear will champ his jaws. He will kind of whine and hum at the same time, and when you hear that sound you had better get your shooting irons. He will roar! It is impossible to describe the rage of a great grizzly tortured by pain and mad for vengeance. There he stands weighing more than half a ton, as powerful for his size as an ant is for his, and his power doubled and trebled by a rage inconceivable to man.

This grizzly flung the big steel trap on his right forearm against the crevice into which I was backed; he seemed forgetful of the pain. With his free paw he tried to break off chunks of the stone. He bit at the stone with the jaws he had already torn on the steel. He tried to squeeze gradually into the opening. He lunged into it, and it seemed to me that the claws of his hand, which looked as big as a ham, reached an inch or two nearer my body. People who have not had opportunity to observe cannot realize what power is in the hand or paw of a great bear. I have seen a grizzly slap lightly the head of a bull, and knock him to the ground with a broken neck.

I do not know how long I stayed in that rock crevice, facing the grizzly. It seemed hours, but it might not have been more than fifteen minutes. He did not relent for a second, so as to give me time to raise the gun and shoot. It looked to me as if the rocks would melt under his white-hot rage. I thought of the way I'd heard Apaches spread-eagle a man down on his back, face up, tying beside him a big rattlesnake by a rawhide thong, just short of striking distance, and then, while they enraged the snake, dropping water, drop by drop, on the rawhide, until it at last expanded enough for the fangs to enter the face of the man. I thought of this and other slow ways of death. When I was a boy I had read Poe's story, "The Pit and the Pendulum."

Finally the bear stood off a second, seemingly to consider some new way of attack. Until I went to raise the gun, I did not realize how weak I had become. As I raised it the grizzly came again, but he was too late to miss a shot in the belly and not quick enough to grasp the barrel. A bear that's merely shot through the belly can live a long, long time. If possible, this one became more furious than ever, but I soon saw that he was weakening.

Before long he kind of hunkered down. I put a bullet through his head. When I shot that last time his eyes were closed. Now they opened like a bear's always open when he is dead. I had to sit down a long time before I had strength to stick him and start skinning.

The Grizzly Mother

Enos Mills

The renowned naturalist Enos Mills contributed a great deal of literature on the grizzly bear, much of it from his personal observations. He was a perceptive and sympathetic student of bear behavior, as this narrative illustrates. I include this passage because of its unusual view of the grizzly, who most often attracts notice by its violent reaction to the threats of man. Here the formidable female bear is shown in her natural role of caring mother, rather than as a wrathful protector.

TWO HUNTERS and a number of dogs made camp one evening near the headwaters of the St. Vrain River. They were after grizzly. There were grizzlies in these rugged mountains. But with numerous high, rocky ridges, deep, rugged canyons, and miles of forest, most grizzlies avoided being seen, and escaped the hunters even when dogs were used.

Off to the north, up a steep mountain, a mother grizzly had her cubs. The bayings of the dogs, or the scent of the far-off hunters, reached her the next morning after the hunters' camp was made. A grizzly mother takes no chances with the cubs. Generally her keen senses warn her of the approach of a hunter while he is still far off. The instant she scents danger, she hurries the cubs far away, out of the danger zone. But one of the cubs of this grizzly was crippled by the fall of a tree limb and could not travel.

The mother grizzly appeared in the hunters' camp just as they were finishing breakfast. Instantly everything was in an uproar, and twenty dogs were after her. Away she fled tu the south — away from her cubs. But she did not succeed, did not, after an all-day struggle, lead dogs and hunters away.

The following morning mother grizzly reappeared near their camp. Again hunters and dogs pursued. Miles to the south she ran. This time she led them far from her den and cubs. She zigzagged, circled, waded three miles up a mountain stream, concealed her trail, and escaped. The bewildered dogs were left at the foot of the mountain.

She should be safe now. But a grizzly ever assumes itself followed and ever is watchful for ambush. The breeze was behind her. Coming to a low ridge, she peeped over. The way appeared safe.

But, the instant she reached the skyline, the hunters opened fire. The grizzly was out of sight in a few seconds. Miles she ran toward the southwest, away from her den. Late in the afternoon the pursuing hunters paused on a high spur. In the distance they saw the bear pacing back and forth on a pass.

She was more than twenty miles from her den. But the cubs were not yet safe. These hunters and dogs must be led farther off.

It was possible for her to cross to the other side of the Continental Divide, and, over a rough and roundabout way which dogs could not follow, come back to the den. This would mean perhaps fifty miles of travel. The grizzly stopped pacing. While the hunters were watching, she crossed the divide.

A little while after mother grizzly had left her cubs, an enormous landslide slipped from the mountainside and carried the bear den and surroundings down into the bottom of a canyon. From my camp I heard the slide and saw the dust it threw off. I did not then know that the mother was away from the den, seeking to lead the dogs off. I feared that the entire grizzly family had been carried down by the slide, and started out to make a search.

The second morning following the landslide, the grizzly returned. She probably had traversed the western slope of the high divide, to a point opposite her den, then climbed over the summit. I was on the mountainside near where the den had been. Through the glass I watched her shuffling rapidly down the long, treeless slope. While still a quarter of a mile from the place where her den had been, she appeared to realize a change. Perhaps she saw some of it, and scented the fresh surfaces and crushed trees. She stopped, stood on her hind legs, drew her paws up to her breast, leaned forward, and, with nose pointing here and there, looked over the changes in the place.

A stupendous pile of chaotic wreckage lay in the canyon. Uprooted trees, boulders, broken rocks — many of enormous size — were flung in wildest confusion. In this debris and along the slide's destructive way, I had searched and searched for the cubs and the bear.

The grizzly showed surprise and interest in the landslide, but no fear, no alarm. She approached the torn edge cautiously, looked at it for a moment, then plunged down in the canyon and began searching for the den. Then she raced here and there, her nose down like a dog, searching for the cubs.

I hurried on down to where the slide had plunged wildly over the canyon rim. Later, the grizzly came hurrying along. In the channel and on both sides she galloped, searching with eyes and nose.

She caught my scent, put her nose in one of my tracks, and rose on her hind legs, with neck bristling. She scented man danger for the cubs. Ordinarily, man scent causes a grizzly to rush from the locality. But her attitude was defiance, not retreat. Intent on the search, and steaming with warmth, she passed near without detecting me. Down into the canyon she went, searching among the landslide debris.

At the bottom, almost on the edge of the stream, she unearthed a lifeless cub. She fondled it, licked its body clean, laid it down and looked at it with a puzzled expression. She lifted it upon the bank. Gently, ever so gently, she pawed and pushed it about as if trying to awaken it. She pushed it against a boulder and backed away, watching it. Then she turned and climbed back up the landslide's torn track, as if there to search further for the other cub.

Fearing that mother grizzly might come upon me in one of her wild dashes, I started for camp. About a mile down the mountain, I stopped to look around.

While I stood upon a log in the woods, a dirty little cub came from among the trees and walked slowly toward me. Neither sight nor scent warned him of my presence. After smelling and sniffing by the side of the log, he began digging. He found nothing, raised his head, and whined. He was a lost, hungry cub — the one for which the mother was now searching. He took a few steps, then stopped as if uncertain which way to go.

I grabbed the cub. He fought me, clawing, biting and struggling. He was weak — he had not nursed for two or three days — and weighed only a few pounds. I pushed him into the pocket of my coat, where he snuggled down.

There I stood with the grizzly cub in my pocket. Any instant the mother might appear, having trailed me down the mountain, or, more likely, having trailed the cub to this place.

But, before the mother found the cub, it might perish from hunger. The right thing appeared to be to carry him up the mountain and place him close to the dead cub, where his mother would be likely to find him. This would be taking desperate chances, with the mother so close. But I took the chances and started up through the woods with the cub.

Carrying a long-lost grizzly cub toward its desperate mother is walking into the zones of adventure and suicide. If she came upon me with the cub in my possession, no explanation would save me. I did not carry a gun, and I was baiting a grizzly bear — the female of the species.

Rushing muffled footfalls on my left startled me. A heavy animal was approaching. Unable to see far because of thick tree growth, I threw myself down on the pine needles to look beneath the low hanging limbs. Nothing could be seen. But the animal could be heard circling around me and coming closer.

The cub set up a bawling. He seemed determined to tell the passer-by that he was being carried off by a kidnapper. I slipped a raisin into his mouth. He became quiet. *Thumpety-thud*, a deer ran by me.

Knowing that this cub outburst might have reached his mother, or that it might be repeated, I made ready to separate myself from him instantly. But, after I had waited a minute or two behind a tree, the forest seemed so peaceful that I went on.

Crossing the stream in the canyon a little below the dead cub, I saw that the water was filled with sediment. Was the mother digging in the landslide debris above? Behind a rock I waited and listened. I was ready to drop the cub and vanish, or to shoot up a tree if the cub whimpered and mother *Ursus horribilis* appeared.

Eager to be rid of the cub, I hurried up the canyon. Startlingly fresh mother-grizzly tracks were by the dead cub. The crumbling track edges showed that one minute earlier there would have been a different story. I dropped the live cub by the dead one.

It was no place to linger. Mother might return suddenly. I headed for camp; but, as I hurriedly climbed out of the canyon, I looked back. The little cub was snuggling up to his dead brother.

As I reached the top of the canyon, it came to me like a flash that I was not yet out of danger. Grizzlies have a keen nose. My clothes were filled with the scent of the cub, and as mother grizzly rushed here and there, she might come close enough to catch this cub scent. If she caught it, she was likely to see if the cub was concealed in the clothes. I hurried from the place.

Down the slope I stopped to look back and listen. A gigantic grizzly coming stealthily behind along my trail was almost upon me. I was in an opening, and it did not seem safe to run, although the bear was approaching as if to pounce upon me.

By the tree nearest to me the bear stopped, and rose on tiptoe to look me over. It was the mother of the cubs. She was steaming with warmth. She put her forepaws against the tree, as if to steady herself. She moved her head slowly from side to side, as if she could not see plainly; then she moved her nose up and down, as she looked me over. Suddenly she dropped on all fours and started toward me. I was less than twenty feet away. After the second step, she stopped. Again she stood on her hind feet.

There was no show of anger. She plainly was greatly puzzled over something. This close approach and apparent hesitation — neither attacking nor retreating — was extraordinary action for a grizzly.

She had caught the scent of the cub. This scent was her first clue of the lost cub, and she was certain to follow it up. I wondered if she would not come up and take hold of my clothes; and what her next move would be on finding my coat full of strong scent of the cub — and the cub not with me.

Perhaps she would allow me to escape, if I threw her my cub-scented clothes. But she might assault me instead. She wanted the cub.

I would have climbed a tree had any been within reach. But it did not seem wise to move toward one, or to move at all. So again I stood still when she started toward me, and resolved not to move unless she growled or charged. Fortunately she concluded to walk entirely around me. This she did deliberately, stopping a few times to stand still for a better look, and to sniff her nose. Not seeing the cub, she again came to a standstill, and finally sat down dog-like, keeping her eyes upon me.

Apparently she intended to stay until I delivered the cub to her. Although there was no suggestion of anger or fierceness, some unexpected thing might arouse her in a second. If the cub should walk out of the hollow log nearby, or come out of the clump of bushes between us, she might assault me in an instant. Grizzly mothers insist that men keep far from their cubs.

So I thought to edge slowly toward a tree. She watched me, but with no show of resentment. When almost to the tree, I concluded to try running away. After many steps I stopped by a boulder, to find out if she was following. She was, and was close to me.

Again I ran. Looking back over my shoulder, I saw her following, a little to one side and at about my speed. She was watching me curiously.

She was trying to find the cub. Its scent being upon me, but no cub in sight, evidently mystified her.

Plainly, the only thing for me to do was to lead her to the canyon near the cub — that is, if she would follow my leadership. If she caught the fresh scent of the cub, I should escape.

I made a dash for the canyon; full speed I ran, without looking back. For several seconds I could not hear her. Suddenly she leaped into an opening in front of me, as if to head me off from the canyon. She stood up, sniffed and sniffed, and acted as if blind. But there was no cub to be seen.

Footfalls on our left disturbed us both. She dashed off, but after a few jumps came to a stop behind a clump of firs. I stood still. The footfalls, perhaps those of a passing deer, had ceased. A woodpecker was tapping far off, a Clark's crow was noisily clamoring in the top of a pine, and close to me a squirrel was just bursting with curiosity.

In a most leisurely fashion the grizzly came walking back. She stopped, and I hoped that, in the silence, the cub would whine or the breeze would bring his mother a message from him. But nothing happened.

Another short run brought me close to the edge of the canyon, above the cubs. I had hoped to reach the rim in this advance, but the grizzly placed herself before me, a short stone's throw from the canyon. She looked and sniffed. She growled. Her neck fur bristled.

In a flash she changed to furious, aggressive motherhood. I now was in danger. She was about to charge me for coming so close to her cub. Fortunately she had not yet seen the cub, and trying to see it delayed her charge. But, bristling and furious, she edged sideways toward me. The cub, near, but out of sight, was climbing out of the canyon toward us.

I had stopped by a tree, up which I could quickly swing if the grizzly charged. If the cub failed to appear, the mother might sit at the bottom of the tree and keep me up indefinitely.

With jaws working and teeth gnashing, she looked at me and gathered herself to spring. A brush nearby snapped. She gave a terrific growl.

I swung free of the earth and up the tree. In her leap she turned and plunged toward the canyon.

Looking down from a high tree limb I saw her lift and hug the little cub.

The Grizzly and
the Golden Rule

James Oliver Curwood

In this collection of stories in which man kills bear and bear kills man, I have tried to present the various phases of man's contact with the fiercest of the North American animals, and the various stages of the struggle for mastery that took place when the intelligence of man was pitted against the instinct and strength of the grizzly bear.

James Oliver Curwood made a business of killing big game for years; at one time, in British Columbia, he killed three huge grizzlies in less than two hours. He took great pride in his trophies. From early childhood until his meeting with Thor, he had hunted small and large game with the love of killing in his heart. His mastery of Thor was to be the crown to all his grizzly-bear conquests. But Curwood's experience proved to be a turning point in his life. He never killed for sport again but campaigned vigorously against the exploitation and slaughter of wildlife, appealing for coexistence and urging man not to become a menace to all other species. To this effect, he wrote a lyrical romance of the wild, The Grizzly King *(New York, 1926), which is based on his experience with the singular and forgiving Thor.*

AT THE PARTICULAR TIME I am going to write about, I was on a big grizzly hunt in a wild and unhunted part of the British

Columbia mountains. I had with me one man, seven horses, and a pack of Airedales trained to hunt bears. We had struck a grizzly-and-caribou paradise, and there had been considerable killing, when, one day, we came upon the trail of Thor, the great beast that showed me how small in soul and inclination a man can be. In a patch of mud, his feet had left tracks that were fifteen inches from tip to tip, and so wide and deep were the imprints that I knew I had come upon the king of all his kind. I was alone that morning, for I had left camp an hour ahead of my man, who was two or three miles behind me with four of the horses and the Airedale pack. I went on watching for a new campsite, for the thrill of a great desire possessed me — the desire to take the life of this monster king of the mountains. It was in these moments that the unexpected happened. I came over a little rise, not expecting that my bear was within two or three miles of me, when something that was very much like a low and sullen rumble of faraway thunder stopped the blood in my veins.

Ahead of me, on the edge of a little wallow of mud, stood Thor. He had smelled me, and, I believe, it was the first time he had ever smelled the scent of man. Waiting for this new mystery in the air, he had reared himself up until the whole nine feet of him rested on his haunches, and he sat like a trained dog, with his great forefeet, heavy with mud, drooping in front of his chest. He was a monster in size, and his new June coat shone a golden brown in the sun. His forearms were almost as large as a man's body, and the three largest of his five knifelike claws were five and a half inches long. He was fat and sleek and powerful. His upper fangs, sharp as stiletto points, were as long as a man's thumb, and between his great jaws he could have crushed the neck of a caribou. I did not take in all these details in the first startling moments; one by one they came to me later. But I had never looked upon anything in life quite so magnificent. Yet did I have no thought of sparing that splendid life. Since that day, I have rested in camp with my head pillowed on the arm of a living grizzly that weighed a thousand pounds. Friendship and love and understanding have sprung up between us. But in that moment my desire was to destroy his life that was so much greater than my own. My rifle was at my saddle horn, in its buckskin jacket. I fumbled it in getting into action, and in those precious moments

Thor lowered himself slowly and ambled away. I fired twice, and would have staked my life that I had missed both times. Not until later did I discover that one of my bullets had opened a furrow two inches deep and a foot long in the flesh of Thor's shoulder. Yet I did not see him flinch. He did not turn back, but went his way.

Shame burns within me as I write of the days that followed; and yet, with that shame, there is a deep and abiding joy, for they were also the days of my regeneration. Day and night, my one thought was to destroy the big grizzly. We never left his trail. The dogs followed him like demons. Five times in the first week we came within long shooting range, and twice we hit him. But still he did not wait for us or attack us. He wanted to be left alone. In that week, he killed four of the dogs, and the others we tied up to save them. We trailed him with horses and afoot, and never did the spoor of other game lure me aside. The desire to kill him became a passion in me. He outgeneraled us. He beat all our games of trickery. But I knew that we were bound to win — that he was slowly weakening because of exhaustion and the sickness of his wounds. We loosed the dogs again, and another was killed.

Then, at last, came that splendid day when Thor, master of the mountains, showed me how contemptible was I — with my human shape and soul.

It was Sunday. I had climbed three or four thousand feet up the side of a mountain, and below me lay the wonder of the valley, dotted with patches of trees and carpeted with the beauty of rich, green grass, mountain violets and forget-me-nots, wild asters, and hyacinths. On three sides of me spread out the wonderful panorama of the Canadian Rockies, softened in the golden sunshine of late June. From up and down the valley, from the breaks between the peaks, and from the little gullies cleft in shale and rock that crept up to the snow lines came a soft and droning murmur. It was the music of running water — music ever in the air of summer. For the rivers and creeks and tiny streamlets gushing down from the melting snow up near the clouds are never still. Sweet perfumes as well as music came to me; June and July — the last of spring and the first of summer in the northern mountains — were commingling. All the earth was bursting with green; flowers were turning the sunny slopes and meadows into colored splashes of red and white and purple, and everything that had life was giving voice to exultation — the fat whistlers on their rocks, the pompous little gophers on their mounds, the squirrellike rock rabbits, the big bumblebees that buzzed from flower to flower, the hawks in the valley, and the eagles over the peaks.

Earth, it seemed, was at peace.

And I, looking over all that vastness of life, felt my own greatness thrust upon me.

For had not the Creator, of all things, made this wonderland for *me?*

I climbed higher up the mountain.

I came to a sheer wall of rock that rose hundreds of feet above me. Along this ran a narrow ledge, and I followed it. The passage became craggy and difficult, and in climbing over a broken mass of rock, I slipped and fell. I had brought a light mountain gun with me, and in trying to recover myself I swung it about with such force that the stock struck a sharp edge of rock and broke clean off. But I had saved myself from possible death, and was in a frame of mind to congratulate myself rather than curse my luck. Fifty feet farther on I came to a "pocket" in the cliff, where the ledge widened until, at this particular place, it was like a flat table twenty feet square. Here I sat down, with my back to the precipitous wall, and began to examine my broken rifle.

I laid it beside me, useless. Straight up at my back rose the sheer face of the mountain; in front of me, had I leaped from the ledge, my body would have hurtled through empty air for a thousand feet. In the valley I could see that creek, like a ribbon of shimmering silver; two or three miles away was a little lake; on another mountain I saw a bursting cascade of water leaping down the heights and losing itself in the velvety green of the lower timber. For many minutes, new and strange thoughts possessed me. I did not look through my hunting glasses, for I was no longer seeking game. My blood was stirred, but not with the desire to kill.

And then, suddenly, there came a sound to my ears that seemed to stop the beating of my heart. I had not heard it until it was very near — approaching along the narrow ledge.

It was the click, click, click of claws rattling on rock!

I did not move. I hardly breathed. And out from the ledge I had followed came a monster bear!

With the swiftness of lightning, I recognized him. It was Thor! And, in that same instant, the great beast saw me.

In thirty seconds I lived a lifetime, and in those thirty seconds what passed through my mind was a thousand times swifter than spoken word. A great fear rooted me, and yet in that fear I saw everything to the minutest detail. Thor's massive head and shoulders were fronting me. I saw the long naked scar where my bullet had plowed through his shoulder; I saw another wound in his foreleg, still ragged and painful, where another of my soft-nosed bullets had torn like an explosion of dynamite. The giant grizzly was no longer fat and sleek as I had first seen him ten days ago. All that time he had been fighting for his life; he was thinner; his eyes were red; his coat was dull and unkempt from lack of food and strength. But at that distance, less than ten feet from me, he seemed still a mighty brother of the mountains themselves. As I sat stupidly, stunned to the immobility of a rock in my hour of doom, I felt the overwhelming conviction of what had happened. Thor had followed me along the ledge, and, in his hour of vengeance and triumph, it was I, and not the great beast, who was about to die.

It seemed to me that an eternity passed in these moments. And Thor, mighty in his strength, looked at me and did not move. And this thing that he was looking at — shrinking against the rock — was the creature that had hunted him; this was the creature that had hurt him, and it was so near that he could reach out with his paw and crush it! And how weak and white and helpless it looked now! What a pitiful, insignificant thing it was! Where was its strange thunder? Where was its burning lightning? Why did it make no sound?

Slowly Thor's giant head began swinging from side to side; then he advanced — just one step — and in a slow, graceful movement reared himself to his full, magnificent height. For me, it was the beginning of the end. And in that moment, doomed as I was, I found no pity for myself. Here, at last, was justice! I was about to die. I, who had destroyed so much of life, found how helpless I was when I faced life with my naked hands. *And it was justice!* I had robbed the earth of more life than would fill the bodies of a thousand men and now my own life was to follow that which I had destroyed. Suddenly fear left me. I wanted to cry out to that splendid creature that I was sorry, and could my dry lips have framed the words, it would not have been cowardice — but truth.

I have read many stories of truth and hope and faith and charity. From a little boy, my father tried to teach me what it meant to be a gentleman, and he lived what he tried to teach. And from the days of my small boyhood, mother told me stories of great and good men and women, and in the days of my manhood, she faithfully lived the great truth that of all precious things charity and love are the most priceless. Yet had I accepted it all in the narrowest and littlest way. Not until this hour on the edge of the cliff did I realize how small can be the soul of a man buried in his egoism — or how splendid can be the soul of a beast.

For Thor knew me. That I know. He knew me as the deadliest of all his enemies on the face of the earth. Yet until I die will I believe that, in my helplessness, he no longer hated me or wanted my life. For slowly he came down upon all fours again, and, limping as he went, he continued along the ledge — *and left me to live!*

I am not, in these days, sacrilegious enough to think that the Supreme Power picked my poor insignificant self from among a billion and a half other humans especially to preach a sermon to that glorious Sunday on the mountainside. Possibly it was all mere chance. It may be that another day Thor would have killed me in my helplessness. It may all have been a lucky accident for me. Personally, I do not believe it, for I have found that the soul of the average beast is cleaner of hate and of malice than that of the average man. But whether one believes with me or not does not matter, so far as the point I want to make is concerned — that from this hour began the great change in me, which has finally admitted me into the peace and joy of universal brotherhood with life. It matters little how a sermon or a great truth comes to one; it is the result that counts.

I returned down the mountain, carrying my broken gun with me. And everywhere I saw that things were different. The fat whistlers, big as woodchucks, were no longer so many targets, watching me cautiously from the rocktops; the gophers, sunning themselves on their mounds, meant more to me now than a few hours ago. I looked off to a distant slide on another mountain and made out the half-dozen sheep I had studied through my glasses earlier in the day. But my desire to kill was gone. I did not realize the fullness of the change that was upon me then. In a dull sort of way, I accepted it as an effect of shock, perhaps as a passing moment of repentance and gratitude because of my escape. I did not tell myself that I would never kill sheep again except when mutton was necessary to my campfire. I did not promise the whistlers long lives. And yet the change was on me, and growing stronger in my blood with every breath I drew. The valley was different. Its air was sweeter. Its low song of life and running waters and velvety winds whispering between the mountains was new inspiration to me. The grass was softer under my feet; the flowers were more beautiful; the earth itself held a new thrill for me.

VI

AFTERGLOW

Hunting Stock-Killing Grizzlies

Jack Tooker

When this ambitious young bear hunter took on the challenge of finding two marauding bears he bit off more adventure than he reckoned on. Many encounters between man and grizzly have turned into terrible fracases when the gun has failed to fire at the critical moment, as was the case with Tooker. But luck was with this young man. This narrative is unusual in that the grizzly pair were sociable following the birth of their cubs. Colorado has produced some fine bear stories, and this is one of them.

THIS STORY goes back twenty-odd years. It was April. The bears were out. Grizzlies were killing stock on both sides of the Sycamore Canyon. The D.K. cow outfit controlled all the range on the east side of the Sycamore from the Santa Fe Railroad to the Verde River, and the Bar Cross outfit had the same claim to the west side.

Tom Wagner was part owner and in charge of the Bar Cross outfit. He had a pack of hounds and kept the bears stirred up, occasionally killing a black bear, but with no grizzlies to his credit. The dogs just could not stop the grizzlies. They would not tree or stand at bay as black bears do, but would shake off or kill their tormentors and keep going down into the roughest part of the canyon, where even a dog could not follow.

Reprinted from the March 31, 1934 issue of *The Saturday Evening Post*, © 1934, The Curtis Publishing Company, with kind permission.

The cowmen were of the opinion that the country was full of stock-killing grizzlies, but after a survey of the country and studying the bear signs I informed them that, in my opinion, two bears were doing most of the killing, and that they were, perhaps, mates with cubs. The cowmen had organized several ineffectual hunts for the bears, always in hopes that they would be fortunate enough not to meet up with any of the bruin family; and in this they had been successful, never having bagged bears of any variety.

The acorn crop of the previous year had been sparse, and, added to that, the snow was staying much later than usual this spring, which made a combination of reasons why the bears were driven to seek an exclusive diet of beef.

The killing was becoming so wanton, the stockmen decided to offer a reward for skins. The figure agreed upon was $1100 for the two bears — $700 for the male and $400 for his mate. They made the usual mistake of believing that the male was the worst offender and doing most of the killing, whereas the female grizzly is far the more destructive and dangerous, especially if she has cubs.

Prior to this time I had killed nine grizzlies, and considered it the most adventurous sport I had ever experienced. So, with the thrills of a grizzly hunt in my mind, and the added attraction of $1100, I let it be known that I would try for the reward. I had known of several cases where stockmen had offered rewards for the pelts of certain cattle-destroying animals, but when the skins were produced the rewards had failed to materialize.

I knew this particular hunt would be hazardous — especially since it looked like I would make it alone — so, in order to insure my receiving the $1100 in case the hunt proved a success, as I hoped it would, I rode out to the ranch house to talk it over with Tom.

While riding through the canyon Tom had come across the big bear on two different occasions; just a glimpse of him each time, but enough to see that he was what is commonly called a bald-faced grizzly — having a white stripe on his forehead. Regardless of whether I killed this particular bear, Tom assured me that the money would be mine if I produced grizzly skins.

"This offer stands," he said. "A big skin gets the $700 and a

small one $400 . . . Boys" — turning to some of the riders who
were sitting around the little shack that served as an office —
"You are witness to what I have just told Jack." Turning to me,
he asked, "Is that all right?"

"Sure," I said. "I just wanted to be sure of some kind of an understanding."

"Well, kid," he drawled out, "you may get the bears and you
may not; but if you're goin' down in the canyon to hunt for
them, you better take someone with you. It's a durn fool notion
to go alone, an' you ain't got no business to do it."

I informed him that I had been trying for a week to get someone to go with me and had offered to split the money fifty-fifty.

"And that offer still stands, boys," I said to the cowboys, but
none of them felt the urge for bear hunting at that time.

However, they were all interested in my plans for the trip, although they informed me in no uncertain terms just how foolish
they thought I was to undertake the trip alone, and all the more
so after I began unfolding to them just how I planned to engineer
the adventure.

I had decided I would start the hunt in Tully Canyon. Tom
agreed that was about the best shot, as the bears generally came
up Tully Canyon. My plan was to go down into the canyon on
foot, locate where the bears were doing their killing, and catch
them in the act, if possible. If I had no luck in that, and the snow
stayed on, I could at least track them to their dens and kill them
there.

"Well, kid," Tom drawled, "maybe that's the right way to go
at it, but you're sure takin' plenty chances. Better take a hoss and
stop at our lower cabin. The bears have been workin' near there,
and I'd not feel so uneasy 'bout you if I knew you had a hoss and
a cabin for sort o' headquarters."

I argued that no one had killed a grizzly in several years, using
that method, and I wanted to try my luck with my own scheme.
All I intended to take with me was a sleeping bag I rigged up
myself, two extra pairs of heavy wool socks, my gun, .33 rifle,
two boxes of cartridges, and grub enough to last about ten days.

The more I discussed the trip and my plans with the boys, the
more eager I became to start out as soon as possible.

Tom mentioned that they were going out with the chuck

wagon to one of the camps near the mouth of the canyon in the morning, and I decided to go that far with them.

In spite of my excitement, I slept well and got up bright and early the next morning, eager to be off. For several miles after leaving the ranch, the wagon tires had sung us a merry song on the frost-crusted snow, but now it had warmed up, with splendid prospects for more snow. Arriving at the Bar Cross cabin at about two in the afternoon, we unhitched the team. I put the horses in the barn, unharnessed and fed them, while Tom started a fire in the cabin stove. While Tom got dinner, I carried the stuff out of the wagon, got my own things together, went into the storeroom and packed up enough chuck to last me for ten days — plenty of bacon, as I knew I could always get fresh meat; and the rest of the supplies were the very lightest possible.

Pretty soon Tom called, "Come and get it, or I'll throw it out to the dogs!"

I yelled right back, "Coming!"

While we each got on the outside of a big steak, we talked of my trip. Those steaks were from a fat yearling and had been frozen for a month or more. They were simply wonderful, and so were all the trimmings — biscuits, spuds, and so on — and Tom could make biscuits. I was eating what I thought was my last meal under a roof for ten days or more at least. But Tom had another thought, and it beat mine all hollow.

He asked, "When are you startin', kid?"

"Just as soon as I get through with this steak."

"No," he says, "you get a good night's rest and get the reports from the cowboys when they come in, and when I turn you loose tomorrow you'll have most of the day before you. Why, gol-durn it, if I was to take you down there this evening, it would be dark before you could find a place to hole up for the night."

"Well, Tom, if you're worrying about me, just cut that out. I'll be all right. I'll get a bear, and maybe two, if my grub holds out, and I'll be back."

"Well, kid," he come back, "I'm not worryin' none, but I am goin' to leave you a hoss in the stable at the J.D. Ranch. That's the nearest ranch to the Sycamore Canyon, and I'll leave you some grub in the house in a big can, so the rats won't get it. One of the boys can go by every day to feed and water the horse. You

can make it to the J.D. Ranch from the east rim of the Sycamore
in about one day, if you run out of supplies; and I'm guessing
that if you kill any bears, that's where you will get them. There
ain't been much killing on this side lately. But I saw the D.K.
foreman last night, and he said that the bear was just raisin' hell
over there."

The cowboys soon came in from different directions and reported having seen no bears, fresh bear signs, or kills. It began
snowing about dark. That was ideal and the very thing I had
hoped for. All bear signs would be fresh and would make my
work easier. It was still snowing in the morning.

After breakfast we saddled our horses and left the ranch in
about eight inches of fresh snow. There was not so much snow
lower down, and at Tully Canyon only about three or four
inches. We rode down the north rim of Tully Canyon to the rim
of the Sycamore, and there Tom left me, wishing me luck.

I adjusted my pack, which weighed about forty pounds, gun
and all. I had good shoepacks. I worked along the rim of the Sycamore for about four miles, almost opposite the J.D. Ranch and
straight across the canyon from the D.K. winter camp. I had seen
several lion tracks, but no bear signs; so decided to cross the
canyon. It had stopped snowing when I reached the bottom of
the Sycamore. The brush thickets were wet and the rocks slippery. The Sycamore Canyon is a miniature Grand Canyon, highly
colored, rough and rugged. Many cliff dwellings, sealed caves,
and ruins bear testimony that it was inhabited long before Co-
lumbus discovered America.

By the time I had crossed the bottom of the canyon, which is
wide at this point, I was hungry and tired. So I built a fire,
broiled a steak, made coffee, warmed up some of Tom's biscuits,
and enjoyed a feed fit for a king.

As I had hoped, there were bear signs in the bottom of the
canyon. They had their trails. In some places these trails were just
tunnels through the thickets of brush and undergrowth. But none
of the signs seen so far were made by the species I was in search
of — namely, the ponderous grizzly.

After a little rest, I started to climb out of the canyon and
reached the D.K. winter cabin before dark. I was up in fairly
deep snow again. There were no man or horse tracks, so I knew

there had been no one about since the fresh snow had fallen. I found the cabin well supplied with firewood, so I soon had a fire roaring in the stove and began preparations for supper. As soon as it got dark, the skunks and rats appeared and began to play about the floor. Fortunately for me, the cabin contained an old bed, so I was able to sleep up off the floor and somewhat out of their line of play, but even at that either rats or skunks, or perhaps both, ran over me frequently during the night.

I managed to fall asleep at intervals, for I was very weary. I would wake up with a start to hear the tap-tapping of the skunks' feet on the floor. They were absolutely safe as far as my molesting them was concerned. I was willing to give them full run of the place, and, sensing my indifference to them, they repaid me by refraining from loosing the vicious odor that has made them such a despised and much-to-be-avoided animal. Added to the discomfiture caused by the rodents, the shack was cold, and before morning I froze out. I got up and built a fire, and as soon as it was light enough to see, I prepared a hearty breakfast.

The D.K. people kept a large box of food supplies in the cabin. The box was well lined with tin and kept the rodents out. I used the D.K. supplies as much as possible for my breakfast, saving my own, for I knew that upon those supplies depended to a very great measure my success or failure.

After breakfast I left the cabin, going south on the west side of Buck Ridge, crossing the heads of many little canyons that ran off into the Sycamore. I had traveled until about ten o'clock and was west of Turkey Butte and the old, historic Mooney Trail, when, on crossing the head of a canyon, I came upon two fresh bear tracks. The one was made by a very large bear and the other, though large, was smaller than the big one.

I was growing tired, although I had not covered much ground, but when I saw those bear tracks and the immensity of them, I forgot everything but the thrill of the hunt ahead of me. The tracks had been made the night before and were going straight south. After following them for about two hours, I came to the mouth of a small canyon, where the tracks separated. The big fellow had gone straight down into the main canyon that emptied into the Sycamore, while the smaller tracks led up a little side canyon.

This situation meant a den and cubs to me, but I wanted to be sure. The little canyon was full of rocks and oaks of all sizes. As the wind was blowing from the south, I climbed out on the north side. I did not want the old girl to wind me, for if she had a den and cubs I could get her and the cubs any time I wanted them, but it was through her that I hoped to trap the old daddy bear.

After getting on top, I could see that the canyon came to an end in less than a half a mile. Also, that it was a box canyon all the way, and narrow. No animal — not even a bear — could scale its walls. I went the full length of the canyon, keeping away from the rim so as not to be seen, but frequently I would slip up and peer carefully over to see if the tracks were still there. At the end of the canyon the tracks went into a cave. I could see back under the shelf and into the cave a short distance, but could see or hear nothing. Yet I was satisfied that the cave housed a mother grizzly and her cubs.

I spent the rest of the day in locating a place to camp. I chose a cave in a small canyon less than a mile west of the den, rustled enough dry wood for my stay, then gathered pine needles and boughs for my bed. I had selected a cave without any small holes in the end, so as to be sure that I was not living in a rat or skunk den. As this cave was to be my home for several days, I made everything as comfortable as possible with my limited supplies and equipment. Time seemed literally to fly. It was dark before I had supper over and a small lunch put up for the morrow. Since I had made my bed well back and had a good fire in the mouth of the cave, I slept warm and very comfortably. In fact, my sleeping quarters were luxurious in comparison to my experience of the previous night.

I was up at the break of day and immediately walked to the mouth of the canyon, in hopes that I might catch the two bears coming in from their night's hunt. But I was too late. According to the tracks, they had been there just a few moments before I had arrived. They had come in from a different direction this time. The smaller track had led up the same side canyon as before, but the big one took off in a new direction, and I decided to follow. What a merry chase he led me — over the roughest part of that rough country, and at last wound up in the bottom of Sycamore Canyon, in dense thickets and with no snow for tracking.

I decided I would have to give up the hunt for that morning, and was thinking with no pleasure of the tiresome walk back, when I came to an unexpected clearing. Looking across the clearing I observed a large animal about one hundred yards distant, in the edge of the thicket. It was looking at me and I was vaguely conscious that it had a white stripe in the face. A few cattle, in search of food, had got into the bottom from the east side, so I thought the animal merely a cow.

And then it moved, and now quickly I knew it was not a cow but rather the object of my hunt. I was not ready for a shot, and before I could sight he was into cover. I saw him no more that day. A bear is no fool and I was satisfied they knew I was in their country. They doubtless had crossed my tracks many times.

I gave up, for the time being, the idea of catching them at the mouth of the den canyon and decided, instead, to locate the place where they were doing their killing. I found that they had no regular place to kill. They met each night at a different place. They would each go straight to the meeting point; then hunt together. They picked the roughest places where the stock were ranging. I found partly eaten cattle with broken hips, broken-down backs, sides caved in, and broken necks, showing that these grizzlies had no regular method of killing, as the lion does. In one small canyon I found enough bones to fill a boxcar — all the results of bear killings.

After they had killed and gorged to their satisfaction, Mr. Bear would escort his mate to the mouth of the canyon where the den was located. But when they reached the mouth of the canyon, that was as far as he was allowed to go. According to the tracks in the snow, they had evidently had quite an argument one morning, and I rather suspect that he wanted to go and take a look at the children. But no large bear tracks led up that canyon, so I concluded that Mrs. Bear had upheld her feminine prerogative of deciding what was to be done, and Father Bear had gone on his way without a visit to the children.

Perhaps you are thinking: "What a simple matter to catch those bears at the mouth of the little canyon!"

True, it would have been, except for the fact that all their movements were made under cover of darkness. It is hazardous enough to meet one grizzly bear in good light, where your sights are plain, but to meet two of them in the dark, and one of them a mother, with cubs near — well, that would be recorded as a plain case of suicide.

I spent six nights in my little cave, and five mornings found me at the mouth of that little canyon at daybreak, but always I was just too late. We had little squalls of snow almost every day, and I spent most of the daylight hours trying to track down or locate the male bear. But my efforts bore me no success. He led me in different directions and to different places each time. Once he took me down the Mooney Trail four or five miles, and still another time he took me to the very bottom of Secret Canyon. How cleverly he managed always to elude me!

My supplies were getting low and I was growing discouraged. I decided to try once more to catch them at the entrance of the den canyon.

It was still dark that early April morning when I took my stand. I had barely settled down to wait when two dark objects came lumbering down the main canyon. They looked larger in the shadows than they actually were. I could discern them plainly enough, locating their heads, bodies, and limbs, but although I tried again and again, I was unable to see my sights.

My impulse was to fire regardless, but my experience told me that a wounded grizzly, even in good light, is one of the most dangerous assailants on earth; so I forebore my impulse and contented myself with watching them.

The bears parted as usual — the mother hastening to her cubs and the old male going back the way he had come. I knew it was useless to attempt to track him in that shadowy light, so I rested where I was until the sun lighted the eastern sky. Then, following the same route I had taken when I located the female's den, I went directly to the cave, staying well upon the rim.

As I neared the cave, I could hear the cubs. They must have been quarreling over their breakfast. Several times a chubby little fellow wobbled to the mouth of the den, and at last the mother herself stuck her head out. I was almost straight above her, close enough that I could see her eyes. I moved slightly until I could sight just a little back of her eyes, and then attempted to place a bullet. I was overcautious about striking the shelf rock and did not hold fine enough. The bullet struck her between the eyes, missing the brain. Out she charged like a mad bull, tearing oak brush down, looking everywhere for me. She could not see me, and the wind was favorable, so that she could not smell me.

In her mad charge she went tearing out of sight down the little canyon. In a brief time she came slipping back, stopping every few feet to listen. As she came under my stand I placed a bullet just back of the hump. It ranged down, passing through her heart and tearing it to shreds. She died trying to locate the enemy. I went back down into the canyon and came up to the mouth of the cave where she lay. The cave was shallow and in the very back end were three grizzly cubs. They were about the size of small shepherd dogs. Each cub had a white stripe on his face and a small white cross on the breast, all three being marked like their daddy. I tried to make friends with them, but they fought and scratched like wildcats.

After skinning out the mother bear, I killed two of the cubs and tied up the other one. I wanted to carry him to my cave and take him to town alive. But even with all feet tied he would not cease fighting. It was a hopeless task to carry that biting, fighting, scratching cub, so I was forced to shoot him and skin him, along with his brother and sister.

Taking the large grizzly skin and my bed, I made the D.K. winter cabin early that afternoon, and, much to my surprise and pleasure, found Curly Grey, who had come in the day before with a packhorse and supplies. He was glad of my success and encouraged me to remain longer and try again for the big fellow. He helped me pack more supplies over to my cave and took the three small bearskins back to the ranch with him.

I was very anxious to know what the old bear had done when the mother bear failed to come and meet him, and so I was at the mouth of Bear Canyon at daybreak. He had been there, and when the mother failed to show up, he had gone up to the little canyon to investigate. His tracks showed that he was still there. To follow him would be foolish, besides being very dangerous. The brush was so thick that it would be very difficult to get in an effective shot. Therefore, I decided on a stand on the north side of the canyon, above and about one hundred yards from where he must come out. I had gone only half the distance when I heard the brush cracking. He had come out into the opening, and such a wonderful specimen he was!

As he came to my tracks he stopped short, looking everywhere for me; then he stood on his hind feet, peering at every angle. At last he located me. He stared straight in my direction for several minutes, but as I made not the slightest move, he shifted his gaze. I was filled with admiration for that majestic animal. I would not have killed the mother and cubs but for the fact that they were outlaws, stock killers, with a bounty on their heads. But with this fellow there was no choice.

Doubtless he reasoned that I was responsible for the disappearance of his family and, in all probability, would have trailed me down, for he showed no fear. The hair stood up all over his body; he was ready for battle.

He stood less than fifty yards from me. A body shot at that distance is very dangerous, as a grizzly shot directly through the heart will live long enough to go one hundred yards and kill ten men, should that many be in his path.

As he turned his head to one side, I drew a bead just back of his ear, hoping to break his neck, and pressed the trigger. He fell like a beef.

Believing him dead, I jumped from my hiding place. But the bullet had only creased him. He revived as quickly as he had passed out. As he raised up I had no chance for a head or neck shot, but took a quick side shot for the heart. He charged with surprising speed.

I pumped my four remaining bullets into him in rapid succession.

Any one of the wounds inflicted would have caused death in time, but now his body seemed impervious to them. With a half ton of angry bear charging, time flies; one thinks quickly. Those beady eyes were two balls of fire, his mouth was open and the bloody froth flowing freely. An awful sight to behold, especially in a lonely canyon miles from help.

Slipping a cartridge into the empty chamber of my gun, I held my fire. He had reared up on his hind legs less than ten feet from me. As he lurched forward I thrust the muzzle of my rifle at his open mouth, intending to pull the gun off and then use it for a club, as a last resort. But with a single stroke of his huge gray paw, he slapped the gun from my hand as easily as though he were merely brushing away an annoying insect. My finger was inside the trigger guard, and the jerk discharged the gun, the bullet going wild. The gun was cast aside. He struck at my head; I ducked. Another swing that was so close I felt the wind. He closed in; I ducked under his massive arms. Then something happened — it seemed as if a mighty pile driver had plunged down upon my head, forcing, driving it down between my shoulders.

Late that afternoon I regained consciousness. The dead grizzly was lying on my left leg; my right was broken. I had lain in the slush snow and was wet and cold. It seemed that every bone in my body was broken or crushed. I made several ineffectual attempts to sit up before I finally attained a sitting posture. But it was worth all the effort it cost, for it probably saved my life.

A most welcome sight met my eyes. I had told Curly that I would be back to the cabin for breakfast by ten o'clock. When I did not show up by noon, he had started in search of me. He had tracked me to that point. When I sat up, the movement had attracted the horse's attention; Curly saw me and came on the run. He rolled the bear off my leg, with the aid of a rope attached to the bear's paw and the horn of the saddle.

I must have been a gruesome sight — soaked from head to foot with bloody froth. It took all the nerve I could muster and Curly's help to get me into the saddle. It seemed at times that I could not endure for another moment that long and excruciating three-mile trip to the D.K. winter cabin. After what seemed an eternity, we reached the cabin and Curly put me to bed. He cut my clothes off and bathed and dressed my many wounds as best he could.

After setting an old can filled with water near my bed, he left me to ride to the Garland ranger station at the head of Sycamore Canyon, to phone Dr. Mitchell. The doctor caught No. 8, Atchison, Topeka, and Santa Fe train, and got off at a station called Maine, where Curly met him with a saddle horse.

I was conscious most of the time Curly was gone, but fully expected to be dead and half of my body devoured by skunks and rats before he returned. It would be impossible to describe the inferno they created for me. They ran over my body, across my face, ate holes in my bloody clothes, and made a meal of my boot tops. The only movement I could make was to turn my head slightly from side to side, but that was so painful that the torture of rats and skunks was preferable.

About daylight Curly and the doctor came in, having made the trip down the east side of the Sycamore — some twenty-seven miles — in about seven hours, which was fast time, considering the nature of the country and the snow. After setting the leg and dressing my wounds, they left to examine the bear and skin it. One bullet had torn away part of his heart — no doubt the second shot. He was literally all shot up inside.

When they returned with the bearskin, they asked innumerable questions about how it happened. I told them as best I could, up until the time the bear hit me. I could not tell how long he had lived. I only knew he had lived long enough almost to succeed in finishing me.

Those six weeks I was forced to spend in that rat- and skunk-infested D.K. winter cabin, while waiting for my leg to mend and my wounds to heal, left memories that can never be erased from my mind. The rats never bit me and the skunks made no odor. Why should they, when they had their own way and were not molested? I was forced to invent many time-killing devices to fill in the lonely hours I spent while Curly was out looking after cattle. Before I was able to depart I had most of the skunks named, and prided myself on being able to recognize them at sight.

One of the greatest joys I have ever known was when the doctor pronounced my leg as being in such a condition that I could be moved and could leave the cabin that had housed rats, skunks, and myself for six long, fiendish weeks. My wounds healed in due time, and I regained perfect health, but at times, when going back in retrospection, I can again feel the effects of the terrible mauling I received at the hands of old Father Grizzly.

Notorious Old Clubfoot

F. M. Young

There have been some very well-known grizzlies operating in the Rocky Mountain ranges. Among them was Old Mose, finally brought down on the east slope after he had killed cattle for many years and destroyed several men as well. There was also Big Bear, whose reputation increased with the years, that wily one who was the object of pursuit of many hunters who camped on his trail for weeks but always returned disappointed. Eventually Than Galloway, the Utah trapper and hunter, was invited to Colorado to try his luck with Big Bear. Than got the bear and the reward.

Old Clubfoot must have been a cousin of these Colorado bears, but his range was in southwestern Utah, at the lower reaches of the Wasatch Mountains. Ranchers in that region tried many times to rid themselves of his nuisance, but, like many other grizzlies, he was too canny for most men. No book about grizzlies would be complete without Old Clubfoot; his story is a good one, and I am indebted to Reuben Gardner and J. M. Moody for its details.

THE HUGE GRIZZLY bear, known as Old Clubfoot by virtue of a deformity apparent in the print of one of his hind feet — evidently the result of an encounter with a trap in his youth — ranged in the vicinity of the Grass Valley and Pine Valley mountains for nearly thirty years. The exact date of his first appearance is not known, but he was causing alarm to cattlemen as early as 1884. He seemed to be a phantom bear, because, despite all his killings, very few hunters ever caught sight of him. In this respect he very much resembled Old Ephraim, of northern Utah fame. Very often his tracks and killings were discovered, their appearance indicating that the bear was not far away, but it seemed impossible for any man to catch up with him. Imported as well as local hunters tried their luck, but all came back empty-handed.

At one time, after several fresh killings had been reported on the Grass Valley Mountain, Reuben Gardner, his brother Ozro, and Frank Snow decided to hunt again for the marauder. They left Pine Valley with the intention of spending several days following the bear's trail. The first afternoon out, a fine rain started falling, which prevented much hunting that day. They did find a yearling that the bear had killed and so knew they were in the same locality as Old Clubfoot. That night, to get as much protection from the rain as possible, they made camp under some ledges near what is known as Sheep Pen country. The men had two mongrel dogs with them, and in the night the dogs, with whimpers and whines, crept to the beds of their masters and would not be moved. The rain stopped during the night, and next morning, not more than fifty yards from the men's camp, the bear's unmistakable tracks were found.

With this evidence that the bear was close at hand, the men started on the hunt again. Because of the previous rain, the tracks were followed easily for a while. In a short time the men came to a large rotten log where Old Clubfoot had been digging for grubs. He hadn't been gone long, because the big black ants living in the log were still swarming about after being disturbed by the bear's rooting nose. Old Clubfoot was tracked to a deep canyon where horses could not travel. Since it was then nearly dark, the hunters decided to make a camp in Grass Valley that night and take up the trail again in the morning.

Next morning the hunters were not very successful in picking up the track, and it was only when in discouragement they were on their way back to camp that they happened to come across it again. This was in Mill Canyon. Not far from where the mill was located, the bear had made another killing, this time taking a yearling that Reuben Gardner recognized as his. The bear had eaten about fifty pounds of the animal, apparently with lusty appetite, then dragged away the rest and dropped it into a deep hole of water.

The third day on the trail, Old Clubfoot was followed into Bear Valley. Here he had left more evidence of his work. A cow had been killed, but only so that the bear could get her calf for his meal; for the cow's shoulder had been broken, and she had been knocked into a mudhole, but otherwise she was untouched. The calf was only partly eaten.

Most of the hunts for the bear ended the same way: after the men had spent as much time away from their work as they felt they could, they went home empty-handed, leaving Old Clubfoot victorious and free to live as he pleased.

The bear, if unmolested, usually made his kill about every third day, seeming to prefer his meat fresh. He was known to have attacked and killed a 1600-pound Durham bull with no special effort, but in the last years of his reign he killed mostly yearlings and large calves, perhaps because of his advancing age.

Some of the people of Pine Valley who did not participate in the hunting were rather skeptical of all the stories of the bear and how he was so seldom seen. One man in particular told Reuben Gardner that he thought the men were just afraid of the bear and didn't want to get too close to him. This man gave Gardner the impression that if he were on the trail, the bear would certainly be brought in, dead or alive.

Not long after this talk, Reuben and the same man were taking a wagon to Right Hand Fork, to get snow to make ice cream for the July 24th celebration. They left the main canyon and started up the mountainside, where the timber was heavy and the going rough, to reach the cave where the snow was to be found. They came upon a freshly killed yearling; about one hundred and fifty yards farther on, they found a cow that had been killed about the same time. Both animals had hardly been touched. When the skeptical friend saw evidence of what the bear could do, he hesitated to go on after the snow. Gardner asked if he was afraid. He replied that of course he wasn't, but he didn't have even a pocketknife with him. He was finally persuaded to assist in obtaining the snow they had come for, so the town had its annual treat in spite of the bear. But Gardner's friend had less to say about the bravery of others afterward.

Around 1900, J. M. Moody, the forest ranger of the Pine Valley division, took up the task and trailed the bear from Rencher

Mountain to Pinto, thence to Page's Ranch, and on to Kanarra and Cedar Mountain, a distance of about thirty miles. He found the same destruction of cattle all along the way, but never caught sight of the bear.

In the fall of the next year, stockmen and farmers of the area prevailed upon the Forest Service to engage a professional hunter of widespread experience, a man named Walker, to bring his dogs and find the bear. Moody was assigned to assist him in doing so. The men searched for a discouragingly long time and were beginning to wonder if the bear had quit the locality, when they unexpectedly ran onto signs of his presence. Tracks showed that the bear had been after a large steer and had run it about three-quarters of a mile before he could get hold of it, so the men knew they were on his trail once more. The kill was rather curious. Apparently the bear had been angered by having to pursue the steer so far and had torn off strips of skin, the width of his paw, over the length of the animal's body. After breaking the ribs to get at the heart, drinking the blood and eating only parts of the body, Old Clubfoot had pulled up some brush and covered his kill. He also had piled brush on the snow and was asleep on it when the hunting dogs, which had outrun the horses over the rough country of rocks and timber, started him up.

Walker said there was no need to hurry, because the dogs would hold Bruin or make him climb a tree. But the tracks indicated that the dogs were actually running the bear away from the hunters. Very soon two of the dogs came back, so frightened that the men could not keep them from under their feet. One had an ear almost torn off where the old bear had struck him. There were five dogs in all, two foxhounds, two terriers, and one bullpup. The foxhounds stayed with the grizzly for over two miles, but the others did not seem interested in the chase. As soon as Walker could get close enough, he called the dogs off.

After this experience, the Forest Service decided that dogs were no match for Old Clubfoot, so Walker was dismissed. Together, the Forest Service and the stockmen hatched a plan to offer three hundred dollars to anyone who could catch the prize. This notice was advertised in all local papers, and hunters responded from many parts. But this effort was of little use. On account of the roughness of the terrain and the thick timber covering it, not to mention the cleverness and experience of the grizzly, none of these candidates even caught sight of the prey.

Finally, in July of 1907, after several years of unsuccessful hunting by all who wished to try their luck at outwitting Old Clubfoot, the Forest Service asked Moody to try again, alone. By this time, Moody was probably the most experienced man who had gone after the bear. He pitched his camp on the Pine Valley Mountain, in what he considered the center of the territory where the bear ranged. He took up the trail, following tracks each day until night overtook him. Often he slept on the ground, without food or blankets. Very frequently he would find that the bear had killed two animals in one night but had eaten only a small portion of each and in some cases had only broken into the chest cavity to take the heart or blood. Once Moody found that the bear had killed a yearling, weighing about four hundred pounds, and carried it, presumably in his arms, for about one hundred yards, into some brush, where he covered it up so skillfully that Moody had difficulty finding the place. Covering his kill was one of Old Clubfoot's habits. Moody had previously heard that the bear had killed a cow that would dress at six hundred pounds and had dragged the body for a distance of seventy-five yards before covering it up. It would have taken a good team of horses to pull the carcass to the place where the grizzly buried it. Moody had also seen the carcasses of large steers that the bear had killed by crushing their skulls with his sledgehammer blows. However, Moody found that most of the kills now were younger animals.

Moody's solitary, relentless searching went on. One day he came upon an unexpected scene of slaughter. Just before Moody arrived, Old Clubfoot had attacked a large bull and ripped out its entrails, but Moody's intrusion prevented the bear from eating his meal. The bear disappeared into the aspens. The disemboweled animal was still alive. Moody wished to end the steer's suffering but desired to shoot the grizzly even more, so he waited most of the day, at a distance, for the bear to return to his meat. The bear did not come back, and Moody had to return to camp for yet another night.

The following morning Moody hiked back to the steer, now thankfully dead but still untouched, and again he took up the trail. At dusk he was favored with a glimpse of the bear in the trees and took a shot that must have wounded it, because when he resumed the hunt the next morning he found blood on a rock. All that day he followed the bear down the mountainside and through the canyons but did not see him again. Most of the time Moody felt as though he were tracking a phantom. The one quick glimpse and the blood on the rock were the only tangible evidence of the bear's existence. But on the fourth morning, Moody discovered more evidence: the water was still muddy where the bear had crossed the creek. Moody knew then that he was getting very close to his prey.

He followed the bear up the side of the mountain again, breaking his way through timber and underbrush so thick that in places he had to crawl to get through at all. After Moody had broken through an especially heavy growth of willows, he was startled to find the old bear, almost as though waiting for him, about one hundred feet above him, at a spot where it had evidently been resting. When the bear spied Moody it stood upright; as soon as it did, Moody took a shot at it, hitting it in the butt of the right ear. Moody was astonished when the old grizzly threw both paws over its head and started to bawl. The man waited, alert and unfrightened, to see what the bear would do next; it dropped to all fours and started after him.

Moody had seven shells in his gun when he began to shoot; he put four balls in the right ear, a space that could be covered with a silver dollar, and two more in the front of the head and in the shoulder. The seventh shot hit the bear in the front of the head again, and he dropped on his knees. Since this shot emptied Moody's magazine, he felt for his pistol, which he always carried, but discovered to his dismay that he had neglected to bring it, being confident in the effectiveness of his rifle. Hurriedly, he put more shells into his gun, which by this time was so hot he could barely hold it in his hands, and waited for the bear to come. Old Clubfoot was on his feet again and about four yards from Moody. With extraordinary calm, Moody held the gun ready, waiting until the grizzly's head was only six feet from the end of the barrel, for he knew he had to make the shot count. He did, hitting the bear squarely in the forehead. The bear staggered, coughed blood in the man's face and on his clothes, and fell at his feet. Just the same, for good measure, Moody pumped three additional shells into the head, as it is common lore of the mountains that a man can never be sure about a grizzly.

As soon as Old Clubfoot fell, Moody tried to stick him, to bleed him, as he desired to take the hide as a trophy. He got upon the bear's shoulder to do so, but Old Clubfoot, not yet expired, reached up with his hind foot, snagged Moody's overalls, and threw him about ten feet back. The man picked himself up, unhurt, and decided to stick the bear from the front. The dying grizzly summoned strength to slap with his paw, again and again, but finally had to give up even that feeble struggle. Old Clubfoot's long career was ended.

He weighed 825 pounds when dressed and would easily have weighed a thousand when alive. The gun Moody used was altogether too small for that king of beasts, only a .25-.35 lever-action Remington. But luck had been with the forest ranger. The people of Pine Valley were so overjoyed at being rid of the old tyrant that they gave a big public dinner and dance in Moody's honor, which Reuben Gardner gladly attended. And the Forest Service supervisor raised the flag to the top notch on the pole, in honor of the event.

Grizzly's High-Power Nose

Enos Mills

*In order to fully appreciate this story, one should be somewhat
familiar with the setting. Big Bear had a range of perhaps
seventy-five miles in diameter, extending from the low hills to the
mountain ridges — canyons, bare ridges with heavily timbered
canyon sides, streams, hollows, groves, parks, valleys, and all
that goes to make up a vast slope of the Rocky Mountains. Big
Bear grew up there; he knew every trail and ravine, every short
cut, every cave and dense thicket. In addition, his sensitive nose
always told him where the cattle were and where the hunters
were.*

*Large hunting parties were easily avoided. Very few of these
hunters were in any sense bear hunters; that is, not until Than
Galloway came upon the scene. I knew Than Galloway, and a
good neighbor and friend he was, though I can hardly forgive
him for using the irresistible secret bait he employed to catch old
Big Bear. But it was effective.*

*Enos Mills, the Colorado naturalist who knew the grizzly well,
wrote this appreciative account of a legendary bear.*

A UTAH GRIZZLY rushed from behind a cluster of pines, stampeded a herd of cattle, and killed one of them in the presence of
an astonished cowboy. With a leap the bear threw his right arm
over the neck of a stampeding cow and caught her nose with his

left-hand claws. Going at highest speed, she was thrown, and landed violently on her back.

Away wildly went the herd. The rough country split it into several parts, but the cattle ran with record speed and came to a stop nearly two miles away. Few had seen the grizzly, but many, possibly all, had scented him.

Within the next two weeks a number of cattle on this range were killed, and evidently by this same big bear. The measurements of the tracks corresponded, and the end of the second toe of the right forefoot was missing. Then too, the tracks revealed the same method of killing that the cowboy had seen.

The bear usually approached the herd and his intended victim by stealth. He slipped up, with the wind in his face, so that the cattle could not scent him. By using ravines, advancing from cover to cover, he picked his victim and, when close enough, made a dash for her.

Sometimes Big Bear varied his clever and successful method of stalking. He introduced clowning, mingled humor with murder. With a somersault he would burst into view of a herd, and advance closer with cartwheeling, varied with the chasing of his tail.

This novel exhibition appealed to the curiosity of the cattle, and commonly they advanced to meet him, or wait for him, filled with wonder and astonishment. Of course, this clever performance was pulled off with the breeze blowing from the cattle to him. The herds were large, and many of the cattle had never seen a grizzly, though all knew and feared him from his scent. Hence he worked from leeward, as the faintest scent from him would have stampeded the spellbound audience — and the picked victim.

This picked victim was almost invariably a two-year-old heifer. As soon as she was thrown, the bear broke back her left foreshoulder and tore out her heart. The heart and the blood were eaten, but rarely anything else.

Big Bear never returned to his kill. This probably was wisdom on his part. He may, of course, have preferred a warm drink or a particular cut for each meal, and then he probably enjoyed the fun of the killing. In any case, he easily made a kill every other day for several years.

A large reward was offered for his head, but his depredations went regularly on. His kills were poisoned and surrounded with concealed traps, and approaching trails were covered with batteries of set rifles, in the hope that he would return to his kill. His next victim commonly was caught ten or twenty miles away.

The only thing certain about his movements was that there was nothing certain about them. One time, from a kill, he would cross over a mountain; the next time he would go upstream. Sometimes he followed a given route between two places; then again he did not. Occasionally he went out of his way for a close look at those who were hunting for him.

Attempts were made to entrap him by using live heifers for bait. They were placed near trails which he frequently followed in going from one part of his territory to another; they were picketed, corralled in the end of a canyon, or hobbled, surrounded with concealed traps, and all approaches were guarded. Apparently Big Bear never came close to them. Certainly he never entered an ambush.

The reward was increased to three thousand dollars. Hunters were hired by the month, and trappers by the season. Frequently an independent hunter and trapper came in hoping for glory and three thousand dollars. But Big Bear continued the evil, even, and efficient tenor of his way, and continued it in the same old territory.

His nose, his amazingly developed sense of smell, appears to have been the foremost factor in his success. Of course, he also had brains. He showed strategy, planned two or more moves ahead, had patience, strength, eyes, ears, endurance, daring, caution, and sustained alertness. But his nose, its extraordinary keenness and its long range, enabled him to locate nervous cattle and make frequent kills, and — far more important — to outwit, triumphantly, innumerable skillful hunters, through fifteen consecutive years.

Just what started Big Bear on this remarkable career of killing, no one knows. Not one grizzly in a hundred ever kills a big animal. Big Bear while hungry may have come upon a carcass, or a crippled cow bogged or dying alone from some injury. And, once having tasted, he speedily became addicted to the habit of blood-drunkenness.

His first kill was during the summer of 1898. He was then perhaps five years of age, possibly twice that. Through several years, during five months of each year, he made a kill every other day. But during the fourteenth and fifteenth seasons of his big-animal slaughter he made a kill every day, or oftener. His total killings of cattle were more than twelve hundred head — possibly a few hundred more.

He does not appear to have touched sheep or horses, or to have paid any attention to deer or other wildlife. Nor was he ferocious. He never bothered people. Not a single report or letter which I received concerning him mentions an attack on a human being. He attended strictly to business; he was a cattle killer. He made his kill, went his way — and from day to day killed again.

Rarely did anyone catch sight of him. It is doubtful if, during his entire life, he was seen a dozen times. During the fifteen years of his active, deadly hunting, numerous hunters were constantly seeking him but saw him not. When he was seen, it was by people who were not looking for him.

A homesteader, taking a load of lumber up a mountain road, met him coming down. His fur was dark brown, with a trimming of cream-yellow; his weight was about twelve hundred pounds — a third larger than the average grizzly. With unchanged speed, he came down the road. As he showed no inclination to give the right of way, the homesteader's excited team did so. He went by without a stop, and with just a glance at the busy, agitated driver and the demonstrative horses.

One night he called upon two hunters who were trying to ambush him on one of his much-used trails. They were two of many who were in his territory trying to get a shot at him. They had concealed their tent in a thicket. He circled the tent at midnight, pushed in the door, entered, and calmly ate a number of trout that were to have been served for breakfast. Then he paused to look quietly at the two men in bed. The one at the back was trying to get under the one in front, and the one in front, in order to avoid being pushed over the rail, gave up trying to get back. After observing the deep, emotional nature of the peaceful hunters, the bear drank from a basin and backed out. He heard no comments; there was no pursuit.

True to his grizzly nature, he was eternally vigilant. His trail showed that he always assumed that he was followed. He was never surprised in the rear. His cautious or bold advances showed that he knew the enemy was trying to meet him at every step. But there never was a meeting, though numerous times one was thrillingly close.

Once, just once, when young, Big Bear appears to have got into a trap — and out again — leaving in it the end of the second right-hand finger. He seems to have been right-handed.

There have been other outlaw grizzlies. After skillfully remaining in home territory for a few years they were either driven off or killed. But Big Bear stayed on.

In the struggle for existence, evolution selected home-territory-loving animals to be the ancestors of the ages. Big Bear's intimate knowledge of his territory was valuable beyond thought. He knew every gulch, forest, retreat, cave, ridge, and pass, every vantage point where he could stand to look, listen, and use his unfailing nose. Then, too, he knew every line of possible advance, and all lines of retreat. He must have become acquainted with the eddying and upcast wind currents of the heights, otherwise he could hardly have caught the scent of surrounding, advancing foes, and have escaped through their closing ranks without their scenting or seeing him.

It is assumed, but is not certain, that Big Bear was born in this locality. In home territory he lived a solitary life. Other grizzlies appear to have kept out of his domain. Otherwise, it is likely, as has happened elsewhere, that there would have been other grizzlies feasting along his trail.

Nor did anyone ever discover where he hibernated, where for four or five months each year he fasted and slept, to come forth again with renewed strength and untiring energy and alertness. He is thought to have hibernated in home territory; this is common, and perhaps he did. But grizzlies have been known to hibernate miles from summer territory. Big Bear may have had a winter den one hundred miles away from the scenes where in summer he lived tensely, almost intoxicated with blood.

There has never been a closed season on the grizzly bear. Since Lewis and Clark opened fire on him more than one hundred years ago, he has been pursued day and night through all the seasons. Dogs, poison, guns, midwinter raids on Mother Grizzly and her cubs — all these have been survived by the species.

The grizzly, the greatest animal on the continent, has been misunderstood; volumes of misinformation have been published concerning him.

He is not ferocious. He enjoys life, and avoids fighting man except in self-defense. Then he makes a terrific fight, and shows brains, skill, endurance, and courage.

The pursuit for Big Bear never ceased. For a time one hunter tried his skill, then another. Then a combination of trappers, cowboys, and hunters tried, some of them following the trail day and night. At one time there were seven outfits trying to intercept Big Bear.

When trappers succeed, it is largely by appealing to an animal's sense of smell, with a savory or alluring scent. Trapper after trapper tried a variety of creations. One tried his celebrated wolf scent, a scent that had lured an outlaw wolf into a trap. Marrow bones were burned, honey heated, and stuffs combined that smelled to heaven. Many of these reached the far-off nose of Big Bear. But he did not appear — he did not investigate.

New hunters were brought in, who had been successful against other outlaw grizzlies. One of these collected all the cattle of the territory into herds, and had them kept out of the rougher part of the region. The natural lines of approach to them were guarded. But Big Bear made a kill every day.

One hunter picketed with scarecrow men three of the leading passes by which the bear crossed from one side of the mountain to the other. The bear appears to have accepted scarecrow guards, and for two days or longer to have hidden close to a pair of these dummy men with real rifles.

Was Big Bear a reasoning animal? Frequently he upset carefully made plans, and often outwitted elaborate strategy. Again and again he was called upon to outwit overwhelming numbers of men and dogs, day after day. Could he reason? Often it seemed as if a number of hunters must be in league with him, to prevent his destruction. But all these hunters and trappers were sensitive over their repeated defeats.

To me, the most astounding thing of all is that no one, so far as is known, during the fifteen hunted years, nor during his entire life, ever had a shot at him.

The fourteenth year of slaughter, he made one or more kills each day. In one ten-day period he killed thirty-four cattle. These activities occurred in thirty-four separate places in his territory. All this time, too, hunters were on his trail.

Could any human outlaw, alone and unaided, have continued such depredations in the very midst of active, skillful pursuit? Could any human outlaw have endured one tenth as long as Big Bear? Human outlaws prolong their careers by remaining inactive for long periods, by lying low, and also by changing to a new territory.

But Big Bear followed no such tactics. His numerous pursuers knew where he was. Nor did he discourage them by ceasing operations for a time. Instead of slowing down, or ceasing to kill, for a time he speeded up and occasionally multiplied killings. He did these things in the presence of numbers of hunters, who were trying with the most effective known means to stop him. But man has a poor nose. Big Bear won by his nose.

It is his highly evolved nose that tells the story of his prolonged and amazing triumphs. He detected the odor, the scents, of enemies — men and dogs — while they were still far away, and promptly hurried to another scene before either dogs or men detected him. Of course, this constant activity in the midst of danger called for a capable and overvigilant brain, a stomach that furnished extraordinary energy and physical endurance. His high-power nose was perhaps more useful to him than a dozen human scouts and as many wireless operators would have been to a human outlaw.

Driven almost to desperation by his prolonged and increasing slaughter, the cattlemen organized and launched a stupendous drive. Bear dogs and trailing dogs were brought in by the dozen; numbers of hunters and trappers assembled; camp bases were established and pack outfits put in motion.

When all was ready, the large force of men, dogs, and horses was divided into three detachments, each of which moved through a different part of Big Bear's territory. All worked under orders and in concert.

Scouts — real scouts — were sent in advance; cowboys dashed here and there, with rush orders. Trails were guarded day and night; dogs trailed day and night; every bit of the territory was combed and stormed.

The first day of the drive the bear made a kill within rifleshot of the rear of one of the divisions. The following morning he made another kill, and this immediately in front of, but concealed from, another division. These daring raids stimulated the aggressive interest of everyone to the highest point.

Again and again the bear broke through the lines of men, horses, and dogs and flanked them; then, while a scouting party was trying to locate and corner him, he suddenly appeared miles away, in front of one of the other divisions. Repeatedly he passed within a stone's throw of sentinels and pickets.

The grizzly is a born adventurer. Perhaps Big Bear enjoyed this extraordinary campaign. In the midst of this terrific drive for his death, his business — making a living, killing — went on as usual; every day, as usual, he surprised a herd and made a kill. For seven days and nights the campaign was waged with incessant activity, with the chief actor everywhere present; but not a single individual in the drive so much as saw him.

N. T. Galloway, the famous beaver trapper, hunter, and Grand Canyon explorer, came on the scene. During 1912 he studied Big Bear's habits and became familiar with the territory. He was out for weeks alone; and whether, during this time, he attempted to hunt or trap the bear is not known. But the season came to an end; the cattle were taken from the mountains, and the bear went somewhere to hibernate for the winter.

Early the following summer, 1913, Galloway took the field. He carried with him a bottle of scent of a secret character. This, probably of seasonal odor, he had concocted himself. During preceding years he had successfully trapped beaver where others had said there were no beaver, and he had succeeded simply by means of concocted scents, which reached the noses and appealed to the curiosity or the interest of the beavers.

In the end of a small box canyon he placed a quantity of this scent. Fifty or sixty feet down the trail, in the canyon, he concealed a number of bear traps.

The odor of this strange scent floated afar. It reached the nose of Big Bear. It was promising — bewitching. He advanced cautiously toward it. As he approached, he became intoxicated by it and forgot all caution. It told him that She had just passed that way, in maiden meditation, fancy free. He rushed after — into a masked trap.

Than Galloway's Grizzlies

Than Galloway

Several years ago my friend Dave Rust sent me a letter he had received from Nathan Galloway some years before. Galloway's letter is interesting not only because of the story he tells but also because of his writing style. He was a good penman, but his sentence construction and capitalization are so unusual that I am reproducing the letter in full, with only minor changes.

Than Galloway was perhaps the last link between the old mountain-men trappers and our present day. A master of the arts of hunting and trapping, he trapped the streams running into the Green and Colorado rivers and followed the Colorado from its source to the Imperial Valley. A river runner, one of the first and best, he navigated the Grand Canyon alone. He was one of the first white-water guides. Seasoned and knowledgeable, Galloway had few peers in the wilderness. His offhand account, with its humorous references to punching and poking the bear barehanded, makes light of an adventure that would more than satisfy any other man's taste for excitement.

Greenriver Utah. Dec. 2nd 1901

Mr. D. D. Rust, Esq.

My Friend Dave,
Your two letters Was received A Long time Ago. But As I Was on A Flying trip With A Boat Didnot Stop to Answer them. And Havent Been Near A P.O. Untill yesterday. When I Landed Here

at Greenriver, Utah. Am Glad to Hear From you, And that you Are Following Up the Lines of Education Closlely and Belive it the Best thing For your Futre improvement.

I Havent Much News to tell you onely I Have A Bear Story. This Will probely Be the Last one For a While, So I Will tell you a Big One.

After I Failed With the Large out Law, I told you of, I Moved Further East to Colorado on East Douglas. There Was two out-laws About, Good Duplicates For the Former. They Moved From the Creek, However, the Knight I Moved in, But Beliving they Would Come Back I Set My traps. There was Allso three other Bears Useing the range there, two Small and one Medium Large Black. Very Black and Shining. I Caught the three Small Bears in four Knights, and one of the Large ones Came Back And Went to one of My Small traps, Which Didnot Catch A Good Hold, and After Working a While He tore Loose. The Bears track Masures 12 inches. (The No. 5 trap is 10½"–11" And No. 6 is 14" – 16".) So you See the Bears Foot is too Large For the No. 5 trap. This Was Discouraging. But Finely I Desided to Follow the other one With My No. 6 traps.

I Found His Fresh tracks About ten Miles Back on West Creek, A tribuatary of Douglas, And Near the Line of Utah and Colo. He had Left there and Gon Further West the Knight Before. But I Made Choice of Location And Set My two No. 6 traps And Made My Round in four Days to the Spot Agane. And As I Neared the Furst trap it Was plain that Something Had Hapened there. Evidently the old Boy Had Spied the Front Quarters of A Fine Deer and Had His Mind Fully Made Up that He wouldnot Let it Lay there and Spoil, But Show Us How they Eat it in this country, By the Section. Accordingly He Fastened His teeth to one Side of the Ribs. About that time He Must of Seen ★★★★ For the No. 6 Had Him by the Front Foot.

He Made A Desperate Lunge And tore the Deers Ribs all Loose on one Side and Made His Next tracks With trap and Clog about ten feet Down the Hill. And Judgeing From the Way the Ground Was torn Up, He Had Located a Farm and Commenced the Furst plowing. He Struck the Creek A Short Distance Below and Cleared the Channell of Brush and Logs As He Went.

And the Creek Was Running Smoother And Faster than Ever

Before. A Short Distance Below He Left the Creek Agane, tearing Up Logs, Brush, and Small trees, And Clearing Up His Farm As He Went. Ocasionaly the Clog Would lodge Behind Large trees, when He Would tear off the Bark For Sevral Feet Up, and Sometimes Splinter the Wood out For two or three inches Deep. The Marks of His teeth Somewhat Resemble that of a pick. It Was No trouble to Follow His Trail, As I Could See it as Far ahead As I Could See through the Brush and Trees. I Followed on About one-half Mile With the Dog A Little in Advance. When All of A Sudden the Dog Became Very Excited, Jumping Up and Down, Barking, and tiptoeing it on His Hind Feet. A Few Steps Further Exposed the Bear to My View. He Was Fastned in the Creek Bed, Standing Straight Up Looking My Way Evidently Expecting Visators. I Walked Up A Little Near to Examin the Setuation and Found He Was Well Fastned in Such A Way He Could Not Go Further.

The Dog Soon Came to His Senses Agane and Flew At Him in Dead Earnest, Biting Him on All Sides. I was Compelled to Stop the Dog As the Bear Very Near Caught Him Sevral times. I Knew the Consequence if He Did, As I Will tell you What Hapned Before. I And the Dog had been playing With one of the Small Bears, the Dog Biting Him & Me punching Him With A Club, When the Bear Caught the Dog By the Sholder With His teeth. I Was Compelled to Kill the Bear With the Club, As I Had Left the Gun Some Distance Away.

Well I Walked Up to the Big Bear And punched Him A Few times in the Ribs With the Musle of My Gun. When I Shot Him He Rolled Back in the Creek. It Required All My Strength to Roll Him out Far enough For Skinning pourposes. I Stretched the Skin on the End of A Medium-Sized Log Cabin With But Barley Room to Admit it.

I Will Close By telling you a Few Words of My trip With the Boat, When I Belive you Will be tired of Reading Such Foolishness. After the Bear Chase I Moved on to Meeker, Colo., and there Built A Boat And Started Down the River traping Beaver. My Catch of Beaver is 117 and Some other Skins. And the Distance on Water is Nearly 500 Miles, including that Dismal trip through Desolation Canon of over 100 Miles.

The prospects are Looking Brighter For the Future to Me All

of the time And Balive I Will Make a Success of it. Have Found Grounds Where Most of the Specimons I Wish to Get Can Be Captured. Will Close By Wishing you Success in your persuits, and Will Be pleased to Hear From You Acasionaly.

As Ever Yours,

N. Galloway

History of Old Bruno

Joseph J. Porter

The rugged and remote Escalante country of southern Utah is a natural haunt of the grizzly bear. Ranger Porter's account of a famous predator, Old Bruno, captures the sagacity of this warrior and the effect he had on the men set upon his destruction.

FOR A NUMBER of years an old grizzly bear roamed over the Escalante Mountain, killing stock wherever he went and terrorizing everyone he met. Cowboys, forest rangers, campers, in fact everyone who rode over the mountain, were on the alert for Old Bruno, hoping sometime to meet up with him and get in a fatal shot. Every camper, on retiring for the night, slept, as the old saying is, "with one eye open," watching for Old Bruno, that he might not call on them when they were asleep.

But finally the time came that he did catch two forest rangers asleep in their tent. These rangers were Ambrose Shurtz and myself. They had planned a trip around the head of North Creek, where they were to meet at a certain date, before going to Escalante after supplies. After having been out in his district for about two weeks, Ranger Shurtz arrived. While coming in he passed the Willow Bottom reservoir, which was located at the head of Twitchell Creek, a branch of North Creek. The reservoir was full and the dam was about to break, but he went on down the creek and selected a nice place to camp in a grassy flat by some willows, where a ranch, or rather a dairy, was once located. He hobbled his horses out on the grass, pitched his tent and got camp fixed

From *The Improvement Era*, vol. 29 (March 1926), with kind permission.

up in fine shape when Ranger Porter rolled in about 3:00 P.M.

They had a little chat and luncheon, then decided to go down to the brook and catch a mess of trout to take home the next day. After fixing up the fishing tackle, they went down to the brook, and returned to camp in a couple of hours, each with a nice string of trout.

By this time it was dark and had begun to rain, so the saddles were piled, with guns strapped onto them, at the foot of the bed, to keep them out of the wet. The rangers sat on the bed talking about their luck catching the trout, about their trips through their districts, and about the weather. During this time they had been cleaning the trout, and when they had finished, the refuse from the fish was thrown just outside of the tent door, and the trout were placed just inside the tent.

The rangers waited for some time for the rain to cease so they could build a campfire and prepare some supper, but it continued to pour down, so they decided to go to bed without eating. Just before retiring for the night Ranger Porter stepped to the tent door, and on looking around said, "I'd like to see Old Bruno step out on the flat." "Why?" asked Ranger Shurtz. "Oh," Porter answered, "so I could get on him and take a ride," and laughed.

Porter soon fell asleep. A short time after, Shurtz awakened Porter and wanted to move the camp up on the side hill. He had been thinking about the reservoir at the head of the creek, and thought it would break the dam and come down the canyon and wash them away. After talking hard, Porter convinced Shurtz that they would hear it coming and would have time to move before it reached them, in case the dam broke. Porter was soon asleep again, but it was not long until Shurtz awakened him. Porter asked, "What in the world is wrong with you? Have you the jim-jams?" Shurtz said there was nothing wrong with him, only he couldn't go to sleep. "Something has knocked the guy ropes from the tent and let it fall in my face, and I'm going to fix it," he added. Porter advised him to tuck the tent down around the bed and not go out in the wet, as he might catch cold, "but for goodness sake, let me go to sleep." They lay down again, and Porter was soon asleep, for he was tired from his long day's ride over the range.

In just a few minutes Shurtz gave Porter a sharp poke in the ribs and exclaimed, "Porter, for heaven's sake, look at that big bear!" Porter opened his eyes, and there stood the big grizzly about a third of the way into the tent. Porter covered up his head and thought of all the mean things he had ever done, while Shurtz was trying to crawl under him. "Here! Don't crowd me out of bed," he said, and then got up courage enough to peek out from under the covers. There stood Old Bruno, calmly eating up the fish and looking around at the rangers. The men lay very still and watched him. After eating all the fish, he lapped out the dish and licked his chops with his long tongue, then looked down at the rangers as if to say, "Lie still. I am boss here." There was nothing for the men to do but lie still. The bear was so near that Porter could have reached out and touched him with his fingers. Shurtz had a quarter of mutton hanging on a tent pole, and the old bear would look up at it and then back at the rangers. Shurtz said, "Porter, he is going to get my mutton. What shall I do?" Porter replied, "Well, let him have it. I am not going to try to stop him."

Apparently the bear had only come for something to eat, and began to move off slowly. He had no sooner started than the rangers jumped for their guns, but Porter could not find his gun, and was rummaging frantically for it. "Why, you have hold of it now, pull it out," Shurtz shouted. Porter must have been some rattled.

Bruno had gone about twenty yards when the rangers fired. With a growl and a jump he was gone; the shots had missed their mark.

The rangers sat in the tent awhile talking about the adventure. Shurtz asked, "Porter, why didn't you ride him?" Porter replied, "I couldn't find my spurs." They went to bed, but they confessed that they didn't sleep much for fear of Old Bruno coming back.

Early in the morning the rangers went out to see if they had hit the bear, but could find no trace of any blood. They tracked him across the creek, and saw where he had sat down, scratched around in the dirt and then gone out through the timber. The rangers went back to camp, got breakfast, wrangled their horses, put on their packs, and started for Escalante, feeling sorry about the loss of the fish and the fact that they had missed Old Bruno, but glad that they were alive.

After traveling about twenty miles down North Creek, the rangers came to Escalante, a town of approximately 1110 people. A big baseball game was on, so after taking care of their outfits, the rangers, of course, went to see the game. They told of their experience with Old Bruno, which caused quite a sensation in the crowd, and they gathered around to hear the story. The crowd listened with great interest until the story was finished, then each began to express his opinion and tell what he would have done under the same circumstances. One man in particular, Ranger Shurtz's brother, Don C. Shurtz, said that if he had been there he would have "had old Bruno's pelt hanging on the fence now." Others said they would have thrown a blanket over his head and then cut his throat with a knife. Some said they would have shouted and given a jump at him, and in that case he would have broken his neck to get away. But one old bear hunter said that the rangers had done the right thing by keeping still, and not bothering him, for if they had bothered him, the bear would have killed them. The rangers felt that the old hunter was right, as the bear didn't look to them as if he was a coward.

Mr. Don C. Shurtz seemed the most anxious to get a shot at Old Bruno, so Ranger Porter told him that he was going back in a few days and would like to have him go along. Mr. Shurtz was going on the mountain to take out a load of salt for his cattle, and if Mr. Porter would go around with him he would go with Porter and get the bear; and the plan was agreed upon. Mr. Shurtz was one of the first settlers of Escalante, is a good marksman and quite a sport.

After getting their supplies and outfit ready, Mr. Shurtz and Mr. Porter left Escalante about ten o'clock one morning, going up the right-hand fork of North Creek. After a day's travel they camped at the hog ranch, where Mr. Shurtz's cattle were located. The salt was put out for the cattle, camp prepared, and they sat down to supper. While they were eating, Mr. Shurtz said, "Sit still. Do not move!" Porter did not know what was up. Shurtz raised his gun and fired. Lo and behold, there was a fine big buck deer passing by. As it was dark, the shot missed its mark and the deer got off free.

The hunters soon retired for an uneventful night. Next morning Mr. Shurtz got breakfast while Mr. Porter wrangled the horses and packed up, so they were soon on their journey. After a few hours' ride they came to the spot where Old Bruno gave the rangers the scare. They pitched their tent, took care of their horses, and were soon down at the creek catching a mess of trout for supper. They returned in a couple of hours with a nice string of trout, which they soon had frying over the campfire. These men thought they would eat the fish before Old Bruno had a chance at them. Porter showed Shurtz where they had had their experience with the bear. Shurtz sized up the situation and made the remark that "they would get him tonight if he came."

After sitting around the campfire for a while, talking about the topics of the times, they went to bed to await results. Mr. Porter, thinking Mr. Shurtz would want the best position, suggested that Shurtz sleep at the front of the bed, but he declined, saying he "would not sleep on the side next to the tent door for a thousand dollars." Mr. Shurtz began to show signs of cold feet, and was not half so brave when it came to the real thing. Porter had to take the front of the bed.

In a short time Shurtz was asleep and snoring. Porter lay there awake for probably two hours, when suddenly he heard the underbrush begin to crackle as something came down the side hill. He listened, thinking perhaps it might be one of the horses coming into camp. All at once he heard a growl. He gave Shurtz a poke in the ribs and exclaimed, "There is Old Bruno." Shurtz raised up in bed, grabbing his gun, and said, "Gee! Where is he?" and began to work the lever of his gun and threw all of the cartridges out upon the ground. Being awakened so quickly, he did not know what he was doing. The clicking of the gun had alarmed the bear, and Porter heard him hurry off down the mountainside.

Next morning bright and early Mr. Shurtz went out to see where the bear had been. He thought Porter was just trying to fool him. In a moment Shurtz called from back of the tent, "Porter, come here quick and look." Porter went, and there were Old Bruno's tracks where he had come up behind the tent, then whirled and run.

Mr. Shurtz said, "Now, Porter, if you won't tell this on me, I will give you the best cow I own." Porter thought it was too good to keep, so when they got to town he sprang the story and the fellows gave Shurtz the laugh. Even the little boys would holler at him and ask him if he had Old Bruno's pelt hanging on the fence.

After Don Shurtz had told the experience he had had with Old Bruno, Mr. Andrew Morton and Mr. Ben Tanner decided they were the ones to get him and pledged themselves to each other that they would stay on Old Bruno's trail until he was brought to justice. After equipping themselves with special guns, revolvers, butcher knives, traps and a pack outfit, they started out with brave hearts to find Old Bruno's trail. Not long after reaching the mountain they found fresh signs where the old bear had been. They started in pursuit, thinking every moment they would overtake their prey. But like others who had sworn vengeance on Old Bruno, they camped on his trail for days and for weeks, Old Bruno giving them the slip every time. They trailed him back and forth from Cannon Mountain to the east end of the Boulder Mountain, a distance of about 150 miles, setting traps on his trail, but Old Bruno continued to evade them. Finally they located a place along the trail where the bear would always go through, between two huge rocks at the point of the ledge. They decided to set a gun for him, with a string attached to the trigger, so when the bear came along and struck the string it would set off the gun and kill him. After setting the gun and getting everything fixed in proper shape, they went back into another part of the range to await results. A few days later they returned to see what had happened, or rather to see what success they had had from the snare. There had been a great mix-up. Old Bruno had run into the snare and received the full contents of the gun, and had torn things up until the place looked as if a cyclone had struck it. But Bruno had made his escape. The hunters trailed him for about sixty miles, and although his tracks showed that he was traveling on three legs, they could not overtake him. They decided to go to Escalante for supplies and take up the trail again later. However, while they were away, a storm came up, and when they returned the old bear's tracks had been entirely obliterated. They said that while they had been on the bear's trail they found where he had killed thirty-eight head of cattle in ten days. Being wounded, Old Bruno did not show up for some time. Mr. Morton caught a few small bears while on his trip, but he had to give Old Bruno up.

The time finally came when Old Bruno "hit the dust." In the spring of 1916 Mr. Reuben Jolly and Mr. Chess Riddle, from Coyote, went out on the west mountain to look after their stock. About seven miles from town they ran onto the old outlaw. A fierce fight was soon on. The boys were well armed and began to shoot. The bear took after them, but the boys stood their ground for a while, until he got too close for comfort. They brought him to the ground several times, but Old Bruno would rally and come again. After chasing back and forth through the timber and rocks for about three hours, the fatal shot was fired that put Old Bruno to the bad.

After taking his pelt they made an examination and discovered that they had shot him about thirty times. He weighed 1400 pounds and was very fat.

Mr. Jolly and Mr. Riddle were lucky, as the stockmen had offered a reward of $500 for Old Bruno, which was soon paid. Mr. Riddle, of Coyote, had the old bear's pelt tanned and is using it for a rug. It is a fine specimen to see.

Now, when any one goes out on the mountain they can lie down and sleep without having any fear of the old outlaw bothering them.

There are a great many other circumstances that could be mentioned about Old Bruno, but thinking perhaps you are tired reading this kind of history, I will bring my story to a close.

Old Three Toes
of Monroe Mountain

F. M. Young

Than Galloway's own offhand account of his exploit is the best introduction to the following story. There was no better hunter in Colorado and Utah than he. Than succeeded where numerous other men failed, and it is appropriate, I think, that the last big bear in central Utah was taken by the last of Utah's mountain men. His letter to our mutual friend Dave Rust, written shortly after the event, describes the capture:

July 25, 13

Richfield, Utah
Mr. D. D. Rust.

My Dear Friend.

On Monday last, Myself and Mr. fillmore, was very highly Elated over our Sucesfull catch. For lying in front of us was that Monstrous grizzley Bear, that had Don So Mutch Damage to the Stalk Men Useing Monroe Mt. After considering So Many failures by Expert trapers, Hunters and proctley all with with Some Devise of his own of Sure get him, we felt that we had performed Some greate feat beyond a Shadow of Doupt. Reports Came to Us of this Bear being in the Co. Some 15 years ago as he was Known by his track, as the Second Nole was broken off on his right front foot. He was allso Known as an Exceptioanly bad Specimen, as it required A freshly Killed animal to furnish him With Each and Every Meal, as he never returned for the Second.

On Considering the fact that an Expert trapper was on the Mts. 4 Days ahead of Us, and we returned in Just 7 Days with the pelt of Such a Noted animal it certainley created quite an excitement among Most of the Citizens, and expecily the Stalk Men. As it was quite a relief to hear the animal was captured that had ben Killing thousand of Dollars worth of Stalk Each and Every year.

The bear was caught Saturday Knight and we over took and Shot him Monday about 4 o'clock. This Delay in finding him was Due to heavy rain Storms which oblitereated practley all Signs made by the bear and trap. When the bear was caught if Someone could of insured us the Co. of D. D. Rust, Mr. J. F. Stone and Many others I could Mention, I would willingly of Sit Down and written him out a filty Dollar Check for his reward. The beauty of it all is the bear was caught in one of the traps you brought over to Me. Baliveing you will get a Mutch better report of his capture in the papers, I wil Close with best wishes to all.

                                                                    N. T. Galloway

---

MONROE MOUNTAIN, a big shouldered extension of the Wasatch range, runs north and south between the Sevier Valley and Grass Valley, in the south-central part of Utah. Old-timers remember when bears were plentiful in this mountain range and the sheepmen built bear lookouts in the tops of the trees near their camps. But for a long time there had been nothing larger than a coyote to bother the stock. The broad flanks of Monroe Mountain had been stock range since the first settlers arrived, fifty years earlier. Every pothole and thicket, every spring and small lake, and every patch of timber was well known to residents of the two valleys. Thus it came as a surprise when, in 1898, a grizzly bear took the mountain for his territory and played havoc with the cattle there.

The bear killed one or two yearling heifers about every four days. He would catch his prey by the ear, throw it, and break its neck, then tear off the brisket, open up the thorax, drink the warm blood, eat the heart and tender delicacies first, then make a meal off the flesh. The bear never came back to the same animal to eat, for he liked his meat fresh. He killed during the daytime or at night, whenever his hunger prompted.

He left plenty of tracks on the trails where he stalked his cattle and made his kill. There was no question as to his identity. He made a fourteen-inch track, not counting the claw marks, and the middle claw of his right front foot was gone, no doubt as the result of an earlier attempt to trap him. Thus he was called Old Three Toes.

Many hunting parties were organized to kill or capture Old Three Toes, but nothing came of them. Every summer the hunters, some from distant states, arrived on the mountain and made their camps near the big bear's stomping grounds. But they always came away without seeing the perpetrator of the many cattle murders. Old Three Toes was a crafty bear.

During the summer of 1913 he had killed twenty-five or thirty young cows, a loss which prompted the stockmen of the area to offer a reward of five hundred dollars for the capture of the bear — a fine inducement by any man's measure. Many writers of Western life have declared grizzly-bear hunting to be the grandest of all sports. Whether it was the sport or the reward that lured hunters to Monroe Mountain in 1913 is not known. But hunters, singly, in pairs, and in parties, with full equipment and dogs, began showing up on the mountain to match their wits with the mountain-wise old grizzly.

At the foot of Monroe Mountain, in Richfield, lived Than Galloway, who made his living hunting and trapping. In the fall of the year he would take his boat and traps and camping gear to the Green River and follow it north into Wyoming, taking muskrats, beavers, mink, and an occasional marten on his way up; then he would trap downstream until spring. He was not only a mountain man but a river man, the first since Major Powell to go down the Grand Canyon of the Colorado to the Needles, California. Many men have made the trip since, but Than Galloway showed them how.

The reward offered for the grizzly of Monroe Mountain was attractive to Galloway, and he asked his friend Angus Fillmore to go with him and share in the hunt. Fillmore took his team, wagon, and two saddle horses. Galloway threw in a dozen bear traps, bedding, and grub boxes; and they were ready to go. The first day they climbed to the rim and over to the Magleby Meadows. There they made camp and then rode over to where a party of hunters from Colorado were camped, to inquire about the hunting prospects. They were told that more than thirty hunters were on the mountain, each intent upon taking the pelt of the big grizzly. Galloway allowed that the mountain was getting crowded.

Sizing up the situation, Galloway and Fillmore decided to work the Grass Valley side of the mountain. As they proceeded, they paused to set traps in likely places. Galloway would build an inverted V-frame and hang his bait — a sizable part of a deer — from the apex, then drive sharpened pegs in the ground around and near the trap, leaving the trap clear so the bear, avoiding the pegs, would step into the trap. Than always put a scent on the bait that was a mixture of his own concoction with a beaver base that never failed to deceive a masculine bruin. Baiting is not as exciting as tracking a bear, but it is less time-consuming and risky, and everyone felt that all-out war against this old-time marauder was justified.

After they set several traps in this manner they returned to their camp. It rained all night and part of the next forenoon. About mid-morning they started out to visit some other camps, to learn if anyone had met with success. On the way Galloway said he would just take a look at a trap he had set by a small lake. To his surprise the trap was gone, and rain had obliterated the tracks of the animal that had taken it. The search for the bear began. When Galloway hunted, he assumed the character of the hunted animal: if a bear, he walked with rocking, wobbling gait; if a wolf, he was quiet as a cat and always on the alert. Fillmore and Galloway hunted for the bear in the rain without success and returned to camp again.

Next morning they began the hunt early, and as the weather cleared they found some tracks where the bear had climbed onto a log, near the edge of the lake. Thinking the bear had drowned, they scouted up the forest ranger, who was also active in this general hunt. The ranger was pleased to learn the bear might already be dead, and he gave Galloway and Fillmore permission to drain the lake and search for the carcass. But while Galloway was busy with this task, Fillmore discerned tracks where the bear had climbed out of the lake and gone into a thicket of willows nearby. He called to Galloway to come at once.

The two hunters were soon at the point of the last trace, where they saw a low opening trail into the thicket. They crawled single file into the mesh of willows, and as they came into a small clearing, by a pool of water, they saw the object of their search. Handicapped by the trap and six-foot drag, the old grizzly, who had always been able to take care of himself, was finally at the mercy of his enemies. He raised his head to ascertain the cause of the disturbance. Galloway drew a bead on the head and fired a ball unerringly above the eye into the brain.

It took several men to drag the big animal out of the willows to a dry spot, where he was skinned and stripped of fat. The hide measured twelve-and-a-half feet, from tip of nose to end of stub tail, and thirteen-and-a-half feet across the shoulders and down the arms. When the hide was stretched out on the lawn, the townspeople flocked to see it, and the hunters received the congratulations of the cattlemen for their good work. It was a great relief to them to know that the grizzly bear that had cost them thousands of dollars in slain cattle during the past twelve to fifteen years was at last captured and his hide stretched out at their feet.

The lucky hunters received the stockmen's reward of five hundred dollars, and a state bounty of fifteen dollars in addition, and they sold the hide for one hundred dollars. Mr. Fillmore mourned that they secured only twelve gallons of oil from the fat.

It isn't romantic to trap and then kill, but it will be recalled that in all his years of being hunted, this bear had never been seen by a hunter. Than Galloway's trapping efficiency probably saved the stockmen of the Monroe Mountain range many thousands of dollars, for the intelligent and crafty Old Three Toes had eluded even the most skilled hunters, in the manner of Pine Valley's Clubfoot and Cache Valley's Old Ephraim.

VII

NIGHTFALL

Utah's Old Ephraim

F. M. Young

The story of Old Ephraim has become legend in northern Utah where he roamed. He was the last bear of note to inhabit the Wasatch Mountains, and his exploits were well known. Frank Clark's encounter with him has been recorded many times. The summer following his adventure, I visited Frank Clark at his sheep camp at the head of Ricks' Canyon, on a hill at the head of several hollows, covered with many patches of quaking aspens. He showed me the sage park where his partner, Sam, first saw the bear, and, just over the hill, the bear's mud wallow. He showed me the huge bear trap that weighed twenty-five pounds, the heavy chains, and the .25-.35 rifle he used to kill the largest grizzly of these mountains. He also showed me the evidence of Old Ephraim's violence during that long night. In his pain and rage, the bear had bitten off several trees fully six inches in diameter and had reached up nine feet and four inches to bite nearly through another. Old Ephraim in fact was as large as his legend.

Frank Clark's experience is one of the classic tales of the West. Though it occurred in modern times, when most people had forgotten about bears and the wilderness, it has all the elements of those encounters that occurred in the Old West, when, with little or no advantage on his side, man met grizzly face to face.

AT ONE TIME grizzly bears were very numerous in the Wasatch Mountains and were often encountered by the early trappers of 1824–25 who cached their pelts in the area they called Cache Valley (known to the Indians as Willow Valley). So numerous were the big bears that forty years after the trappers departed

Portions of this story appeared previously in *Western Humanities Review* (Autumn 1950) and in *Selected Papers of the Western Folklore Conference* (Utah State University Press, 1964).

they were still common hazards to the Mormon pioneers who settled in that area. The settlers prevailed eventually, drove the bears out of the willow-green valley, and began running their sheep and cattle far over the Wasatch Mountains, killing any bear that made his presence known. In time the grizzly, like the frontier itself, faded into history, and the ranges and ranchlands became quiet.

Therefore it seemed strange, after the turn of the century, that rumors of a grizzly frequenting those mountains cropped up. Nevertheless these rumors gained credence when the bear acquired a taste for sheep, for huge paw prints were found at the various places of slaughter, fully twelve inches long not counting claw marks, with the middle claw missing on the left hind foot. Only a grizzly could leave such a track. Though many men came to know the bear's work and his pawprint, no one saw the bear.

In time the bear acquired the name *Old Ephraim,* partly because that had been a familiar name for the grizzly bear and partly because Mormons have a special fondness for the biblical Ephraim, the venerable patriarch of noble lineage. Utah's Old Ephraim ranged the mountains between Bear Lake and the head of Ogden Canyon, a large territory more than fifty miles in diameter, and his plundering took on a proprietary character. He would stir up things in sheep camps around Bear Lake, then disappear for a while. When he was missed, one of the stockmen of the region would drop a postcard to a sheepman over in the Ogden country saying, "Watch out, Ephraim is coming over to see you." And the old bear would actually appear among them. Then when his escapades in that country let up, the Bear Lake boys would get the message: "Ephraim must be showing a preference for your mutton, he's gone from here." This sort of jocular exchange went on several years, until Old Ephraim and his journeyings became a legend, catching the imagination of the sheepmen he victimized; yet no man ever saw the bear who made the big tracks.

Naturally, efforts were made to trap and kill the bear. But he was too canny and too experienced to be caught. How he kept himself concealed for so many years is a mystery. He took his meals regularly, had mud baths and naps, and chose a cave for wintering, but all out of sight of man. For many years Old Ephraim was visible only by his tracks.

During those years Frank Clark ran sheep in the range between Cache Valley and Bear Lake. In the summer of 1923 he again put sheep in the high country beyond Ricks' Canyon, a range he had been using for twelve years, after it had been abandoned by other sheepmen because of bears. Clark and his partner, Sam Kemp, had shot twenty-two black bears in the dozen years they had been using these feeding grounds, and they always brought a trap with them. For a few years they had been aware that a huge grizzly made periodic visits to their herds, but they had not seen him and did not feel he posed a menace, their losses being small and infrequent. That summer, as was their custom, they came prepared for bear, bringing two heavy traps, plenty of logging chain to secure them with, and their rifles. Clark's .25-.35 was dependable and effective against the black bears they spotted. The summer passed uneventfully.

One day in late August, Sam was out with the sheep at the head of a hollow; they were peacefully feeding and he was sitting on a log at the edge of a small sage park. Something made him glance around. Looking at him from the opposite edge of the clearing was the largest bear he had ever seen. The bear looked at Sam, looked around slowly, then turned into the trees and walked away leisurely. Sam lost no time in getting back to camp to tell Clark what he had seen. Both men knew at once the bear must be Old Ephraim.

They returned to where the bear had been seen and backtracked a short distance into the aspen, where, to their surprise, they found what was unmistakably the bear's wallow. His big tracks were all around, and it was obvious that Old Ephraim had only recently been enjoying the soft ooze. The well-used look of the sink indicated that he would probably be back to soak in it again. Clark was startled to realize that the grizzly had been so close yet so quiet and unsuspected, and he determined at once to try to take the bear. To trap him at the wallow seemed the most obvious strategy. That same day he set one of the traps at the wallow, attached the chain to a heavy log, and carefully covered his own tracks, a procedure he had followed successfully on other occasions when he had had to trap a bear.

Two days passed without any sign of bear. When Clark rode up to the wallow to check the trap he found that Ephraim had recently returned, using his famous stealth, for the trap was lying next to the drag log, right-side-up and unsprung. Clark set the trap as before, but this time with a sense of challenge that made him smile.

It was time for Sam to ride down to the valley for supplies. Clark told him he was sure he could manage alone for two or three days. Though the bear was in the area their herds remained unmolested. When Sam rode off, Clark went back to check the wallow; there he found a surprise from Old Ephraim. The wallow was dry, the exposed trap sitting where Clark had placed it. But there was a new wallow immediately below the other. Old Ephraim had scratched a channel, allowing the water to drain into his new sink, and it was evident that he had already taken a mud bath in it.

Clark could not refrain from admiring the bear's cunning even as he cursed it. It was obvious that this bear's craftiness called for new tactics. He went back to camp for the second trap and a log chain about eleven feet long. First he situated the twice-spurned trap in the new wallow, as he had done before; then he placed the second trap at the wallow's edge, fastening it to the longer chain, which he secured unobtrusively to a heavy drag. His plan was for the bear to sniff out the wallow cautiously — for though Clark's tracks might be covered up, his man-smell would linger — discover the first trap as before, then step back, less warily, into the jaws of the second.

After these preparations Clark made a small camp for himself at the head of the hollow, in order to be at hand when the bear was caught. Before settling into his bedroll that night he made sure his gun was in easy reach and that his pants next to it had extra cartridges in the pockets. He could hear the familiar clank of the hobble bell from the horses grazing nearby. The knowledge that Old Ephraim was in the vicinity, though still unseen, filled Clark with mounting excitement at the prospect of challenging him, and he lay awake a long while before he finally fell asleep, his little dog Jenny hunkered comfortably alongside him.

He was awakened suddenly, perhaps two hours later, by an unearthly noise, a reverberating sound at once a bellow and a groan. In the first nerve-racking moment, jolted from his sleep, Clark could not imagine the cause. He had never heard such turmoil. He sat up straining to see in the moonless dark. The awful roar and bellowing was repeated, this time even louder, and he realized that whatever made the din was coming nearer and that he had better move. He flung aside the blanket and fumbled to pull on his boots. Then, seizing his rifle, he crept through sage toward the entrance of the hollow, which seemed to be in the general vicinity of the roaring. And then he realized what the sound must surely be, and his heart hammered in his ears. He was sure the bear had stepped into one of the traps. But he could not understand why the bear sounded so close, when the wallow was nearly a mile up the draw. The horrendous howling told him the grizzly, in his fury, was headed down the hollow and would soon overtake him. Clark was mountain-wise and stolid and had experienced many things in his lifetime, but never, he vowed later, had he felt such an overwhelming sense of helplessness and fear. Somewhere in that dark night an engine of destruction was crashing toward him.

Yet there were intervals of silence, almost more terrifying than the appalling bellowing. Clark walked cautiously into the entrance of the main hollow and advanced about two hundred yards, feeling exposed and vulnerable and listening intently, knowing that the dark was no protection against the bear's acute sense of smell. He became aware of his dog cringing against his legs, as he stepped slowly and deliberately up the trail. Then he heard another great roar, even more chilling to him as he realized it came from behind him and that the grizzly must have passed him only moments before in the moonless night. For once in his life fear possessed him, and he scrambled up the hillside and climbed into the first big tree he could find. There he waited for the next sound or move from the bear.

He was afraid to go back to his tent, for the beast was between him and his camp. There was no safe place. In the heavy calm between the bear's outbursts, Clark tried to account for the turmoil and the wailing and for the fact that the bear had passed so close without attacking. Far down the draw he could hear the horses; nearby the little dog whined softly. Clark decided to wait where he was until light of day. He shivered as the moments passed slowly, and he discovered that he had forgotten to pull on his pants when he sprang from camp. This meant he would have no extra ammunition to replace the cartridges in his rifle. Clark knew he would have only seven shots to bring down the big grizzly when the moment came for them to meet, if he wasn't ambushed before then. Still, he thought, seven shells would be sufficient. So he waited out the night.

When it was light enough, he mustered the courage to step down to the trail again. Everything was quiet — almost too quiet, he felt. He could not shake off the feeling that Old Ephraim was hiding too and was, like Clark, alert to every sound and movement. Clark was hesitant about returning to camp by way of the trail in the main hollow and thought it wiser to go through the shallower and wider draw on the other side of the ridge on which he had been waiting. Cautiously he made his way over, stopping often to listen and watch. Though the churning fear he had felt the previous night had passed, he was nonetheless oppressed by the knowledge that somewhere near, possibly in the very clump of alder or chokecherry he was brushing past, was the huge grizzly that men had been seeking for many years, a cunning adversary now undoubtedly wounded and thus filled with a grizzly's terrible wrath.

Suddenly Clark was stunned by that awful roar once more, and he knew that the bear was in the same draw, on the farther side but very near. He knew now that he was committed to action. He set his gun and stepped boldly toward the willows where he estimated the bear to be. Almost at once he discerned a patch of gray or brown in the willows about ten yards away and fired a shot at it, the bullet twanging in the still air of early morning.

Instantly a huge shaggy back reared up above the willows, looking at least fifteen feet high, to Clark's dazzled eyes. Though bears were no strangers to him, never had he seen anything to equal this giant. The bear turned slowly, snuffling the air for the scent of his enemy, and Clark nearly froze with consternation. The night's terrible outburst was now clearly explained: on the bear's left forearm hung the big trap, its steel teeth buried in flesh; and wrapped around that arm was the heavy eleven-foot chain. The bear's mouth was horribly bloodied from his efforts to bite through the chain and trap. In his agony and rage Old Ephraim looked unbelievably fearful.

He saw Clark and, still upright, crashed ruinously toward him through the willows and bushes. Clark somehow steadied himself enough to pull the trigger. The bear dropped down at once but, shaking froth from his muzzle, continued forward with lurching but powerful strides. Again and again Clark fired. Each time the bullet found the target, for the bear fell to the ground; yet each time Old Ephraim struggled to his feet and, implacably and seemingly indestructibly, narrowed the gap between himself and the man. Six times Clark shot for the heart; unbelievably, the bear fell six times, only to pull himself up and plunge forward again.

When the bear was less than two yards away, Clark turned and ran up the side of the hollow, pulling himself through the scrub growth, heading for the aspens above. Close at his heels followed the relentless bear, on all fours but hindered by the injured arm dragging the trap and chain. Clark had not traveled more than fifteen yards when he heard a familiar yet strange noise. It was Jenny, barking wildly. Clark risked a quick glance behind him and saw Old Ephraim, perhaps ten yards downslope, with Jenny, who had been silent and afraid until this moment but was now nipping recklessly at the bear's hind legs, with restored courage. The bear had paused and was striking at the dog. This distraction, however brief, detained the bear long enough for Clark to steady his gun against a tree, draw a fine bead behind the bear's ear, and fire the seventh and last shell. Old Ephraim sagged to the ground and did not rise again.

Shaking and spent, Clark looked with incredulous eyes at the fallen giant for a long time. He had come face to face with legend and could not believe he had survived. Jenny ran up to him, giving his numb hands occasional hurried licks, while deep in her throat little growls rumbled her gratification. Clark did not approach the carcass but went back to camp and waited for Sam to return. Then together they examined the bear. Old Ephraim was nine feet and eleven inches long, nose to tail. They found that two of Clark's bullets had actually pierced the heart, and Clark learned by experience what he had heard old-timers claim: an enraged grizzly is much more difficult to kill than an unexcited one. So powerful was Old Ephraim that only the final lucky shot in the brain felled him for good. The men buried the remains, a singular honor for a bear, perhaps. But there were practical considerations, for even his carcass inspired terror, and the horses could not be kept in camp until all trace of the big grizzly was gone.

Although glad to be alive, and aware of the long depredations of Old Ephraim, Clark never boasted of his exploit. Too much of himself had been spent in that morning's confrontation. Nor was he afterward fully at ease in the mountains, where he continued to do his job each year in those same ranges. In the fall he was glad to come down to the valley, more eager than in previous years. At least once each summer, however, he made a special point to ride over to Old Ephraim's grave, which he had marked with a blunt testimonial written on a piece of old board: HERE LIES OLD EPHRAIM. HE GAVE FRANK CLARK A GOOD SCARE.